KD

ALSO BY MARCUS THOMPSON

Golden: The Miraculous Rise of Steph Curry

KD

Kevin Durant's Relentless Pursuit to Be the Greatest

MARCUS THOMPSON II

ATRIA PAPERBACK

New York • London • Toronto • Sydney • New Delhi

ATRIA
PAPERBACK

An Imprint of Simon & Schuster, Inc.
1230 Avenue of the Americas
New York, NY 10020

First Atria trade paperback edition November 2019

ATRIA PAPERBACK and colophon are trademarks of Simon & Schuster, Inc.

Photo of Durant with trophies by Trillicon Valley/Khristopher "Squint" Sandifer

For information about special discounts for bulk purchases, please contact Simon & Schuster Special Sales at 1-866-506-1949 or business@simonandschuster.com.

The Simon & Schuster Speakers Bureau can bring authors to your live event. For more information or to book an event, contact the Simon & Schuster Speakers Bureau at 1-866-248-3049 or visit our website at www.simonspeakers.com.

Interior design by Dana Sloan

Manufactured in the United States of America

1   3   5   7   9   10   8   6   4   2

Library of Congress Cataloging-in-Publication Data has been applied for.

ISBN 978-1-5011-9781-9
ISBN 978-1-5011-9782-6 (pbk)
ISBN 978-1-5011-9783-3 (ebook)

To the people from my neighborhood, Sobrante Park in East Oakland, and every 'hood like it in this country, who believed strongly enough and worked hard enough to excel despite the shackles and trauma of poverty you inherited. What you pulled off was indeed amazing.

CONTENTS

INTRODUCTION

KEVIN DURANT'S SIGNIFICANCE had reached a ceiling.

While he had as much name recognition as any current player outside of LeBron James, his connectivity to the NBA fan base always had a limitation. Durant was a good guy, and good guys don't always move the needle so strongly. His physical frame seemed to stretch to the heavens but the packaging of his personality came off as inconsequential. Even though he was from Chocolate City, having spent most of his time in the spotlight in midtier markets—specifically Austin, Texas, and Oklahoma City—Durant was lacquered in small-town sauce.

He was birthed by a metropolis, a product of the D.C. area, and was no doubt a phenom of a player. His game was a gift, with fluidity and drive that paired perfectly with his gangly frame. Durant entered the league at a time when the celebrity of NBA players was peaking. Allen Iverson's career was winding down, Kobe Bryant was in his prime, and LeBron James was the obvious next star on deck. The three of them took the baton from Michael Jordan and carried NBA superstardom further into mainstream culture. Their lives, their personalities, their dramas became as much a part of the packaging as their dominance on the court. Durant had the game, but he didn't have the illustriousness to draw fervent loyalty from the masses. He had the personality of a midrange jumper—respectable, effective, reliable even, but so unremarkable as to be negligible.

But overnight that changed, and he became the source of historic drama and a lightning rod after making one of the most controversial free-agent decisions in the history of the NBA. His next era would be defined by new polarizing heights of fame.

Durant had played eight seasons in Oklahoma City, nine seasons with the franchise all told, including his rookie year in Seattle before the Sonics were moved to Oklahoma. That was the same amount of time LeBron James had put in with Cleveland the first time around. Durant signed his rookie contract extension in 2010, for five years and $89 million, without even testing the free agency market. He'd given the Thunder more than enough. Six weeks after the Golden State Warriors knocked Oklahoma City out of the 2016 playoffs, Durant joined them. And overnight he went from humble superstar to a controversial figure who the league is still trying to figure out.

"I'm just not built like that," former Boston Celtics star and future Hall of Famer Paul Pierce said on the ESPN television show *The Jump*. "I'm not a guy who goes into the neighborhood, gets beat up by the bully's gang, and then now I want to join your gang. That's just not me. I want to fight. Let's go. I'm gonna stand up for myself."

Watching Durant, it was always clear he was something special: a point guard on stilts, a center with the fluidity of a shooting guard, the essence of a 1970s scorer in the body of a 2000s stretch-five. Still, his aw-shucks veneer presented him as too simple to investigate. He was harmless, immensely likable, yet lacking the texture that inspired fervor. But when he decided to leave OKC and sign with Golden State, all that was stripped away and the world saw the real

KD. Still a once-in-a-generation player, but hungry, passionate, and very human.

Long gone was the media adulation and admiration that wrapped its arms around Durant as he spoke lovingly about his mother being the "real MVP." He lost his glow as the antithesis to the entitled, diva athlete. With one decision he was exponentially more significant. And Durant had to exist in his new skin. A skin that would need to thicken overnight.

Hall of Famer Charles Barkley on Durant: "Kevin is a terrific player, he's a good kid. But [I'm] just disappointed with the fact that he weakened another team and he's gonna kind of gravy train on a terrific Warriors team. Just disappointed from a competitive standpoint. Because just like it meant more to LeBron to win one in Cleveland, it would mean more to Kevin to win one in Oklahoma than it would be in Golden State."

Stephen A. Smith, the popular ESPN analyst who hosts the *First Take* debate show athletes watch faithfully, called it the weakest move he's ever seen from a superstar: "Kevin Durant is one of the top three players in the world. And he ran away from the challenge that he faces in order to jump on the bandwagon of a team that's a little bit better."

Durant was no longer the humble superstar.

He announced his free agency plan to join the Warriors via a letter he wrote on the *Players' Tribune*. It featured a now-famous black-and-white image of Durant in a sleeveless white T-shirt surrounded by trees, the most serene of expressions on his face. The headline read: "My Next Chapter," and he looked like one who was at peace with his move. But the ensuing days brought only agony as his decision set off a national controversy.

Durant's first time addressing the media since his earlier decision to join the Warriors was at the University of Nevada, Las Vegas, where he was taking part in the Team USA training camp in preparation for the 2016 Summer Olympics in Rio de Janeiro. He was still processing the sports world's reaction.

"The two days after I didn't leave my bed because if I walk outside somebody might try to hit me with their car or say anything negative to me. I thought people would react to me a little differently. I never had this much attention," Durant told reporters. "I just stayed in and tried to process it all. I wanted to be around family and positive support. It felt different, obviously. I had been somewhere for so long and made a change no one saw coming and didn't think I would do. Of course I didn't know how it would be received afterward. But at some point I said, 'Life goes on, and I can't hide forever.' So I had to face it."

Durant was now on the other side of the initial storm. His vibe was so smooth and unbothered that he'd even gotten a tattoo during the camp.

He had worn blue sleeves over his calves for two days at camp, an accessory also worn by Carmelo Anthony and a few others. But on Day 4 of camp, Durant's legs were bare beneath a pair of gray shorts. A sheet of plastic clung to the left side of his left leg, on the expanse between his knee and his ankle. Beneath the Saran wrap was a glimpse into the depth that was before hidden. Durant could have worn pants to this practice. Even with the heat, Nike assuredly had some Dri-Fit sweats to keep him cool yet covered. Instead, Durant wanted to reveal his new tattoo, or at least wasn't interested in hiding it. And with the peek at his new artwork, a portrait of slain rapper and actor 2Pac, Durant gave a glimpse behind the veneer of himself.

In hindsight, as Durant's layers have been peeled back, the artwork depicting the late rapper makes sense. Sure, 2Pac's music career took off in the Bay Area, and that was where Durant was headed. Even the image inked on Durant's leg was a photo taken during the filming of 2Pac's "Brenda's Got a Baby" video by Gary Reyes of the *Oakland Tribune*, the former flagship newspaper where Durant would be playing his home games. But the connection was even deeper, much more spiritual than geographical. He didn't have Steve Wiebe, the celebrity tattoo artist who does ink for numerous players, engrave the West Coast hip-hop legend on his leg to announce a regional allegiance.

"To be so young and say the things he said," Durant explained. "Who is thinking like that at that age?"

It is reasonable Durant would be drawn to such a figure. Bingeing on Tupac Shakur's catalog is like hearing the mind of an artist with undiagnosed dissociative identity disorder. He is one of the most celebrated rappers in the history of the art form. He sold more than 75 million albums worldwide—at a time when people bought CDs. In a music career that spanned five years in earnest, 2Pac released five albums, the last one coming shortly after his death. Another five albums were released posthumously, curated from unreleased tracks, remixes, and remastered classics. His work ethic was stuff of lore. He was known for cranking out song after song in studio sessions. He had so much to get off his chest, so many thoughts and feelings.

He was also a conscious artist during the height of the gangsta rap era, championing the causes of political prisoners such as Geronimo Pratt; Mumia Abu-Jamal; and his father, Mutulu Shakur; while espousing Black empowerment and encouraging the youth. Some of his most famous songs are uplifting women or shining a light on women's issues. "Keep Ya Head Up" and "Dear Mama" and "Brenda's Got a Baby" are hip-hop classics. But 2Pac also had songs filled with rage and revenge. He had the arrogance to taunt and ridicule rappers by name. The braggadocio dripped off his words like sweat from a brow as he aggrandized being shot five times in New York in 1994 and surviving. The same man also had the humility to discuss his own mortality and reflect on his regrettable behaviors and appeal for forgiveness from women, from fans, from God.

The secret ingredient to 2Pac was his passion. He is not mentioned among the greatest rappers of all time simply because of his lyrical skills or the millions of records he sold. He remains preeminent because of how much he poured himself into his music. He made you believe in him. He had a way of making the listener feel what he was saying no matter the topic. His artistic range allowed him to tug on heartstrings with touching songs, yet he was just as adept at tapping into machismo and promoting rowdy aggressiveness. He could provoke thought and contemplation as easily as he could intoxicating fun and violent rage. That's because 2Pac was all heart. Whatever emotion or affection he shared was turned up all the way, be it contemplating the afterlife or boasting about his sexual exploits.

"Tupac was known for being woke, being politically incorrect, having a voice, and standing up for himself, standing up for what he believes is right," Durant explained to the *Mercury News*. "He expressed that in his music. He expressed that in interviews. He expressed that through his movies, through his artistic work. It's way bigger than him being an artist or making a hot-ass song or having a No. 1 record. It's that at that age, for you to be thinking about the stuff you were thinking about, at 22, 23 years old, and he died at 25, like . . . young people don't think like that. So for him to have that type of mindset at that age . . . today [he] would've been like Gandhi, you know what I'm saying? Or like Nelson Mandela–type intelligence for our culture, our people, our voice as being from the neighborhood. He meant so much to having me just think a different way."

Durant and 2Pac are relatable in both the intensity of their feelings and the diversity of them. Durant's decision to join the Warriors started the tearing down of his facade and the revealing of the complex and varied personality beneath. Like 2Pac, KD is one who experiences the gamut of emotions, whose assorted feelings and perspectives are like strong currents swaying him in multiple directions. Perhaps Durant wanted to exercise the same freedom as 2Pac to be controversial, mimic the moxie to take criticism and smile, mimic the audacity to do things his own way. His lyrics must have appealed to Durant as he wrestled with his own history. The language and stories of hip-hop have long been a bible for generations of inner-city youth. Many have used the music to process what was happening within them and around them.

It makes sense Durant would be moved by 2Pac's storytelling in songs like "So Many Tears," the clashing of spiritual overtones and carnal vigor in "Hail Mary," the rebellion of "Ambitionz Az a Ridah," and the affection and repentance of "Letter 2 My Unborn."

Durant's been through so much. It makes sense that, like 2Pac, he also comes across as having multiple personalities, a divulging unearthed by his departure from Oklahoma City. He spent years developing and managing his one-note persona. His absence of complication made him unlike other stars. He took pride in being different from typical household NBA names. He bandied Jesus' name around in interviews, kept his mother close and up front, endeared himself to the community, avoided run-ins with the law. Durant was simple. Down home.

But his move to the Warriors yanked back the covering and revealed an entanglement of characters. He had been exposed by making the most stunning decision. Through it all, the revelation of Durant is still how "regular" he actually is. His normalness was once epitomized by the simplicity of his persona. Now it is his complexity that makes him ordinary.

Yes, he is a down-to-earth guy who appreciates the priceless elements of life: friendship, laughter, generosity, community. He also has a larger-than-life chip on his shoulder that demands elite status and recognition. Yes, he is thoughtful and compassionate, connects with people, and cares about people. He is also aggressive and vengeful, willingly confrontational and inclined to fire back at anyone who wants smoke. Yes, he has stratospheric confidence, which drives this pursuit of his to be the best basketball player in the world. He is also acutely sensitive to criticism and admonishment, which is typically a by-product of insecurity and self-esteem issues.

These diverse attributes underline a truth about Durant, one that draws a kinship to the author of *Thug Life*: Durant feels. Deeply. Enough to break down in tears in front of the cameras when Thunder assistant coach Monty Williams lost his wife in a car accident, and all he could say was how much he loved Williams. Enough to really be warmed by hearty moments and allow the stinging ones to linger longer than would be advised. Enough to invest heavily in communities across the land, much of it without fanfare.

Months after winning his first championship, Durant had a new version of his Nike KD 10 signature shoe released. It was called "Finals MVP"—a royal-blue sneaker with gold accents. The unique feature was inside the shoes.

The blue insoles had messaging on them, all in handwritten fonts. On the left insole it read "16-1" and "2017 CHAMPS" in yellow, the Warriors' postseason record en route to the first title with KD. On the right insole, also in yellow, were Durant's statistical averages from the five games in the NBA Finals with the words "FINALS MOST VALUABLE PLAYER" on the heel. In black writing on both insoles, underneath the yellow, was a list of the insults that had been hurled at Durant. "Lame." "Quitter." "Follower." "Snake." "Soft." "Arrogant."

"Pathetic." "Cursed." "Undeserving." "Traitor." In total, thirty-one insults were listed.

This shoe was Durant stepping on his haters.

One fan commented on Durant's YouTube page, which featured a video of the new sneaker. The commentator declared Durant shouldn't be worried about what other people say. His status as an NBA star and champion should make him immune to such taunts. Durant, though, responded by defending his ordinariness. His reply in the comments was from one who didn't want to surrender his regularity to his popularity.

"I play basketball. I got acne. I grew up with nothing. I'm still figuring myself out in my late 20s. I slide in DMs. I make fun of my friends. I drink beers and play Xbox. I'm closer to you than you think."

. . .

Durant is now a champion. He grinded his way from the Seat Pleasant Activity Center, the gym in his hometown where he learned to play, to the upper echelon of NBA greats. He has transformed from a lanky kid with the strength of a fawn into arguably the greatest natural scorer the league has ever known and, inarguably, one of the most dominant players in the game today. He is on pace to become the eighth NBA player to reach 30,000 points, a mark he should hit in the next five years. He already has as many NBA Finals MVP awards as Kobe Bryant, Larry Bird, and Kareem Abdul-Jabbar, and Durant is still in the prime of his career.

It has been quite the road to get here. He has survived poverty and a broken home. He wore six uniforms in six years at one point, before Oklahoma City became home. But Durant has made it. He has long been a prodigy destined for these levels. His package of height, shooting, and ball handling have long left scouts and analysts salivating.

His combination of skills seemed to make NBA success only a formality. However, these things don't happen automatically. Potential isn't always realized. And it wasn't enough to just be an All-Star: he wanted to be the greatest.

His relentless pursuit of that greatness forced him to realign and reckon with his personality. Yet Durant's status hasn't transformed him into a commercial presentation of superstardom.

When athletes get to this level, they are often public relations concoctions. They are molded, groomed, and polished by corporate interests and mogul motivations. Their true thoughts get choked out, their blemishes Photoshopped away. They become choreographed brands beholden to investors. Image is everything and must be procured and protected like priceless works of art. Perception is reality and therefore is relentlessly manipulated.

But Durant refuses to acquiesce. Perhaps he is unable. The grander his fame has grown, inevitably exposing him to more criticism and attacks, the more he has chosen to lean in to his true self. Superstars are taught to have thick skin, to brush off insults and quips like dandruff. Durant, though, spurns the idea that he doesn't get to feel anymore, that normal human reactions don't apply to him, that he must fold up the totality of him to fit in a marketable package. He clings to his unalienable right to bite back, to question the status quo, to have flaws—all privileges granted to noncelebrities.

Four days after officially re-signing with the Warriors—his third straight two-year contract with an opt-out after one year—Durant was browsing Instagram. He came across a post from an account dubbed @Bucketscenter. It was run by Kalyb Champion, an aspiring sports media member. It featured a photo of Durant, Kawhi Leonard, and Anthony Davis with the following analysis: "Three elite two-way players but don't elevate a team quite like LeBron and Steph due to their playmaking/leadership deficiencies."

Durant took exception: "Bruh go sweep ya dorm room, u don't know hoops. Stop tagging me in this trash."

The account responded by calling Durant "insecure." Two posts later, the account posted screenshots of private messages with Durant. In the exchange, Durant called him a "Middle school/knock off Stephen A" in reference to the ESPN analyst and debate specialist Stephen A. Smith.

Champion rebutted: "You know it's true. That's why your insecure ass responded to me. Why don't you actually prove you can LEAD a team to a championship? Not even in the same galaxy as LeBron."

Durant apologized for the dorm room and fake Stephen A. retort. But he voiced his disagreement with the analysis and made sure to point out he had given the guy what he wanted.

"You took it real personal," Durant responded. "Relax bud, it's just basketball. You've been tagging me in posts for months. I respond and you finally speak your mind. Nice."

This exchange embodied the clash of Durant's status with his person. He makes $30 million a year from Nike, nearly as much annually from his NBA salary, and untold amounts in his investment portfolio. Yet he is willing to argue with teenagers on Instagram.

Yes, Champion was 17 at the time of their spat, which only made Durant's engagement that much more unfavorable. But Durant feels the stings no matter who throws the dart. They come from everywhere, every day. He can't appease these away, can't redirect them by turning up the humility. Especially in the social media age, where anonymity has created an impersonal audacity, Durant can't perform enough good acts to quench the bloodthirst of cyberbullies.

His adaptation has been to nix pretenses. He is resolved to just be himself, to rip away the facade and be the unadulterated version of Kevin Durant. The parts people love. The parts people can't stand. The parts that inspire. The parts that irritate.

Perhaps the most interesting part about the diversity of Durant's feelings and his governing of them is how it has crystallized the constant in his life. Ultimately, there is one refuge where he can escape being swallowed by his increased significance, one retort he can issue to all naysayers and trolls, one reward for all his supporters who rode with him to this rarified air. Dominance.

If 2Pac poured his heart and soul on wax, working out his multiplicity of emotions and passions through music, Durant does the same on the court. He pours his all into the game. Basketball is the sacred realm. Not the money or the fame, not even his behavior. Basketball.

Which is why his decision to join the Warriors has elevated Durant's game to new heights. There is no denying that playing alongside three other All-Stars is an ideal way to maximize his performance. Durant enjoys space unparalleled in his career. His attack is as versatile as it has ever been because of the talent he gets to play with on the Warriors. He's with a collection of veteran players who are as cerebral as they are physically gifted. He looks to be a better passer because his teammates know how to get open and finish. He looks to be a better defender because he's part of a unit on a string and a lighter offensive burden reserves energy to invest on defense. All of his talents are taken advantage of in Golden State coach Steve Kerr's system, which employs a philosophy of body movement and ball movement as a way of engaging all of the options on the court.

But the pressure on Durant wasn't lessened by his decision to join the Warriors, even if the obstacles in his way were. For the first time in his life, failure was not an option. Being really good was not satisfactory. He had to be great. That required evolving as a player. It required being willing to adapt. That, Durant did.

He seized the moment. The rung of NBA superiority was right there for the reaching. And, man, did he leap to it. He made the jump from incredible scorer to incredible player. He matured from unstoppable to unbeatable. His minutes dropped to the lowest averages of his career with the Warriors, so his numbers aren't as gaudy as they were with the Thunder. But in his first two seasons with Golden State, Durant set career highs in field goal percentage, rebound rate, blocked shots, postseason 3-point percentage, and postseason offensive rating. He became known for his defensive abilities, even garnering Defensive Player of the Year talk for the first time in his career.

But the most notable improvements came in the postseason, when Durant shifted to another gear. He never looked more like the best player on the planet than during the championship runs in 2017 and 2018. It had the aura of a destiny being fulfilled, a basketball prodigy earning his knighthood. The Warriors are arguably one of the best teams the NBA has ever seen. And in the postseason, in the Finals especially, under the most pressure and against the best opponents, Durant has risen above all others. During the regular season and even at the core of their union, the perception is that Durant has been lifted to these heights by the Warriors. He joined a team that won a record 73 games and was two shots from winning back-to-back championships.

But in the biggest moments it has undeniably looked as if Durant was the one lifting the Warriors. He proved that when he is on his game, when his focus is maximized and his talents are fully exploited, he deserves mention among the all-time greats.

Now he has the hardware to prove it. The player who once was defined by scoring titles and his 2014 regular season MVP award now has the résumé that validates his greatness: two Finals MVPs and two championship rings. It took him a long time to get there, seated among the legends of the game. But the skinny Maryland kid—Durant, not 2Pac, who lived in Baltimore for two years of high school—with a textured life and a warm heart finally made it to the place destiny had carved for him. It took him surviving and growing. It took admirable discipline and a work ethic that matched his talent. It took everything he was and everything he had to be: The Rose That Grew from Concrete.

1 | THE EARLY YEARS

LEN BIAS BELONGED TO PRINCE GEORGE'S COUNTY through and through. He hailed from Landover, Maryland, and learned how to play basketball there at the Columbia Park Recreation Center. It was his city before the Washington Redskins moved to town in what is now FedExField.

Bias also starred at Northwestern High School in Hyattsville, then played college ball a mile away in College Park at the University of Maryland. When he wanted to get away from the pressures of the Atlantic Coast Conference, he'd walk the mile or so to Northwestern to work out at his old stomping grounds or see his childhood coach, Robert Wagner. The kids knew him for encouraging them to stay in school. Blacktop hoopers knew him for getting up shots on the outside courts at Columbia Park. Everybody knew him as Frosty.

So, when Bias was drafted in 1986 by the Boston Celtics, all of PG County won—especially the rougher parts where victories don't come so often. He turned an area known for being a hoops hotbed into a basketball blaze. The Washington, D.C., area has produced some basketball legends, such as Dave Bing, Elgin Baylor, and Adrian Dantley. PG County, specifically, took pride in producing greats on its own even though it blends with the basketball scene of the neighboring metropolis. DeMatha High, with one of the most renowned high school basketball programs in the country, is in Hyattsville about two miles south of Northwestern High. Some real talent has come through those parts, but none had been as touted as Bias. He was slated to be the NBA's next star. The NBA belonged to the likes of Magic Johnson, Larry Bird, and Isiah Thomas. Michael Jordan had just finished his second season. Even though he missed 64 games with a broken foot, he was clearly a budding superstar after scoring 49 points and 63 points in back-to-back playoff games against Boston. Bias was expected to join Jordan as a flag bearer of the new era of the NBA, and Bias was PG County's own in every sense.

For parts of the county that had been written off, that knew struggle, Bias was a point of pride. He was an inspiration for kids who walked the same streets he walked. He was evidence for the generation before him that the future had hope. Not since boxing legend Sugar Ray Leonard, who grew up in Palmer Park, had PG County produced a star who shined as brightly as Bias was going to shine. So when he died—on June 19, 1986, from a cocaine overdose, two days after being selected No. 2 overall in the NBA Draft—it was a gut punch for the whole region. He was supposed to carry the banner for PG County across the nation. He was going to be an All-Star, an MVP, a champion, and his people would be as well, right along with him. That was taken away in a dorm room in Washington Hall at the University of Maryland.

"I can't see why we would lose someone like this, someone so important to us," Wharton Lee Madkins, then-director of the Columbia Park Recreation Center and one of Bias's earliest coaches, told the *Washington Post*.

Bias's friend, Brian Tribble, who was with Bias when he died, was accused of supplying the cocaine and charged with drug possession and distribution. That set off a trial and an ensuing circus. Bias remained in the media cycle. Politicians got involved, ramping up the rhetoric and the stakes. For a year the residents of PG County grieved in the background of a national court drama. The fallen hero they had been certain would become legendary wound up a cautionary tale in a public discourse about drugs and crime.

In June of 1987, Tribble was acquitted of all charges. But it wasn't the end of Bias's time in the public eye. In November 1988, Congress passed into law the Anti-Drug Abuse Act of 1988. It was an extension of the act first passed in October 1986 as part of the War on Drugs, which created mandatory minimums for drug offenses. When Bias died, the initial rumors spread like wildfire that he died smoking crack cocaine. At the center of the War on Drugs was the crack epidemic taking over inner-city neighborhoods, like the ones in PG County. Crack was being blamed for rampant crime and violence. It wasn't long after Bias died that it was learned his overdose was on powder cocaine, the more expensive form of the drug used primarily by people with means. But the initial rumors had already fanned the roaring flames about crack and the need to get it under control. With the 1988 presidential election in full swing, crack was back on center stage. One of the Anti-Drug Abuse Act amendments made crack, already the most harshly penalized of drugs, the only substance with a mandatory minimum penalty for a first offense of simple possession. It was dubbed the Len Bias Law. Two years after his death ripped the hearts out of the people of PG County, Bias was still the focal point of a political war. Worse than that, he was being used as a poster child for what was wrong with their community.

But amid the grieving, a birth would represent PG County's resilience. Before Bias's star had completely faded from view, another star was being forged.

Like Bias, he would be their very own. Their culture would shape him. Their environment would mold him. Their struggles would engrain in him their brand of toughness. Their people would uplift him. They would be able to touch him, to know him.

Like Bias, he would reach incredible heights in basketball and leave jaws dropped because of his unique collection of skills. Eventually, PG County would get its basketball icon, its very own superstar who would raise the bar of what's possible. He would be mesmerizing. But he would do what Bias wasn't able to do—grow into a figure renowned enough to remove the lid from the dreams of children.

Like Bias, he would be imperfect. But that wouldn't diminish his value to home; instead it would validate his tangibility. Like parts of PG County itself, he would be rough around the edges, gruff in appearance, yet unquestionably good and worthy at the core. His foibles would make him more real, more human, which matters to those who have been routinely dehumanized.

It's rare to get two global superstars harvested from the same locale. If Bias was groomed and destined to be that superstar, perhaps it was too much to expect another. Shooting stars don't appear so close together. But PG County would indeed get the ultimate reprieve.

On September 29, 1988, Kevin Wayne Durant was born.

． ． ．

Decades before he was a load to deal with on basketball court, he was a load to his mother: 8 pounds, 3 ounces, 22.5 inches. Her first son, Anthony Durant, had been born two and a half years earlier, and six months before Bias died. Kevin was her second child.

"I remember it. Exactly. And I had natural birth with him," Wanda Durant said in the documentary *Still KD*. She closed her eyes and shook her head. Just thinking of that birth caused a chill. "Woooo."

The boys were given the surname of their great-grandfather, Troy Durant, from whom Wanda gets her maiden name and from whom her oldest son, Anthony, gets his middle name. Kevin's middle name is that of his biological father, Wayne Pratt.

Wanda, twenty-one, and Wayne, twenty-two, had two young boys and were starting a family together in the shadows of the White House as the Ronald Reagan administration was ending.

Prince George's County, the suburbs of D.C., was in the middle of interesting times when Durant was born. It was really two worlds colliding. The county is the second largest in Maryland. In the 1970s, Blacks migrated to PG County, many of them with government jobs in D.C. Blockbusting—real estate agents selling to one race and using the fear of that race taking over the neighborhood to get others to sell—opened up whole neighborhoods. The Blacks who were moving into PG County were affluent and educated. Between 1970 and 1990, the median household income in the county grew to more than $30,000. In 2014, Atlanta Black Star listed five neighborhoods from Prince George's County among the richest Black communities in America.

But in the '80s, as with many other inner-city neighborhoods, the crack epidemic robbed the county of its innocence and affluence in several areas. Crime rates shot up and once-scenic neighborhoods were rampant with poverty, a primary contributor to crime and violence. Seat Pleasant was one of the cities especially ravaged. Affluent parts still existed, but PG County suddenly had other-side-of-the-tracks neighborhoods.

"The train tracks in this case was the Beltway," said NFL front office analyst Jimmy Halsell, who grew up in Clinton, in PG County, just south of Andrews Air Force Base, and worked as a salary cap guru for the Redskins. "Outside of the Beltway, subdivision neighborhoods in Fort Washington, Upper Marlboro, Bowie, and Mitchellville represented the fact that PG was the most affluent, predominantly Black county in the nation at the time. While inside the Beltway, in neighborhoods like Seat Pleasant, Fairmount Heights, and District Heights, Blacks endured many of the same criminal and economic challenges as their neighbors in the District. Drive any five-mile stretch of PG and you could see the full range of the Black socioeconomic spectrum. From Huxtable-like economic and professional success to disenfranchisement and violence. It was all there for one to experience in PG."

Data from the police department shows a 62.8 percent increase in crime between 1984 and 2004. In 1985, 43 homicides were committed in PG County. By 1989, there were 120. By 1991, the count was up to 134. Some parts were still beacons of the middle class: the family, the kids, the stable jobs and owned homes. Other parts were impoverished and rife with drug addiction and broken families. Unlike some of the roughest 'hoods in America, PG County wasn't a compilation of dilapidated high-rises. These were houses and duplexes of hardworking people who had forged a good life but their homes had deteriorated into distress.

Crack hit the entire Metropolitan D.C. area hard. The nation's capital's homicide total rose to 369 in 1988, 60 percent of which were estimated to be drug related. It jumped to 434 in 1989 and 483 in 1990. Even the mayor was arrested for drug possession. Marion Barry was a civil rights activist who transitioned to big-time politics. He gave the nomination speech for Jesse Jackson in 1984. But in 1988 he was caught buying crack from a former D.C. employee, Charles Lewis, at a Ramada Inn. A 1989 sting by the FBI and Metropolitan Police Department, with cooperation from Lewis, caught the mayor on video smoking crack at the Vista Hotel. Barry had served three terms running D.C. He ended up serving six months in a federal prison for his crack habit.

It was around this time that it was essentially determined on which side of the tracks Durant would exist. He would end up part of the struggle side. When Durant was about a year old, his father walked out. Wayne Pratt left Wanda a single mother with two baby boys. Wayne didn't go far. He was in the vicinity, working in D.C., hanging out in PG County, still in his same circles. He just didn't want to be the head of this particular household, leaving Wanda to assume that role.

"I felt like I was immature, selfish, I was young," Pratt told the *Washington Post* in a 2012 interview. "I didn't know what I was getting myself into."

So Wanda did what so many Black women have done: she made it happen. She also did what many other Black women have done: leaned on their own mothers.

Barbara Davis—one of sixteen children by Troy and Esther Durant, who migrated to the D.C. area from Sumter, South Carolina—was the life raft Wanda needed. Her home became the epicenter of Durant's life, tucked at the dead end of Quire Avenue, a nondescript four-block stretch in Capitol Heights. Positioned on a hill, only the top half of the house was visible from the entrance on Quire Ave. The front porch, covered in a carpet resembling a putting green, didn't have any steps, as it was level with the street. There was always a place to sit on the porch—a rocking chair, a worn couch—and the largest tree on the block, driven right through the center of the front yard like a stake, made for perpetual shade. The years and the weathering chipped away at the luster this single-family home once had. The banana-yellow vinyl siding didn't glow as much anymore against the brown trim of the windows. The white screen doors, gutters, and decorative rods holding up the roof of the porch were tinted with the grime of life. But this little house had character in its grooves. It had a soul, concocted by family arguments and Sunday dinners, by celebration, by death. It was the home base for the family. Where uncles and aunts and cousins and family friends could crash while they got on their feet. Where cousins played with each other. Where hard conversations were had and tears were shed. Where kids were schooled in banter by smooth talk and catchphrases dished from adults. Where emotional wounds and gaping issues were sutured with fervent prayers. Durant used to run down the hill on the side of the house, where the descending grass revealed the mint brick that made up the bottom half of the house.

This residence shaped Durant as much as any. It was a hub of his maternal family. Its comforts warmed his soul. Its shabbiness prompted his dreams. His grandmother's sister, Pearl, lived there, too. But before it was all that, it was refuge for his childhood while his mother got her bearings.

Wanda eventually landed a job at a post office about a ten-minute drive south near the Suitland Federal Center. She started by loading mailbags onto trucks, making her best effort to get her and the boys a place of their own. When she was at work, Barbara filled in, picking the boys up from school and making their peanut butter and jelly sandwiches. Durant also spent a lot of time with Aunt Pearl. They watched cartoons and movies together. She made his lunch sometimes and helped him with his homework.

Durant's formative years were shaped by these three women: his mother, his grandmother, his grandaunt. Three unique kinds of love. The unconditional love of a mother, the spoiling of a grandmother, the companionship of an aunt. It's why he had "Wanda" tattooed on his left pec, near his heart, and "Barbara" on his right. Aunt Pearl gets a pair of his signature shoes dedicated to her every year, often with a floral pattern as an ode to the robe she wore around the house.

Eventually, Wanda secured them their own apartment. The first one they moved into had no beds or furniture. Yet they were a joyous family of three. Durant would later call this one of his favorite memories, them hugging on the floor. In their minds, they'd made it. But not quite yet. They hopped around quite a bit in PG County. Often the money didn't stretch enough for all three to eat, and Wanda would go to bed hungry.

Durant and his brother were boys, so they needed to play. They needed to be around men. Wanda needed something for them to do after school, so she enrolled them in the Boys & Girls Club in Capitol Heights. At age seven, Durant was the tallest kid there. He played football first, then switched to basketball when the season ended.

During basketball season, a grandmother of Durant's teammate suggested he play for a man named Taras Brown. Everyone called him Stink. He was the coach of the PG Jaguars, an AAU team that practiced at the Seat Pleasant Activity Center. Wanda recognized the place. It wasn't far from where her mother lived. Once she was taking the boys for haircuts and came across the Center again, so she signed them up.

Durant was eight when he first visited the Center. He described his first day walking through the doors as like entering an amusement park. Kids everywhere, running around, sounds of fun bouncing off the walls. The pattering of feet. The squeaky yells. Kids were free to be kids there. That's when he met Charles Craig.

Known as "Big Chucky" or "Chucky," he worked with Stink on the basketball team. Craig became Durant's first coach and mentor. But he was also a real lifeline. He'd give Kevin and Tony money for snacks. He would pile them into his van and take them to the movies with other kids. He'd even take them to his mom's house for some home cooking. Craig always made sure the youth got home safely. Like most youngsters, young Durant didn't fully comprehend the aid he was getting from people like Craig.

Hindsight and maturity bring appreciation for the hard times. But a preadolescent tends to only feel the absence of comfort in his life. The peace that comes with a stable and consistent home, with a mother and a father working in unison—Durant noticed early on he didn't have that.

. . .

"We moved so many different places growing up," Durant said in his famous MVP speech. "It felt like a box. It felt like it was no getting out."

Even his grandmother's house represented the lack of stability in his life. Whenever he lived there, it was because life wasn't working according to plan. When he wasn't living there, it was a rest stop on his journey, wherever he was going, an always-available fortress. For all the love and life that happened in that house, it was also a reminder how he longed for a permanent tent and the traditional family structure to go with it. And even in that house, heartache would come.

When Durant was eleven, his aunt Pearl died. As detailed in an ESPN feature, the whole family was on Quire Avenue hanging out. Suddenly she started coughing up blood. It must have been terrifying for Kevin, but for the rest of the family it wasn't so shocking, as she was home on hospice care. Breast cancer had ravaged her, but she didn't want to spend her last days in a hospital. She wanted to be home.

"She didn't want to pass away anywhere else," Durant's older brother told the *Oklahoman*. "She wanted to be there because that's where all the memories that we had were. That's where everything started. That's the foundation of me and Kevin. We learned a lot of values in that house so it's very important."

When Aunt Pearl died, her body was cleaned and remained peacefully until the coroner arrived. Durant climbed in the bed next to her. He lay with her. He knew she was gone but he didn't really understand. It was as surreal as it was sad. He knew death came knocking. It had showed up at the doors of several in his neighborhood. He had heard tales of lives suddenly ripped away. But what was he supposed to do now that death touched his family, hovering over the house that had been a safe space? Imagine what crossed the mind of the eleven-year-old as he cuddled with the lifeless body of his grandaunt. This preteen now had two significant voids to walk around with: Wayne and Aunt Pearl.

That void explains why Durant spent so much time at the Center. After school, he would stop at his grandmother's house and then make the hike to Seat Pleasant. He'd walk across Faye Street and up Sultan Avenue, taking a shortcut through the parking lot of the Capitol Heights Metro Station. He'd cross East Capitol Street to get to Southern Avenue and walk the street parallel to the border of D.C. and Maryland. He'd pass the Watts Branch baseball field, now the home of the $14 million Marvin Gaye Recreation Center, and venture into D.C. territory by veering left up Sixty-Third Street. He was back in Maryland with a right on MLK, putting him two blocks from the beginning of Addison Road, on the corner of which is the Center, sunken just below street level.

On weekends and in the summer, Durant was there more than the employees. The gym opened at 10:00 a.m. and closed at 5:00 p.m. for a break. Then at 7:00 the evening hours would begin. This was the premium time for Durant, who enjoyed the night basketball leagues and advanced-level pickup games. But he didn't want to make the trip back to his grandmother's house during the two-hour closing window. So he found a spot behind a curtain and sprawled on what amounted to a yoga mat. He'd sleep those two hours away. If he couldn't sleep, he'd just lie there and think. Just about every day he spent at the Seat Pleasant Activity Center. Playing. Practicing. Escaping.

He didn't know it yet, but he was building the foundation of a Hall of Fame career. With a couple boys to run with, Charlie Bell and Devonte Young, he would become a bona fide basketball junkie. He ran up and down the court as if his problems were chasing him.

He took shot after shot, falling in love with the accomplishment of watching the ball go in, addicted to the swish of the net. Each shot made was a thrill, each bucket a victory. He stacked them up like cinder blocks, fortifying himself from the world.

At a Nike event in 2013, his mom told a story about him playing with a set of Hot Wheels. Every day he was playing with those cars, but not how they were meant to be enjoyed. He wasn't on the floor *vroom-vroom*ing with them like most boys. She couldn't tell what he was doing, so she asked. His answer: coming up with basketball plays.

Basketball gave him friends, purpose. It also became the common ground for him and his father when his dad returned to his life.

Durant remembers a story from his childhood, the kind of tale that paints a picture of the psychological impact an absentee father leaves. According to an interview in *GQ* in 2015, he was in the car headed home one day. Wanda was driving. Durant casually surveyed his surroundings as they eased into a light. He looked at the car next to theirs. In it he saw his father with some friends. His dad saw him and didn't say anything. He told his mom to look and pointed out the man whose face resembled his own. But Wanda had no interest in talking about it. First he had been abandoned by his father before he could understand he had one. Now he was fully aware who his father was, and that same person wouldn't even acknowledge him.

Pratt said his sons always wanted him around. Their eagerness for him to be in their lives compelled him to return. But the reconciliation wasn't smooth. Sometime after that moment at the intersection, Wayne started coming to Kevin's AAU games and middle school games, establishing a consistent presence. The easy conclusion was that Pratt returned because he knew Durant was a basketball prodigy. He must have heard about how his son was starting to look like a future star on the court, and Durant was already taller than all the other middle school kids. In fact, he was so tall, his coaches had to carry his birth certificate because opposing parents always thought he was older. Yet the NBA hype didn't really stick to Durant until high school. So the timing of Wayne's return preceded the prodigy years.

"I didn't think I would be in the NBA," Durant said of his childhood thoughts in his documentary. "I didn't know for sure. I didn't plan on anything else since I was, like, nine. I was humble enough to know it may not happen, but I was arrogant enough to be, like, 'I have no choice but to make it.' "

Either way, Wayne Pratt had a long road back into the lives of his sons after leaving them back in 1989. On top of that, Pratt had two other children, Rayvonne and Breana, while he was away. He was now a father of four children, working as a security officer at MedStar Health.

The pertinent question: Why would Durant allow him back? It would have been normal if his hurt feelings and young resolve had erected a steel wall around his heart. Many boys in his situation have sworn off their biological dads. The anger and the emptiness from being abandoned leaves a wound that doesn't always heal. But Durant's response tells a lot about him. He valued wholeness over hate. His desire for love, to appease the yearning he couldn't shake, overwhelmed whatever anger he had from his dad leaving in the first place. Durant had the chance to reunite with his father, and he took it.

"Kevin, he is a loving, generous, kind person," Wanda said in Durant's documentary. "He's the kind of person that believes that everyone is inherently good. Just how Kevin is."

Durant wasn't even in high school yet and he had already dealt with his fair share of trauma. The chance to have a father in his life had to be enticing. He got a dose of it initially. His dad started picking him up from school. Wayne and his boys would chill together and play video games. He would take them to eat before taking them home, winning them over with quality time and tasty grub. Durant didn't have many friends. But for about a year and a half he relished having a cool dad.

                              .   .   .

But then all that stopped. Wayne disappeared again.

"I was really hurt," Durant told *GQ*. "That was the first time I'd ever been hurt by anything. I'm always used to, like, keeping it inside, and it'd go away in a day. But I was like, 'Damn, man, so we can't play video games together no more? We can't laugh at jokes? We can't wrestle?' We would wrestle every day in the living room and shit. It was the coolest thing. And then, like, when he left, it was just like, 'Damn, we can't do all that stuff no more?' It's boring now. Because I'm by myself."

Nothing fills the void of a father in the heart of a young man. Durant did, however, have a couple of father figures in his life who tempered the emptiness. Big Chucky looked out for him, put wise words in his ear, and made sure he knew someone cared about him. His support and praise instilled confidence in Durant. It was Chucky who made Durant believe he was the best player on the floor. He would watch the NBA Draft with the players and tell Durant he couldn't wait until it was his turn to be drafted into the NBA. Chucky was good with all the kids, but he was noticeably closer to Durant, which gave the kid a sense of how special he was.

Taras "Stink" Brown became a godfather to Durant. He didn't put the ball in the kid's hands, but he sure put it in his heart. Stink taught him work ethic and discipline. He once even kicked Durant out of the Center and told him he couldn't come back. Durant ran home crying. Of course Stink let him back in, but the lesson about accountability was learned. Stink taught him teamwork and sacrifice.

"He was there when I wasn't there . . . ," Pratt told the *Washington Post*. "And I continually thank him for that, because he didn't have to do that. He did the things that most men wouldn't do; I thought that was very noble of him and [the] selflessness that he showed."

But even Chucky and Stink, as gracious and as committed as they were to Durant, couldn't replace the magnitude of his real father. A young man's identity is connected to his pops.

Absentee fathers were an issue in the African-American community in those days. According to the U.S. Census Bureau, in 1991, about two years after Pratt left, 46.7 percent of Black children were being raised by a mother in a single-parent household. The national average was 21.2 percent. The number of single moms in Black households jumped to 52.3 percent by 1996 but dropped down to 47.7 percent in 2001, which is around the time Wayne came back.

Studies have linked all kinds of issues to an absent father. According to the Census Bureau, children in father-absent homes are almost four times more likely to be poor. Research has linked fatherlessness to drug and alcohol abuse, and increased truancy and incarceration rates. But while Pratt once epitomized a common problem in his community, he ended up part of a trend that would take place over the next decade: he re-upped his bid to get back into the lives of the Durant boys, as Black men across the country did the same with their own children.

A 2013 Centers for Disease Control report, covering 2006 to 2010, revealed how African-American fathers were among the most involved in their children's lives, including fathers who didn't live with their children. For children ranging five years old to seventeen years old, Black fathers were more likely to take their children to and from activities several times a week, talk with children about what happened during their day, and help them with their homework. Undoubtedly, the push in the Black community to encourage fathers to handle their chief responsibility produced increased involvement. Then-Senator

Barack Obama encapsulated this popular message and movement with his Father's Day speech in 2008 imploring Black fathers to step up with lines like "We need fathers to realize that responsibility does not end at conception. We need them to realize that what makes you a man is not the ability to have a child—it's the courage to raise one."

Pratt's resolve to get back into the lives of his boys was emblematic of a cultural shift. That doesn't mean Pratt didn't have to work to reclaim his post. He said his approach was relentlessness. If they ever needed him somewhere, he was there. If they needed anything, he worked to provide it. And this time he didn't disappear.

There is profound messaging in a father clawing his way back. For a teenager like Tony or a rising teen like Durant, a father making an aggressive push to be part of his life was probably tough to resist. The formative years of a young man are largely a search for self-identity, confidence, and value. The desire to belong is strong; the need to be protected is real. These feelings have prompted many youngsters to turn to gangs. People like Chucky and Stink all over the country were dedicating their lives to address the sense of belonging and security at local rec centers, churches, and schools to keep youth out of gangs. Their love and consistency lured Durant away from the streets. But now he had his father fighting for him.

For a sentimental youngster like Durant, his dad's efforts had great value. Being pursued was as uplifting as being deserted had been damaging.

Pratt's presence didn't dramatically change their financial status. They were still a working-class family with little room for error. But Durant did not let the opportunity pass to have a dad. He also got a half-brother and half-sister in the process.

"It's never too late to be your kid's father; it's never too late," Pratt said. "You have to try, we all make mistakes. But, you have to get back in there and fight. These young men really need us."

2 | DMV HOOP

THE CEREMONY FOR OPENING NIGHT 2018 was over. NBA commissioner Adam Silver was in his seat. The Warriors had received their championship rings. The banner commemorating the 2017–18 title was unveiled and the introductions were completed. It was time for tip-off.

The Warriors' starters unzipped and peeled off their white hooded Nike jackets with black trim and gold accents, revealing their white home jerseys, and yanked off their all-black tear-away pants. Quinn Cook made his way to the scorer's table and stood near half-court. The third-year point guard brought his effective shooting off the bench for the Warriors, so his warm-ups weren't coming off yet. But he was getting in position to start the new season with a tradition.

Durant, before tip-off, embarked on a series of high-energy salutes as he does every game. Ball boys. Assistant coaches. Team security. Statisticians. Teammates on the bench. He gave low-fives to security personnel. He slapped hands with assistant athletic trainer Roger Sancho before the two embraced in a brief but emphatic hug. He did the same with Shaun Livingston, followed by a high-five for Andre Iguodala. Then Durant went down the line, one by one, slapping hands with all of the coaches on the bench. Then a pat on the chest for newcomer Alfonzo McKinnie. Then a hug for reserve big man Jonas Jerebko. At the end of the parade of daps, after Durant made his way from the baseline out toward half-court, Cook was waiting for him.

Durant and Cook have their own choreographed handshake, a series of hand slaps and movements they've got down to a science. Cook has a special place in Durant's pregame routine: right at the end of the line. That's because Cook was there with him at the beginning.

Cook is still amazed by it all. Not that the six-foot-two, 184-pound guard made it to the NBA. Not that he is playing for the world champions and has a ring to show for it. But that he gets to experience this with Durant, his big brother from his second family.

"It's crazy when you really think about it," Cook said. "How does it work out like this?"

This family, though, chose each other. They don't share blood, but they do share roots in the same soil. They are bonded by the same spirit. Nobody knows that better than Cook. Because not too long ago, he needed that family to get through the worst experience of his life. That family showed up in a way that lasts forever. When his father died in 2008, Durant and other basketball brothers-in-arms were there for Cook years before he made the NBA.

Up until then, Cook was one of the lucky ones, at least where he was from. He was born in Washington, D.C., where he lived until he was eight. The family moved to a suburban home in Largo, Maryland, in Prince George's County. They were a traditional nuclear family. Two parents, Ted and Janet. Two children, Quinn and his older sister, Kelsey. A dog. A little yard. His life didn't resemble the lives of his peers.

And Cook was super-close with his father.

The Cooks had multiple businesses. There was 4th and Goal Sports Bar and Grill in D.C., a fifteen-minute walk from the White House.

There was Pure Sunshine, a lemonade stand, and a deli called Talking Turkey, both in Union Station. His family ran a concession stand at Washington Redskins home games. Quinn happily wore his burgundy polo to sell chicken fingers and fries as part of his father's staff. He spent a lot of time rolling with his dad. When he wasn't in school or playing basketball, he was his old man's sidekick.

But something was going on with Ted's colon. In February of 2008 he had surgery to fix it. Complications during the surgery stopped oxygen from getting to his brain. He was on life support for two weeks.

On March 3, 2008, Ted Cook died. His boy was no longer a lucky one.

Losing his father put Cook in a dark place. His family lost its pillar. He lost his hero, his protector, his inspiration. The trauma made him even more connected with his peers. So many of the young Black boys in PG County were forced to go through their formative years without the example and guidance of their father. They lugged an emptiness through their teenage years and young adulthood. It's a life-altering burden, like a backpack of bricks they can't take off but are just expected to overcome. Fatherlessness was common enough among them to be considered normal. But with respect to all the father figures, big brothers, mentors, and coaches who step up in the lives of young men, the void of an absent dad is never filled. Now Cook had the void too.

He spent hours on the phone with Nolan Smith, a freshman guard at Duke. Cook was six years old when he met Smith. They were in Memphis, part of the same Amateur Athletic Union program, when Smith adopted Cook as his little brother. And when he lost his father, Smith was his first call. And Smith, who lost his father at six, knew the words to say.

Cook was held out of school for bereavement but didn't grieve alone. In addition to Smith, Victor Oladipo, who was Cook's teammate at DeMatha High School before becoming an All-Star for the Indiana Pacers, was pulled out of school also. He was with Cook in the gym, sweating out the grief, trying to focus on the rim instead of the crumbling of the Cook family empire.

Cook was fourteen years old and faced with being the man of his house. The hurt, the questions, the anger—they gnawed at him. It's hard to think straight when such darkness is burrowing a home inside. A year later he found himself in a bad place.

He was injured shortly after his father's death. A torn meniscus caused him to miss the whole summer of AAU ball. While his friends were playing, he was hanging out. He did what most fifteen-year-olds whose lives were falling apart do: rebel. Fight against what they know is right. Like so many, that landed Cook with "the wrong crowd."

"I was doing a lot of stuff that I shouldn't have been doing at that age," Cook said. "I caught myself. You know, you can make two choices. You can go this way or that way. And I kind of caught myself. But I had guys around me who never let me go that way."

Oladipo stayed in Cook's ear. So did Smith. Visiting his adopted big brother at Duke was an inspiration for Cook.

He had another big brother who inspired him in Durant.

When Durant played AAU ball for the PG Jaguars, Cook was on the younger team. They became friends as their games grew. Durant went on to Texas and the NBA. He was playing for the Seattle Super-Sonics when he got the news about Cook's father. Encouraging words from an NBA player are especially meaningful to a fourteen-year-old in despair.

Over the years Durant kept a line to Cook. With Durant as a mentor and brother figure, Cook's reason to stay on the right path was tangible.

When Cook was a freshman, getting little playing time at Duke, Durant sent him text messages telling him not to bury his head because body language is important. "Be a pro," Durant would tell him. In the summer of 2013, Durant invited Cook to come work out with him in Oklahoma City. The next year Durant won the MVP of the 2013–14 regular season. Cook helped lead Duke to the 2015 NCAA championship.

So Cook kept at it. And now he has made it in the NBA. And he's with his homeboy.

Cook is part of a rare community inside a unique culture. Every major city, every metropolis region, has a basketball fraternity. New York City. Los Angeles. Chicago. Atlanta. Pick one and there will be an impressive list of basketball alumni. There will be an anthology of stories about grimy courts, legendary games, and ballers who would have made it if life hadn't gotten in the way. One of the most underrated of these cultures is the DMV basketball fraternity. Durant is the unofficial president.

DMV stands for "D.C., Maryland, and Virginia." This region has a noteworthy alumni association. But hoop in this area also has its own signature style, a stamp on the players it produces. Making it even more special is the interconnectedness among the players, which functions like a brotherhood. They all have varying levels of success, but those levels don't dictate the relationships.

To understand Durant is to understand this basketball community in which he was reared and for which he is now chief ambassador. His game, his personality, his perspective—they were all shaped by this culture in the District of Columbia and its surroundings.

Getting addicted to hoop in the D.C. area does something to one's basketball DNA. Basketball in these parts comes with an unwritten code. Really, it's a value system. There is pretty much one way to be revered here, to garner the kind of love that all ballplayers in the neighborhood crave: get buckets.

In New York, basketball is about the ball handling. Dribbling with flair, embodying the arrogance of the area, has always been a surefire way to build a reputation in New York City. Because New Yorkers adore their point guards. From Tiny Archibald and Pee Wee Kirkland to Kenny Anderson and Stephon Marbury to Rafer Alston and Sebastian Telfair—they were basketball deities in New York because they were magicians. In Oakland the greatest currency is toughness, grinding out wins and never backing down. Bill Russell. Gary Payton. Jason Kidd. Antonio Davis. Damian Lillard. The style of play didn't matter; respect came with grit and resilience. In Chicago, explosiveness was premium. Maybe it was because they grew up on Michael Jordan. But leapers, speedsters, bangers—there is something physically imposing about Chicago hoopers. Isiah Thomas. Tim Hardaway. Ronnie Fields. Derrick Rose. Anthony Davis.

In the streets of D.C. and Maryland—even Virginia, which has produced the likes of Allen Iverson and Dell Curry—worth is connected to the ability to score. No matter how it looked or how it was accomplished, putting the ball in the basket has always been the gold standard.

"A lot of scorers come from our area," said Charlie Bell, Durant's childhood friend and current manager. "If you make it from our area, nine times out of ten you know how to put the ball in the hole. So that's really what the DMV about. Look at Kevin and Mike Beasley, Steve Francis—everybody's about getting a bucket from back home."

No matter your height, athleticism, age, or weight, to be considered good, to be chosen in pickup games, to be adored by the crowd, required being able to score. And because of that, skill was a requirement.

Pickup basketball, especially on blacktop, increases the difficulty of scoring. From physical and heated full-court games to every-man-for-himself, offense takes a certain savvy. Durant was raised in the era of streetball, when blacktop hoops reigned. This version of basketball was usually more gritty than pretty. The ability to handle the ball is a must at the highest levels. Even nonshooters become adept at shot making. Innovation and creativity are how the best distinguish themselves.

Of course, players from other areas could score. Getting buckets is a universal trait of great basketball players. But players from DMV seem born to do it. The most refined players from this area score with an effortlessness, an expertise groomed from years of practice. They aren't one-trick ponies with it, either. They score in a multiplicity of ways. They make tough shots seem monotonous. They have a knack so prominent, they tend to treat other parts of the game as irrelevant.

"You always want to have that bop to your game," says Jarrett Jack, a veteran NBA point guard from Fort Washington in PG County. "So I think, even if it wasn't natural, you worked on it. You couldn't really go to the park and just be a big dude. Because then you've got to wait for somebody to give you the ball. I think everybody wants to be able to manufacture their own shots. So you go out there and just work on your stuff. Say if you're in the park—you ain't gonna just work on jump hooks. You're going to get out there in the park and you're going to go put some moves together. And you're going to try to add some pieces to your game."

Back in middle school Durant was still all knees and elbows, a skinny kid with a Louisville haircut who hadn't fully lost his baby cheeks. He didn't have his father to show him how to shoot. He didn't develop and refine his skills at summer camps. Instead he played at Seat Pleasant every day, working on his game.

Durant started picking up skills immediately. He found touch early. The thrill of watching the ball go in the basket was like a sugar rush every time. He'd play contests with himself, seeing how many times he could make it in a row without touching the rim or how many shots he could make before the full-court game that was going on came rummaging back his way. Unbeknown to Durant, he was developing a skill that would make him a unique scorer in NBA history. And it was about to make his name ring out in his area.

. . .

It was the summer of 1999. Durant was ten years old, still weeks from his eleventh birthday. He was one of hundreds meeting up at RFK Stadium, former home of the Washington Redskins. The famous Hoop-It-Up 3-on-3 Tournament was going down in the parking lot. Hoop-It-Up was like the AAU tournament for the blacktop. It was the event that allowed players to build a reputation in their city and get some hardware to back up their trash talk, as winners received trophies and medals. Especially for those who couldn't afford to play on traveling teams or weren't interested in organized hoops, Hoop-It-Up was a veritable proving ground. This event wasn't about plays or coaching schemes, the shoes players wore or the newness of the ball. This was streetball, where a few screens and a makeshift ref were the only aids to one's skills.

Durant was too young to play officially. The youngest age division was for twelve-year-olds, and Hoop-It-Up required registration and payment. So Durant couldn't compete. But a few of the many courts erected in the football stadium's parking lot were reserved for unofficial pickup games. There were no age restrictions, just open run on blacktop courts that faced the entrance of the D.C. Armory.

So Durant's Hoop-It-Up experience came in a chaos of ballers. In the DMV, they play 33: every man for himself, first one to 33 points wins. It was like an inner-city basketball version of Royal Rumble. In this mass of hoopers, Durant stood out.

You want your name to spread like the flu in February? This was how you did it, by being seen making baskets. Rack them up until people started asking questions about who you were and where you were from, until they started whispering about what you were doing.

"I remember it like it was yesterday," said Michael Beasley, an NBA vet from D.C. who met Durant when he was nine. "KD went off for, like, 19 straight. Crossover, crossover, jump shot. Crossover, crossover, split two defenders, jump shot. At, like, eleven. And the guy on the mic was like, 'Who the fuck is this kid? Get this motherfucker an agent.' I'll never forget it."

Durant put together similar performances at the Center. Wednesday night was Teen Night. The gym would stay open late for teenagers to get in some open run. Some of the best players in the area would come through Seat Pleasant. Durant wasn't even a teen yet and he was dominating. That elongated right-to-left crossover, then crossover back to the right, worked every time. Losing on Teen Night meant a long wait to get back on the court. Durant rarely had to wait. Mostly because he won. But even when he lost, the waiting team would quickly add him to their squad.

Durant had another spot that didn't close. He and his brother Tony hit it up all the time. They called it the King Dome. It was about a fifteen-minute walk from the Seat Pleasant Activity Center up Addison Road. Once they crossed Sixty-Second Avenue, they were in Fairmont Heights, a town in PG County right above Seat Pleasant and hugging the Maryland-D.C. border. At the end of the walk, just before Addison curved into Sheriff Road, was Fairmont Heights Park, aka the King Dome.

This park was a five-minute walk from Melvin's Crabhouse, where the late Melvin Roberts put up a court and lights and hosted some legendary games, visited by the likes of Bernard King and Moses Malone. Greg "Mr. G." Sanders—a six-foot-six lefty shooter with seemingly unlimited range, who is St. Bonaventure's all-time leading scorer—is one of those local legends who worked, hung out, and played at Melvin's. But Roberts shut down the hoop games in the '80s and the local action moved to what Durant called the King Dome. The cars driving by on Sheriff Road would slow to a crawl or just stop and watch the hoopers.

Sometimes KD would go all day at the Center and then afterward head to the King Dome and play until midnight. He'd shoot by himself if he didn't feel like going home. That was where Durant honed his blacktop game. On that court, where the older kids played, Durant had to earn his time and make a name for himself.

"Only the strongest survive out there," Durant told reporters during a 2013 tour of the park when Nike launched his new shoe. "They didn't care who you were, how old you were. If you were on the court you were playing. And I was a skinny twelve-, thirteen-year-old out there playing with grown men sometimes. And they wouldn't take it easy on me. But that built toughness. I always wanted to win. I would lose so much out there but that just molded me into who I am today."

This was Durant learning the ropes in DMV basketball and just beginning his ascent as the pied piper of the region. He was molding the foundation for his Hall of Fame career by first being indoctrinated by the very culture for which he would become the face.

The list of basketball icons from D.C., Maryland, and Virginia is impressive. Elgin Baylor, Dave Bing, Adrian Dantley, Grant Hill, and David Robinson are all claimed by DMV. John Thompson Jr. is a coaching legend—scratch coaching; his prominence is too great to be qualified—from his days leading Georgetown and being a molder of young Black men. DeMatha High's Morgan Wooten was the first high school coach in the Hall of Fame. Red Auerbach started his coaching career at St. Albans High in D.C.

But even within the DMV circle is another fraternity, a brotherhood of inner-city hoops. This culture has bred Carmelo Anthony and Ty Lawson, Randolph Childress and Steve Francis. They follow in the lineage of Chicken Breast Lee, a six-foot-one playground legend who once grabbed a towel off the top of the backboard. And Will Jones, a Dunbar High star famous for talking trash while scoring relentlessly, who once dropped 54 in an NCAA playoff game.

DMV basketball doesn't have the regard that other basketball beds have gotten, but it has a worthy résumé. This area is full of legends, players with track records of great feats, memories of epic games in the sweltering heat before lit crowds. They all find their roots in the work of Dr. E. B. Henderson, known as the grandfather of Black basketball, who was inducted into the Basketball Hall of Fame in 2013.

Henderson was a product of D.C., save for a six-year stint in Pittsburgh, and was a standout student athlete at M Street High School in Northwest D.C. As outlined in a 2013 *Washington Post* article, he pitched for the baseball team, was an offensive lineman on the football team, ran track, and was also an honor roll student.

In 1904 he was the top-ranked graduate from Minor Normal School, the training ground for teachers in D.C.'s Black public schools. He studied basketball at Dudley Sargent's School of Physical Training at Harvard. This was connected to the YMCA in Springfield, Massachusetts, where the first basketball game was played in 1891. At Harvard, Henderson became the first Black man certified to teach physical education in public schools in the United States, which would become his life's mission.

The U.S. Supreme Court's "separate but equal" ruling in *Plessy v. Ferguson* in 1896 gave teeth to segregation. D.C. schools felt the burden. Blacks were barred from competing in the established athletic associations and barred from most facilities. And by 1910, well over a quarter of a million Blacks lived within a fifty-mile radius of the nation's capital. Henderson believed the density of the Black community was an impediment to physical education.

In 1906, Henderson was one of six visionaries to create the Interscholastic Athletic Association of the Middle States, a high school league of sorts for Black schools. By the end of 1908, Armstrong and M Street of D.C., Colored and Morgan Prep of Baltimore, Bates of Annapolis, and Howard of Wilmington were competing in the ISAA in football, baseball, track, and basketball for the "cultivation of a healthy social environment and worthy use of leisure through sports," as Henderson wrote in his 1913 manual, *Official Handbook, Interscholastic Athletic Association of the Middle States*.

Henderson also put on the first-known Blacks-only game in Washington, D.C., at True Reformers Hall in 1907, where a team of high schoolers beat Howard University. That prompted the start of the basketball league on Saturday nights at the hall. Then he created and starred on the Twelfth Street YMCA team. They won the 1909–10 Colored World Championships by beating the Alpha Club in New York on Christmas Day in 1910 at the Manhattan Casino. In 1912, after raising $25,000 for the national YMCA and having it matched by the Rockefeller Foundation, the Twelfth Street branch of the Metropolitan YMCA opened. Blacks had a place to play basketball in D.C. And so began the lineage that leads to Durant.

In his 1980 dissertation for Louisiana State University on the history of national basketball tournaments for Black high schools, Charles Thompson's research showed that first national tournament was won by Armstrong High in D.C. in 1929. At the Hampton Institute in Virginia, Armstrong—the first Black high school in the country to have a gymnasium—defeated Douglass High of Huntington, West Virginia.

The lineage grew and grew. In 1975, Stacy Robinson was named Parade All-American from Dunbar High. But before that, he dominated for three years at Crossland High. Rob, as they called him, was known for being an unstoppable playground legend. He grew up in Peppermill Village, a neighborhood on the opposite side of Seat Pleasant from the rec center where Durant learned the game.

This was the air Durant breathed, the spirit that possessed him. He and his friends would go watch games in the Urban Coalition basketball league and games at Dunbar High. They hit up Barry Farm in D.C., Kenner League of Georgetown. They saw local legends like Curt Smith, Lonnie Harrell, Lawrence Moten, and Victor Page. Durant was too young to see Walt "the Wizard" Williams before he made pro. But before Iverson's crossover became famous, all the kids who grew up in DMV were trying to emulate Moten's elbow-high, long, sweeping crossover and wearing high socks like Williams did.

Durant used to watch one baller in particular with awe. His name was Cortez Davis.

"You should've seen this guy," Durant said. "He was such a beast. I just knew he was going to the league."

A six-foot-eight superathlete, Davis was a load. About five years older than Durant, Davis looked like a grown man the way he imposed himself on the court.

Davis was a beast at Friendly High School, about fifteen miles southwest of Seat Pleasant. After getting grazed by a bullet in a local shooting, he transferred to a high school in Maine for his senior season. He did one more year at Laurinburg Institute, a prep school in North Carolina.

"One time we were playing at the University of Maryland," said Bryan Harrod, a Fort Washington product who played with Davis on the PG Jaguars AAU club and at Friendly High. "He was just so talented and lanky. He had glided from, like, two steps over the free-throw line and just dunked on this dude. I think that's when his stock went up from there. I think we was, like, in the tenth grade going into the eleventh-grade year. After that, he had almost every college team in the country on his lap."

Davis committed to play at Maryland and then Memphis before actually signing to play at Rutgers for the 2002–2003 season. He lasted a year in New Jersey before his basketball promise fizzled out. He never made the league, going unpicked after entering the 2004 NBA Draft. But he still made a contribution to DMV basketball if only by setting the bar for a future star in Durant.

This came at a time in Durant's life when physicality wasn't on his repertoire. He was tall for his age, but he was always rail-thin and lacking strength. And basketball where he roamed had a tendency to prey on weakness of any kind.

To understand Durant's basketball makeup is to understand the D.C. area when Durant was being reared. Violence was part of the ambiance. Being in the wrong place at the wrong time could be a life-threatening mistake. In the early '90s, D.C. was dubbed the murder capital of America with a homicide rate of 77.8 per 100,000 residents, the highest of any American city, per FBI data. A record 703 murders were committed in the Washington area in 1990—605 of them in D.C. and PG County—even as drug-related crimes started declining. Police in the areas, according to a 1991 *Washington Post* article, were concerned about the greed and rampant disrespect for life.

"In my personal conversations with young people who have been involved in violence, there is no remorse, there is not the first tear, there is no sense that this is wrong," Police Chief Isaac Fulwood Jr. told the *Post* after a drive-by shooting killed a six-year-old girl in D.C.

The District set a homicide record for four straight years from 1988 to 1991. By the time Durant's third birthday rolled around, D.C. was well on its way to a record 489 homicides in 1991. The murder rates started declining after it became a national issue and a priority in the area. But the decline was gradual, and the effects were still present in Durant's upbringing. PG County's record for murders was 158 in 1991 and dropped below triple digits in the late 1990s. But in 2002, the year Durant entered high school, the homicide count was back up to 137.

The D.C. area was no joke. Everyone walked around with their head on a swivel. Surviving required hardening. It was volatile and dangerous, characteristics that trickled from the drug game to the hoop game.

Poverty already demands a minimum standard of resolve. Deprivation attacks one's hope, dilutes ambition. Being challenged was inevitable; the only question was how severe and whether one could hold up. On top of that, leaving the house came with it a risk of harm. Death had a real and yet random presence in the 'hood. Call it desensitized or just brave, but kids in neighborhoods like Durant's had to make a conscious choice not to be deterred from living life. And neighborhood hoopers were especially brazen about not being deterred, trekking from turf to turf in search of competitive games. They did that knowing that leaving their own neighborhood often meant dropping the protection they had with their own. They did that knowing they would share the court with real thugs who had impulse control issues and things could go south quickly.

Durant was part of this hoop collective who chased the thrill of basketball into unsafe zones. And his own physical frailty made him an easy target for bullies.

On the basketball court, Durant was given the unflattering nickname "Cookie." As good as he was—and everybody knew he was good—he was still relatively feeble and couldn't power through the elbows and shoves, hip checks and swipes. He was physically inferior. So when they wanted to mess with him, talk trash to him, they called him "Cookie" because he crumbled with forceful contact.

Thinking back on those days, one of Durant's close friends— NaVorro Bowman, the veteran NFL linebacker who was a four-time All-Pro with the San Francisco 49ers—is still amazed that Durant ended up where he is now. Bowman grew up in District Heights, not far from the Pennbrooke Apartments, where Durant's family lived for a spell. Bowman starred at nearby Suitland High a few years after

Durant's brother went there. Bowman was one of those with Durant who followed their basketball jones all across PG County and D.C.

But back then, Durant wasn't the dominant player he has become in the NBA. When Durant came to the Warriors, Bowman started frequenting games at Oracle Arena to watch his childhood friend. They'd hang out together afterward. They'd be chilling, just like they did years ago, and Bowman would find himself shaking his head at how it had all turned out.

Not that he made pro but that Durant did, too.

"We used to go over [to] each other's house after school and shit," Bowman said. "And he made it to the NBA. That shit is wild. We all played. But as far as him outgrowing everybody and being able to handle the ball like that, I ain't gon' lie: I didn't see this coming."

When they were kids, Bowman was the local standout. He matured early physically. He would end up a six-foot, 242-pound chiseled machine with the speed of a sports car who starred at Penn State before going pro. But before that he was a dominant basketball player growing up in PG County. He was a physical point guard who defended with aggression and used his supreme athleticism to score with the best of them.

Durant had the skill and the height, but Bowman had the skill and the physique, which against teenagers made him a tough foe. Durant's father, after returning to his son's life, would get frustrated with Bowman because he didn't pass the ball enough when the two played together in middle school. But Bowman was a rock who could get where he wanted on the court. He was difficult to stop. He had the mentality and the body.

"I was that man! I'm trying to tell you," Bowman said with a grin as he rubbed his bare tattooed chest in the Oakland Raiders locker room.

In comparison, Durant was the opposite. Oddly enough, it worked to his advantage. Until his muscles grew, his mental toughness had to hold him up. His work ethic gave him the advantage his girth couldn't. Something about getting pushed around made him not want to get pushed around.

"He wasn't no punk or nothing," Jarrett Jack explained. "It wasn't that. He was just real skinny. What was he supposed to do? Wasn't nothing he could do but get stronger. The game, it's always about finding the edge, and with him you knew you could be physical with him. It was just something he had to deal with."

The answer for Durant wasn't to start a fight. No doubt, responding to elbows with fists was the natural reaction. But the real response by Durant, the one that would shape him forever, was to not be broken. He refused to fall apart mentally even though physically he might crumble. His retort wasn't to get mad. He wasn't the kind of hothead whose pride would prompt him to take the action off the court. He knew this wasn't the answer early on. His talent placed him in the athlete lane of inner-city life.

One of the unwritten codes of the 'hood is that people who are not in "the life"—those who didn't choose to participate in illicit activities—get a certain level of exemption. To be sure, everybody is under the umbrella of danger, and being in the wrong place at the wrong time has been the explanation for many untimely deaths. But the probability decreases for those who aren't in the life. That probability declines even more when one becomes known for having a special talent. Again, it doesn't mean harm can't touch them, especially if that talent inspires envy. But generally even the seediest of characters in the worst of neighborhoods allow for special individuals to play out their hopes for escape. That could be in music or sports or scholastic prowess. Either way, there is usually a recognition of the special talents in the 'hood and respect for their aspirations to something greater.

That offered Durant some peace, as the real thugs steered clear of the sports stars, even helped them out. He and other athletes had a certain type of immunity that allowed them to go from neighborhood to neighborhood to play ball. It also meant hoopers like Durant had to stay in their lanes. Being an athlete means just being an athlete, not doubling as a dealer or gangster. That's also why Durant laughs at the number of players in the NBA who claim to be so hard-core. He knows what it really means to be hard, what that looks like and what it entails. He saw it live. Many NBA players from rough neighborhoods enjoyed the same pass he received, and many aren't from regions nearly are as dangerous as D.C. and PG County.

The pass doesn't mean things can't and don't happen. Even Bryan Harrod, Cortez Davis's teammate, took three bullets in his arm while running away from an attempted robbery two months before his junior season.

One of the most well-known tragedies in the DMV is the story of James Board, one of Durant's childhood friends. They called him "Silent" because he was known on the court for quietly killing his opponents. For whatever reason, he never got the breaks, and, on December 29, 2012, was found with a bullet in his forehead. Durant wrote "RIP SILENT" on his Nikes when the Thunder visited Houston that night.

Things just go wrong sometimes, no matter what exemptions you have. Bad decisions at suboptimal times are enough to alter trajectories. The margin for error is thin, and talent isn't always a ticket out. It often must be combined with other elements: discipline, a level head, key breaks.

Durant was never confused about who he was or about his purpose. He didn't have a stint with a gang, didn't try to prove he was the hardest dude on the block. Durant wasn't about carrying guns or selling drugs. He was all about basketball. Most real DMV hoopers were. They weren't above hanging out and blazing some trees, playing video games and shooting their shots with the ladies. But basketball was the epicenter.

That was the spirit of DMV basketball: the love of the game trumped all else. The sport never got boring. They didn't get so distracted by the pursuit of other things that they wanted to pull away from the game.

"We went everywhere," said Beasley, who is in his eleventh season in the NBA. "We'd play basketball all day. That kept us out of the streets. But some of us still got into a little bit of trouble here and there. But it would have been way worse had we not had basketball, had we not had each other. Like, Kevin was probably one of the biggest influences in my life. Because Kevin always, like always, knew there was a better way to do things. Whether that be basketball, whether that be walking to school, Kevin always knew there was a right way to do things. And he always prided himself in doing things the right way."

DMV basketball made Durant tough in the truest sense. He couldn't much help being thin, but he could compensate with drive and heart—and skill. And Stink, his AAU coach, started working on those elements early.

During Durant's first few seasons with the PG Jaguars, Stink had him playing in the post. But when he got to middle school, he switched Durant to the wing. This required Durant ramping up his perimeter skills, a significant task that made for a rough winter. The ten-year-old Durant went through drill after drill—shooting, passing, dribbling—often by himself in the Seat Pleasant gym. He hated it, but he loved it. That was when he got the quote that has since been etched on his soul:

Hard work beats talent when talent fails to work hard.

Stink made Durant write that hundreds of times on a piece of notebook paper. He even prohibited Durant from playing pickup for a while: Stink saw it as a way to develop bad habits. And Durant, who was honing his shot and his handles, couldn't afford to get sidetracked or lean on old tricks. So while his homies were running full-court games at the Center, Durant was doing workout drills and practicing his shooting. This was also when Brown introduced Durant to "the Hill."

On a random street in Fairmont Heights is where Durant's determination got the training it needed. Coming up Addison Road, two blocks before the King Dome, was L Street. It zigged a bit, past the Sylvan Vista Baptist Church and continued east toward the Cedar Heights Community Center. But when L Street got to Balmsamtree Drive, it rose sharply. It's a mile between Balmsamtree Drive and Cedar Heights Drive, and it arches to a peak high enough to see downtown D.C. on the horizon. Durant would run to the top of the hill and backpedal down. Up the hill again, backpedal down.

When Stink wasn't drilling him, Durant's mother would take him to the hill. Wanda said she would sit in her car and read while her youngest son crested the hill twenty-five times. And if she wanted more quiet time, she'd make him do another set of twenty-five.

Stink estimates Durant ran that hill over a thousand times between ages thirteen and eighteen.

"I knew that it would make me better," Durant told a throng of reporters from the U.S. and China who visited his neighborhood in 2013. "I really just did anything that he told me to do. I had to if I wanted to get better. I hated it at the time, but I knew it would make me better in the long run. It built up that work ethic and that discipline, and it's a big reason why I'm here today."

Durant never actually got the Bowman physique. But he developed that leathery toughness that makes DMV proud. This is the blood that courses through him now, the clay from which he was molded. And now it's in him, woven into his genetic code. It was home that pushed him to the brink, which built his confidence when he didn't break. It was home that tried him, broke him down, challenged his fortitude until it measured up.

That's why, even when Durant turned pro, he kept a steady presence in D.C. and PG County. He had to return to the quarry from which he was chiseled, to bring his refined game back to the rough courts that made him. This was how he paid homage. He wasn't just refusing to forget where he came from. Durant refused to let where he came from forget him. In the process, he wasn't just giving back to a community but elevating one.

He probably didn't even do it intentionally, but he validated DMV basketball. His presence made basketball in the area special. Sure, he was on hand to offer advice, donate funds, and lend his name for promo. But he was also living, breathing, tangible evidence of what PG County could produce. He wasn't alone but he was reaching the highest heights, and was clearly the most special of the region's players.

They got to see him and touch him, to play with him and against him. Cook. Oladipo. Markelle Fultz. Many professional players make appearances on the playground here and there. But Durant lived on the playgrounds. When his season ended in the NBA, his off-season began on the blacktop. Durant, Bowman, and others used to watch games at the Goodman League at Barry Farm Recreation Center in D.C. as kids. Durant couldn't wait to dominate the summer pro-am staple. He spent his summers in high school playing at Barry Farm, right across the Anacostia River from the Navy Yard. He kept that tradition going even while he was an All-Star for the Oklahoma City Thunder. Before the bleachers were added and the sponsorships draped the fence, Durant was at Barry Farm draining pull-up jumpers. This was his rite of passage: to make the NBA and come back to fulfill his destiny as a local legend.

These blacktop moments validated Durant nearly as much as the fame and the scoring titles he was racking up in the NBA. Because this was how he fought back. Along with the millions of dollars, winning these hypercompetitive quests for the rawest of supremacy was also his reward for the resolve and work ethic he showed.

How else does a young man shackled by poverty rage against the machine? What does he do with the frustration, the angst—the pain— that lives inside him through preadolescence, the teenage years, and young adulthood? A young man needs to fight, to release that aggression built up from a life of struggle, break down the wall of insecurity hoisted by circumstance and failure.

Durant wasn't going to fight with fists or guns and squander his potential. He wasn't going to drown away the agony with hard drugs. He fought on the court. That was where he could kill without being a killer. That was where he could serve without being a dealer. On the court he was free to be a monster because off the court he couldn't be a gangster. Day after day, on court after court, Durant treated his defenders like they were the embodiment of the life that attacked him so relentlessly. He took back his confidence, his future.

This is the core of Durant, his basketball soul. It was molded and infused by and for DMV.

3 | BECOMING A PHENOM

BASKETBALL FANS FLOCK TO THE ANNUAL McDonald's All-American Basketball Games to see the best high school players in the country. A future star is likely among this crop. Of course, those attending the game at San Diego State in 2006 had little idea who it would be. If they had to guess, most would've probably predicted seven-foot-one center Greg Oden, headed to Ohio State, had the brightest future of the bunch. By the time the game was over, it was clear all were treated to a preview of an NBA star in the making named Kevin Durant.

Jarrett Jack was watching the game on ESPN in the Portland Trail Blazers' training room with Kaleb Canales, Portland's video coordinator, and rookie forward Martell Webster.

"Yo, my man is playing the McDonald's game," Jack said, recalling his conversation from 2006. "He is the best player in the country. He's going to be the rookie of the year. He's nice. Like *nice.*"

Jack had been convinced Durant was going to the NBA since Durant was about fourteen. Jack, one of the old heads from PG County, already knew about Durant's perimeter skills. But once he had his growth spurt, giving him the height scouts coveted, Durant had what he needed to overcome being so slim. Jack was certain NBA trainers could put some weight and strength on Durant.

When Jack made his proclamation, Durant was still six months shy of his eighteenth birthday. He was listed at six-foot-nine, 205 pounds, for the McDonald's All-American Game. He could play. But anointing him NBA Rookie of the Year before he even played a game of college ball?

"For real? He's that good?" Canales asked with skepticism.

"Kaleb," Jack said, doubling down on his prophecy, "lights out. He's an All-Star. Easy."

If anybody knew how lofty of a measure that is for a young player, it was Webster. He was a ballyhooed prospect who had made the jump from high school to pro. He had experienced firsthand the pressure of NBA expectations. He held up underneath the weight of his hype but he wasn't Rookie of the Year. That went to Chris Paul, who played three years at Wake Forest.

"He's good, man, but I don't know," Webster said while watching Durant. "You think he's good like that? I don't know if he's like that."

Jack didn't tone it down or even try to qualify his projection.

"It's not even debatable," Jack said.

Durant lived up to Jack's prophecy. He scored a game-high 25 points to go with five rebounds, four assists, and two steals. He was the best player on the floor, and the two rosters had no shortage of talent. Of the twenty-four players on both rosters, twenty made it to the NBA; seventeen were drafted in the first round. The Lopez twins, Brook and Robin, D. J. Augustin, Wayne Ellington, and Thaddeus Young are all still playing in the league. While Durant became the biggest star from the West squad, the East featured Mike Conley Jr., who went on to become an All-Star point guard and is the face of the Memphis Grizzlies franchise.

None of them shined like Durant, who wore No. 3. He shared co-MVP honors with Chase Budinger, who was in his hometown, but the display Durant put on made him the undisputed most outstanding talent.

He made ten of his seventeen shots in the game. His collection of baskets illustrated the versatility of his offensive arsenal. He had four dunks, all of them coming in transition, showing off his ability to run the floor, be a slasher, and finish strong at the rim. He also knocked down two 3-pointers, a nod to his range. The McDonald's All-American game is more like an All-Star game, more free-flowing and playground-like than a typical game. Still, Durant came off screens and hit two midrange jumpers, both in half-court sets. He also had a driving layup he created off the dribble and an offensive rebound he put back in traffic.

Durant became a player to watch on the high school circuit while he was at Oak Hill Academy. After this McDonald's showing, he was now among the ranks of incoming college stars and future NBA prospects. He was officially a phenom.

· · ·

The KD 2, Durant's second signature shoe, was the release that legitimized his line. It was a bit lower up the ankle than the high tops he had for KD 1. It also featured a strap over the middle of the shoe, tightening the feel around the foot. It helped that Durant was en route to his first scoring title. He finished the season averaging 30.1 points per game, a nearly 5-point boost on his average from the previous season. He also led the Thunder to the postseason for the first time.

Toward the end of that season, Nike announced the release of a new color scheme for his KD 2 shoe. The sole with Nike's Zoom technology was all white. The strap was also white, with KD's logo in black.

The upper portion of the shoe was black leather. The Swoosh and the accents were . . . purple and gold? Why was Durant releasing a pair of shoes in Los Angeles Lakers colors?

The shoes featured purple and gold, but they weren't repping the Lakers. Those were the colors of Durant's first AAU team. The shoes—coincidentally released a day after the Lakers eliminated the Thunder from the first round of the playoffs—honored the team that got Durant's hoop dreams started in earnest. They were called the Nike KD 2 "PG Jaguars."

Those shoes celebrated the beginning of the journey for Durant. His route to phenomenon status was as unique as his game. Basketball became a serious part of his life during his preadolescent years, starting with his time on the Jaguars. But at that age, Durant first learned a vital lesson while playing middle school ball.

He was on the team at Drew-Freeman Middle School in Suitland-Silver Hill, Maryland. His dad was back in his life then and NaVorro Bowman was his teammate. Oddly enough, Durant back then was always hesitant to shoot. Bowman would have to urge Durant to let it fly, break out of his passive shell.

"And at a young age," Durant told the Associated Press, "NaVorro being such a leader that he is, he knew that I had some pretty good talent at that age and he just told me, 'Go out there and just play.' As a kid, you need that, you want that validation from your teammates. Especially starting off early when I started to take basketball really, really serious. Just a couple words from him meant a lot."

This transition to the perimeter, and the lessons on aggressiveness from Bowman, were critical, because the Jaguars had two other players who were also big: Chris Braswell and Michael Beasley, both already tall and athletic. Stink needed somebody to play on the perimeter, as he already had two inside players.

Braswell wound up a six-foot-nine forward who committed to

Georgetown before switching to UNC Charlotte. Beasley became a six-foot-ten forward who starred at Kansas State and was drafted No. 2 overall in 2008. Durant ended up six-foot-nine, 225 pounds by the time he landed at Texas. None of them had gone through their growth spurt yet when they were together on the Jaguars, but they were physical marvels for their age group. Together, the trio was ridiculous.

Once, they beat a team from New York 98–7. The Jaguars used a pressing defense that for most twelve-and-under teams had to feel like dribbling through an Iowa cornfield.

"You see how long Kevin's arms are now?" Brice Plebani, who traveled from affluent Montgomery County to play with the PG Jaguars and is still friends with Durant, told *Deadspin* in a 2014 interview. "They were just as long in middle school. No 12-year-old is going to throw over Kevin Durant."

The Jaguars traveled the land during the summers, blitzing teams with their combination of physical prowess and skills, racking up trophies and winning championships.

In August 2001, the Jaguars won their second consecutive Youth Basketball of America Tournament (YBOA). Led by 22 points from Carl Scott III, the tournament MVP, the twelve-and-under team from Prince George's County demolished the Titans from Temple, Florida, 75–46 in Orlando.

Over a three-year span, which for Durant was at ages nine, ten, and eleven, the Jaguars amassed a record of 123-9 overall with seventeen tournament championships. In the YBOA national tournament during that three-year span, they were 20-1 with two championships. Durant scored 16 in the second half of the 2001 title game and won the Mr. Hustle Award. He was about seven weeks from his twelfth birthday but he was now sure about what he wanted to do with his life. When he returned home from the tournament, he revealed to his mother that the NBA was officially his dream.

At this point, though, Durant was still more potential than prodigy. He was tall for his age, standing six-foot-three by the time he was fourteen, tall enough to be teased often and make him self-conscious. His mother would ask teachers to put him at the ends of lines so he wouldn't stand out so much. Durant did have nice touch with the ball and he knew how to move on the court. He was already figuring out angles and how to use his length to his advantage.

His body, however, prevented him from dominating. That, of course, prompted Durant to build up his skill. Because he had the bug, for sure. He treated basketball like a job, working out for several hours a day. In the winter he played for Drew-Freeman. He would go from practice at school to Seat Pleasant and practice more.

His father, Wayne Pratt—now firmly back in KD's life—saw it in the winter of 2001, months after Durant was named Mr. Hustle and had his breakout second-half performance. He watched his son play a middle school game. He and NaVorro Bowman were eighth graders.

"That's when I first knew he was a special basketball player," Pratt told *The Undefeated*.

Durant eventually leveled up to the D.C. Blue Devils when he was fourteen, a select AAU team in the nation's capital. The Jaguars squad that dominated was split up, a decision by Stink not to hold the boys back from greater competition.

Beasley switched over to the D.C. Assault, a popular AAU club run by a well-known supporter of local athletes named Curtis Malone. Bowman played for the D.C. Assault, too. So did Nolan Smith, who went on to Duke.

Durant, heeding the advice of his father and others, stayed away from the Assault. Stink recommended him for the Blue Devils. In 2014, according to the *Washington Post*, Malone, cofounder of the Assault, was sentenced to one hundred months in federal prison for pleading guilty to distributing large amounts of cocaine and heroin.

Durant didn't make the Blue Devils' top team to start. He didn't even start for the B team. He came off the bench, playing shooting guard and small forward, for the team that fed into the traveling squad.

"When we first started, he wasn't that good," Richard Wyatt Jr., who played with Durant at Seat Pleasant, told the *Gazette*, a PG County–area community newspaper, in 2007. "He had to work at it. Everything you see in Kevin is because of his hard work. He lived in the gym."

Hard work beats talent when talent fails to work hard.

Durant got his feet wet in the faster pace of the higher age group. He started his high school life at Suitland High with Bowman, the same nearby public school his older brother, Tony, attended. But Charlie Bell, Durant's childhood friend, orchestrated a workout for Durant in front of Trevor Brown, the coach at National Christian Academy. Durant switched to the private high school in time for basketball season.

He started on junior varsity at National Christian. It didn't take him long to compel coach Brown to do what he usually didn't: put a freshman on varsity. The pieces were coming together in his game. And he was getting taller.

Durant became one with the maroon rubber court at National Christian. And when he was done working on his game at the high school, he found a ride for the twenty-minute drive to Seat Pleasant for more hoop. When he returned to the Blue Devils in the summer of 2003, he had sprouted to six-foot-seven. His height and work ethic started producing an impactful player.

One story, revealed by the *Austin American-Statesman*, has Durant playing in Virginia with the Blue Devils. He was struggling. His mother tracked down the coach at halftime and gave him explicit permission to light a fire in her son.

" 'You need to get in his ass,' " Blue Devils coach Rob Jackson said, recalling Wanda's message. " 'You coach my son.' "

When Durant told his mother he wanted basketball to be his life, he wasn't playing. He was all in. This was his passion, his escape, his fun, his career.

He returned to National Christian for his sophomore season ready to dominate.

Early in the 2003–04 season, Durant played with his high school in a then-annual event called the War on the Shore. This random tournament would change Durant's life.

Each year some of the best high school basketball programs in the country would travel to Milford, Delaware, to take part in this premier tournament. Russell Springmann was there scouting for the University of Texas, where he was an assistant. Like most scouts, he spent this late-November weekend getting a good look at Dorell Wright. The Los Angeles product had just come off a dominant AAU season in the spring of 2003 and put himself on the map. Instead of entering the 2003 draft, the same class as LeBron James, Wright did a fifth season at South Kent School, a private boarding school in Connecticut. At six-foot-seven, he was an exceptional athlete who was unstoppable on the open court, easily a five-star recruit for the class of 2004. Springmann had eyes for small forwards and big guards with the skills to make plays. So imagine how they lit up when he saw a six-foot-eight sophomore smoothly drill a corner 3-pointer.

"I didn't see much of the game, to tell you the truth," Springmann told the *Austin American-Statesman*. "But that was the one thing that stood out."

That sophomore was Durant. It was early in his breakout season at National Christian Academy, so he wasn't on Springmann's radar yet. But the Texas scout watched Durant more closely, noticing his versatility, how he played the perimeter on offense and in the paint on defense. He took notes, highlighting his ability to handle and shoot. He also wrote down Durant's skinny frame, lack of strength, and sketchy shot selection. But he was a sophomore and infinitely intriguing. Durant now had a player profile in the University of Texas recruiting portfolio.

Springmann was from Silver Spring, not quite around the way—about ten miles northwest from Durant's stomping grounds, and a zero or two more on the median income. But Springmann is DMV, so he understood what Durant had pumping through his veins. He knew the area, played in the area, and still had connections. He saw beyond the skin and bones. He saw Durant the center, Durant the guard, Durant the forward. He saw Durant's drive. His talent. His heart. He saw Durant before Duke and Connecticut and Kentucky and North Carolina did, and perhaps before Durant even saw himself. And what Springmann saw was a boy with greatness dripping from his baggy jersey. He called Durant's high school coach at National and started the recruiting process. It didn't take long for the offer to come.

There was no way Durant, who'd just turned fifteen about two months before Springmann first saw him, could know what was happening, how the stars were aligning to orchestrate his future. This turned out to be a crucial tournament, because Springmann got in the door first. That would pay off big for the Longhorns.

National Christian made school history that season with a 27-3 record. For seven years Durant had poured himself into basketball—or perhaps, more accurately, poured basketball into himself. The evidence was starting to show.

Abdulai Jalloh was the star at National Christian that season. He was the six-foot senior point guard who would end the season named First Team All-Metro. Future NBA players Jeff Green, a senior at Northwestern High, and Sam Young, a senior at Friendly, were also First Team All-Metro. The Player of the Year was a six-foot-nine senior forward from Archbishop Spalding High named Rudy Gay. And on the list of honorable mentions was Durant. He landed outside of the twenty-five players who made All-Metro, including Georgetown Prep senior center Roy Hibbert and Bishop McNamara sophomore point guard Ty Lawson, both of whom made it to the NBA. But in his sophomore year Durant made sure there was no question that he was the future. He was the reason National Christian's makeshift gym, converted from a sanctuary, was at its seating capacity of five hundred people practically every game. Fans had to find a spot on the stage once the seats were gone. Durant played center on defense because he was the tallest. On offense, he played on the wing because he was so skilled. The letters from colleges recruiting him were rolling in.

When the high school season ended, he returned to the D.C. Blue Devils. That summer between his sophomore and junior years of high school, Durant was on the traveling team. He was becoming a beast.

Their AAU team played in a 2004 Memorial Day weekend tournament in New Orleans. They split the four games they played. One of their losses was to the Georgia Stars squad that featured future NBA sharpshooter Lou Williams. Durant averaged 18 points and eleven rebounds.

"As he gets stronger and more mature physically he can really be great," Blue Devils coach Rob Jackson said in a 2004 article on the Maryland Varsity recruiting site. "He more than held his own, inside and outside, against the best competition in New Orleans."

The NBA was becoming less of a pipe dream and more of a possibility. And Durant felt the potential while visiting the gym of Oak Hill Academy, the next step in his rise as a phenom.

Mouth of Wilson is an unincorporated Virginia city on the North Carolina border. The woodlands from the Blue Ridge Mountains spill down into the city, which got its name from the location where Wilson Creek feeds into the New River. The central hub of Mouth of Wilson is a 240-acre campus, an intimate collection of brick buildings spread out on landscaped grass peppered with trees. Oak Hill Academy is a Baptist-affiliated coed boarding school with a mission of pulling the best out of unmotivated and struggling students. It's a second-chance high school, a sanctuary for harnessing untapped potential. It is also a haven for hoopers who need to get their academics together so they can play college ball. Over the years, the prominence of the basketball program and it's gaudy alumni list have made it a go-to spot for players to get exposure, which helps them land scholarships and get on the radar of NBA scouts.

Before his junior year of high school, Durant visited Oak Hill Academy with Lawson and Jackson, his D.C. Blue Devils coach. It's a six-hour drive from where Durant's life was centered, yet closer to the dream he harnessed. In 2001–2002, Carmelo Anthony played on the same floor where Durant stood. Anthony came to Mouth of Wilson to get his grades up and prep for the ACT college admission test, which he would need to go to Syracuse. Between the time he left Oak Hill and Durant's visit, Anthony won a national championship, was named first-team All-Rookie with the Denver Nuggets, and joined LeBron James as one of the top young stars in the NBA.

Oak Hill offered Durant the kind of visibility and competition he wanted. The program played nationally televised games and traveled the nation to face the best teams. Durant was coming into his own as a star prospect. This would be his chance to measure himself against the best in the country. And if he balled, with the exploding popularity of high school hoops, everyone would know. This was the benefit of all the obsessive work he put in, the reward for the convergence of his skill and height. He was becoming more and more a coveted commodity.

During his visit, Durant worked out with Josh Smith, who had just come off leading Oak Hill to a 38-0 season (along with point guard

Rajon Rondo). Durant was fifteen years old at the time and Smith was about to be the Atlanta Hawks first-round pick straight out of high school. During the workout, Durant was holding his own against Smith, a spectacular athlete who was physically superior.

Durant ended up making the switch for his junior season. Lawson joined him at Oak Hill, leaving Bishop McNamara.

"It's in the middle of nowhere, first off," Durant told ESPN in a 2009 interview. "It's right dead-center in a bunch of woods. But it was great exposure. We played on ESPN three times, went to the biggest tournaments in the country, had the best coaches and got to play with the best players. It's good for your game. Like I said, it's in the middle of nowhere, so all you can do is play basketball and go to school."

The Oak Hill Warriors were in Hillsboro, Oregon, about fifteen miles west of Portland, in December of 2004. This is one of the perks of playing at a prominent high school such as Oak Hill, whose program offers the opportunity to galavant across the nation. Durant was still new to the national scene. But he was six-foot-nine and 190 pounds, so the expectation was for him to exist in the paint. But at the Les Schwab Invitational, Durant let everyone know those expectations were misguided. He handled the ball on the perimeter, taking players off the dribble and pulling up from three.

"At that point no one knew he was a perimeter player," Oak Hill coach Steve Smith told ESPN. "He played a face-up [power forward] for us and no one knew him to make threes. It's funny because now that's what he does."

Durant made another important acquaintance while attending Oak Hill. In 2005 he was approached by Alan Stein, a youth basketball coach from DMV who was trying to make a name for himself as a strength and conditioning coach. He had been working with Montrose Christian basketball teams since 2003 but was doing so as a volunteer. When Stein saw Durant play, he just had to approach the sixteen-year-old.

He told Durant he had all the tools. His game had no ceiling. But if he were to ever maximize that potential, he had to work on his body. It was more than just being skinny. Durant was weak on the court. He could get pushed around, be moved off his spot. He had a vulnerability opponents could go after, a red flag that could make scouts doubt him. He made Durant an offer: one workout. If Durant didn't like it, he would never hear from Stein again.

Durant took him up on that offer. Stein tortured him through the hour-and-a-half session, which didn't feature any dribbling, shooting, or skill work. They worked on his core and his conditioning. They lifted weights and did other resistance work.

"After about 90 minutes," Stein, now at DeMatha High, told the *Oklahoman* in 2013, "he lay there just absolutely exhausted and spent and I said, 'Hey, did you have fun?' And he looked at me dead serious and said, 'No, that wasn't fun. But I know that's what I need to do to get to the next level, so when can we meet again?' That was really when it struck me how mature he was. Because most 16-year-olds don't do things that they don't like to do."

Durant had a new trainer. Stein would drive an hour to work with his new prodigy.

Durant led Oak Hill with 19.6 points and 8.8 rebounds per game that season, both team highs. His father could be heard screaming "Green Room!" from the bleachers, a reference to the waiting area for expected top selections at the NBA Draft. Durant, per *The Undefeated*, pleaded with his father to stop shouting that and embarrassing him. But his dad wasn't wrong. Durant became a Parade All-American after his junior season, named to the second team along with his Oak Hill teammate Jamont Gordon and sophomore phenom O. J. Mayo.

The only juniors to make first team were Greg Oden out of Indiana and Brandan Wright out of Tennessee.

Durant's game was now infused with confidence as he rejoined the D.C. Blue Devils for the AAU season. In April 2005, he lit up the Boo Williams Invitational in Hampton, Virginia, a tournament that featured dozens of the nation's best players, including Dallas' Darrell Arthur, Seattle's Spencer Hawes, and Portland's Kevin Love. Durant and Lawson torched Team Texas—featuring Arthur, the No. 4 ranked player in the country—for a combined 69 points. Durant had 20 points in the first half with five 3-pointers as the Blue Devils built a big lead. Every time Texas would mount a comeback, Durant would silence it.

In life, trauma had a way of mounting a comeback, too. Durant kept having to figure out a way to silence it and not succumb to it. It struck again his junior year while he was at Oak Hill.

On April 29, 2005, according to an extensive report by the *New York Times*, Charles Craig was at a strip mall off Laurel Bowie Road in Laurel, Maryland. It's about twenty minutes up the Baltimore-Washington Parkway from the Seat Pleasant Activity Center where Craig worked. He was at a bar with his two younger brothers and some friends. It was called J's Sports Café. Friday night had bled into Saturday as they hung out together over drinks. Last call was at 2:00 a.m. and the scores of people there took the party outside. It was raining that night. Those who didn't hustle to their cars finished the conversation in front of the bar, in view of the security cameras of A-1 Pawn.

A fight broke out as some woman started hitting a man. It escalated into a street fight involving several people. Craig never got involved in the fight. His friends held him out of the commotion. But he was a large man, which was why he was known at the Center as Big Chucky, and he was wearing a bright yellow polo shirt. He stood out amid the chaos.

The fight eventually died down and the crowd dispersed. Craig left, too. According to the police report, a man walked up behind Craig as he was walking to his car and shot him four times. The man who shot Craig was shirtless, having lost it in the fight, and was later identified as Terrell Bush. He was arrested and charged with first-degree murder.

Durant was in Mouth of Wilson when the news delivered a blow that crushed his spirit. His initial shock gave way to a heaviness on his heart. He had lost his coach. He had lost his friend. He had lost his father figure, his male role model. Big Chucky had believed in Durant. He had supported him, encouraged him, pushed him. And now he was gone.

"He's a person that died for no reason," Durant said back in 2010.

Durant was sixteen years old. This was the second death to hit so close to home. Life just kept gut punching him, leaving him with emotional scars that didn't really heal. Durant just had to learn how to press on. He had no other choice, really, because the only other option was to give in, to be consumed by the loss and abandonment. So he buried this, too, behind his passion for basketball, underneath his hunger. Talent trumps trauma. Potential overpowers pain. It just had to.

Some three months later, he was on the road with the Blue Devils. Durant shined the brightest in a game against Athletes First out of Oklahoma, which featured Blake Griffin and future NFL quarterback Sam Bradford. Years before Griffin became a dunk god in the NBA, soaring for highlight-reel jams and catching lobs, he was dunked on by Durant. Early in the game, Durant caught a baseline pass and flushed it with two hands over Griffin's outstretched arm. Durant scored a game-high 29 points as the Blue Devils won.

"I used to make sure I watched his games," said Mike Conley Jr., who played with Oden on the Indianapolis-based AAU team Spiece Indy Heat. "If we were at a tournament and their team was playing, we were watching. It was just something you didn't see, someone so tall and so skilled."

In the summer before his senior season of high school, Durant had given his college commitment, so he didn't need to stay at Oak Hill, some 350 miles away from home. He wanted to spend his last year of high school closer to his roots. Another transfer, a third high school in three years, was a small price to pay. And he had the added benefit of going to the school where his trainer worked.

So Durant switched again. This time he went to Rockville, Maryland, in affluent Montgomery County.

Montrose Christian rose to No. 1 in the country in 2003. Led by Stu Vetter, renowned for building dominant high school teams, the small private school was a powerhouse that had just landed the new face of its program. As for Durant, he got to come home and be around family. The people he had grown up with, who had helped mold him, could watch him in his new skin as a hot-shot prospect.

It took two trains to get to school in the morning. But Durant used to show up for the early workouts with player development coach David Adkins.

"A lot of times, we'd play one-on-one and he used to bust our ass," Greivis Vásquez, who played with Durant at Montrose before going to Maryland and then to the NBA, told Yahoo! Sports. "And we kept playing and he knew we were going to fight back and he liked that. That got us better."

Sometimes Durant didn't have money for the train. He would sometimes get a break from the commute by staying with teammate Taishi Ito, a Japanese-born point guard who lived nearby. After school, they were regulars at Chipotle.

They went to the movies, hit the nearby mall. Durant would sign autographs, all the while saying he didn't understand why they wanted his signature.

"Some nights, we just talked forever about basketball, girls, life," Ito once said.

Durant created moments on the court, too. On March 4, 2006, three days after the McDonald's All-American game in San Diego, two private schools with elite basketball programs were facing off at a public school in D.C. Durant and Montrose were in a showdown against Durant's former school, Oak Hill.

Montrose was the preseason No. 1 with Durant's arrival. But at the time they met, Montrose was No. 12. Oak Hill was No. 1 in the nation at 40-0, riding a 56-game winning streak. Ty Lawson was still on Oak Hill. Michael Beasley was now, too. So was another Prince George's County product: Nolan Smith. With Vásquez, that was five future NBA players in one high school game.

The hope was to have the game at George Washington or American University, but schedule conflicts prevented that. The Wizards' home arena was considered, but organizers concluded it was too cavernous a venue. So they settled on Coolidge High's four-thousand-seat Frank R. Williams Activity Center. They could've sold out a bigger venue, but the vibe at Coolidge turned out perfect. Tickets were gone well in advance and the lines to get in got long. Even scalpers were working this game, which featured so much local talent.

Lawson controlled the game for Oak Hill, carving up the defense with his penetration and screen-and-roll savvy. Durant got into foul trouble and was forced to sit most of the second quarter. He was helpless to watch his AAU teammate break down his new squad. Things changed when Vásquez demanded to defend Lawson. The intensity of the game picked up as Vásquez initiated the trash talking. Oak Hill was up 61–48 when Lawson and Vásquez had to be separated. They kept jawing at each other, prompting the refs to stop the action and tell them to turn it down a notch.

"I wasn't even Americanized, if you call it, so I didn't really know who Ty was at the time," Venezuelan-born Vásquez told the *Washington Post* in a 2016 interview about the game. "I just knew he was killing us. So I got under his skin, played aggressive, talked trash in Spanish, and it was working."

With just inside of seven minutes left, Lawson lost Vásquez around a screen and tried to throw down a thunderous dunk. He was fouled and it rimmed out, but suddenly the packed house was engaged. Vásquez answered with a 3-pointer and was tauntingly clapping as he defended Lawson. The vibe in the gym started to match the hype leading up to the game.

Beasley grabbed an offensive rebound and dunked it back, putting Oak Hill up 66–55. Durant answered with a driving layup at the 3:59 mark. Beasley came right back and hit a floater. But Durant answered with a deep 3-pointer, cutting the Montrose deficit to 68–60.

A turnover on the inbounds by Oak Hill got Montrose the ball right back and Durant was fouled taking another shot from deep. He made all three free throws, giving him 8 points in forty seconds to pull the Mustangs within 5 points. It was on.

The teams traded big baskets as the game came down to crunch time. Lawson's layup was answered with a Vásquez putback. Lawson threw a sweet pass to Nolan Smith for a layup and a 72–65 Oak Hill lead. They were the last points the Warriors would score.

Ito hit a 3-pointer. Then Durant blocked a layup attempt by Smith, picked up the loose ball, and started a fast break, feeding Maryland-bound forward Adrian Bowie for a transition layup, tying the game at 72 with 1:07 left. Lawson tried to milk some clock as Vásquez tried to bait him with trash talk. A backcourt violation by Lawson, created by Vásquez's pressure, got Montrose the ball for the final shot.

The stage was set for Durant's heroics. He already had a game-high 31 points. Now his team had the ball and was in position to take the last shot. They ran some action for Durant to get the ball at the top. He rushed a contested 3-pointer, but Bowie was right there for the rebound. His putback dropped in as time expired. Montrose players mobbed Bowie, who scored 10 points in the final seven minutes as fans stormed the court.

This was why Durant had come home. He was a full-fledged phenom. If the NBA hadn't just changed the rules forbidding high school players from entering the league, Durant would have gone straight to the draft. That's how good he'd gotten. All those years. All that hard work.

Home needed to see what he'd become.

A month later he was playing at Madison Square Garden. Durant was one of the marquee names in the annual Jordan Brand Classic. He filled up the stat sheet in the showcase: 16 points, seven rebounds, four assists, and three blocks. He earned MVP of the Black Team.

More than ten thousand people showed up, including rappers T.I. and LL Cool J, boxer Floyd Mayweather, NBA stars Vince Carter and Al Harrington, and NFL star Warren Sapp. Of course, the biggest star in the building was Michael Jordan himself.

"I met MJ," Durant's dad, Wayne, told *The Undefeated*, "which was a bucket list request."

4 | HOOK 'EM HORNS

AFTER LEADING NATIONAL CHRISTIAN ACADEMY TO a 27-3 record, the best in the school's history, and then switching to Oak Hill Academy for his junior year for further exposure, Durant was on the NBA trajectory.

Legendary UConn coach Jim Calhoun visited Oak Hill Academy in April to catch him as well as teammate Tywon Lawson. Whatever he said prompted Durant and Lawson to visit Storrs, Connecticut, a week later. It wasn't the normal time for official college visits, but they wanted to experience the school while it was in session. Calhoun played up the Huskies' long track record of wings who make it to the league.

But both Durant and Lawson had their sights set on North Carolina, the storied college program that claimed Michael Jordan as an alumnus. Also, Tarheel product Vince Carter, even though he played in Canada, had developed a cult following with his insane dunks. North Carolina was the dream.

"I'll give you the whole story," Durant told a packed audience during a live conversation at the Center for Sports Leadership & Inno-

59

vation at the University of Texas, where he received the Outstanding Young Texas Ex Award in September of 2016.

"I had 20 offers on the table. I visited UConn, North Carolina. And Texas . . . I would visit them just because I had a relationship with Coach [Springmann], who was from the same area. So I was going to do him a favor. I was going to North Carolina and I told my mom that's where I want to go. She said, 'You promised to visit Texas, and you got to stick to your word.' And I did."

Durant and his dad, Wayne Pratt, officially visited Austin in May 2015. The night of his visit, Longhorns coach Rick Barnes took Durant and his father to Ruth's Chris Steakhouse. Springmann and strength and conditioning coach Todd Wright were there, too.

Durant and Pratt were assured that Durant would be treated like family. And Barnes shared the freedom Durant would have to play his game, not be forced to dwell in the paint because of his height. And Springmann had already made the best impression.

"Out of all the schools, he was the best recruiting assistant I dealt with," Pratt told the *Dallas Morning News* about Springmann.

Trust, in all forms, was paramount. Letting Kevin go meant putting their son's fate, his well-being, his livelihood—his very safety—in the hands of men he hardly knew. A month later Durant committed to University of Texas, spurning UConn and North Carolina. Lawson went to North Carolina.

.   .   .

Durant arrived in Austin a regional nomad, having lived in many places and been to a collection of schools. But in one year at Texas he grew roots that would anchor him for life.

College is usually a gloried benchmark when adults who attended a four-year institution look back on their lives. It's the gateway to independence. It's usually the place where enlightenment happened, where they learned the world isn't just the one they inhabited back home. It's where fun is unadulterated. This is intensified for many athletes from humble beginnings. Many can't handle the experience. They get exposed to another world, one that isn't painted by poverty and struggle, one with resources and access. Texas is where Durant started eating breakfast.

Maryland had raised him but Texas refined him. His basketball genesis was in Seat Pleasant, but his basketball anointing happened in Austin.

Durant came to Texas with such a fresh face that, had it not been attached to his lanky six-foot-nine-inch frame, he might have been mistaken for a lost thirteen-year-old traipsing across the campus's famed Forty Acres. Austin was nothing like Maryland. His classmates were dramatically different than the cats from his 'hood. But one thing was the same: basketball and his drive to conquer it. The game kept him grounded. Basketball was his North Star, guiding him toward his purpose.

Texas teammate Justin Mason remembers Durant's first official day on campus. All the gyms were closed, so Mason thought they had escaped practice, that they were free to go home and relax for the day. But Durant shut that down. He called around Austin looking for any local gyms open. He found a gym by the evening. He and his teammates were getting shots up until after midnight. That became routine.

"Kevin was a whole 'nother beast when it came to putting work in," said Mason, an Amarillo, Texas, native who speaks with a syrupy drawl. These days he looks more like a linebacker than the 185-pound freshman guard he was back then. But his twang is still the same.

"The work that he put in from Day 1 is what made the teams I was a part of special. Him being here for one year—he impacted four years' worth of wins and building blocks of future success that Texas has had."

Mason said none of the other teammates wanted to get shown up by Durant, so they matched his intensity and commitment. He elevated the team's work ethic just by being there. His fellow freshmen— D. J. Augustin, Matt Hill, Damion James, Dexter Pittman, and Harrison Smith—didn't want to look as if they weren't ready. None of the sophomores, such as A. J. Abrams and Connor Atchley, or juniors like Ian Mooney, were going to stand for being embarrassed by the newcomer. And, of course, the team's lone senior, Craig Winder, wasn't getting outworked by a guy who was just in homeroom. Mooney fouled Durant incessantly in practice. Atchley kept the pressure on Durant every day.

Durant loved it. This was why he wanted to play college basketball. He wanted the fire that would mold his game. He wasn't interested in being coddled like a prima donna. Neither were his parents. They made that clear to Barnes. Wanda wouldn't be there to pull Barnes aside and tell him, "You need to get in his ass. You coach my son," as she had told his AAU coach. So she informed him in advance.

And Durant, with all his talent, needed it.

But Durant couldn't fully step into his new life in Austin without bringing PG County with him. And one person in particular had to join him on this new journey: Big Chucky.

On August 28, 2006, Terrell Bush was sentenced to life in prison plus twenty years for the murder of Charles Craig. It had been sixteen months since Durant's first coach and father figure was shot and killed. It was Craig who had seen this for Durant well before Durant did. He would have enjoyed this as much as Durant, too, seeing one of his own make it to the Division I level. Durant would have loved to give that to Craig, who had given of himself to so many kids in their neighborhood.

To honor Craig, Durant decided he would wear No. 35. That was how old Big Chucky was when he died. Durant started a movement of players from his area to wear No. 35 along with him. Durant's brother, Tony, wore No. 35 for Towson during the 2007–2008 season. Braswell, a Capitol Heights native who played with Durant on the PG Jaguars, switched from No. 33 in high school to No. 35 when he played college ball at UNC Charlotte. Even D.C. native Dwight Bell wore No. 35 at Gloucester County Community College in Sewell, New Jersey.

"It feels good to see a lot of 35s from the people I know," Durant would later tell the *Oklahoman*. "It shows that every time we step between the lines, where [Charles Craig] taught us how to be tough, how to go out there and play with passion and play with heart, even though he's up there he's living his dreams through us on the basketball court."

Durant unveiled his new number on Halloween 2006, at an exhibition against Lenoir-Rhyne University, Coach Rick Barnes's alma mater. It was a lightweight disaster. Despite Durant's 16 points, Barnes said he . . . played . . . awful, emphasizing each word like he was pressing on the breaks. Durant's defense? "Really, really bad."

The growing pains were just the beginning. The following film session was longer than usual, and it was pretty much all pointed at him. Afterward the team hit the court. The impact on Durant was noticeable. He wasn't pouting, wasn't mad he had been singled out. But he was in his feelings, down on himself.

Nearly two months later he had another stinker against Tennessee, where Barnes now coaches. Texas lost 111–105 in overtime, blowing a 15-point half-time lead. Durant's 26 was overshadowed by 35 points from junior guard Chris Lofton, who famously hit a deep 3-pointer late over Durant to give Tennessee the lead, erasing a once 17-point deficit. Durant's runner with two seconds left forced overtime. But he missed a chunk of the second half because of foul trouble. His game was just off. He'd made too many bad plays, too many mistakes. The coaches knew. *He* knew.

Durant's dad was at the game. He, too, was upset about Durant's performance. This was right before Christmas break. So Durant stewed on it for days. He came back to Texas knowing what was missing. He probably didn't know what it was called at the time, but Durant needed to get his basketball IQ up. He needed to get better at understanding the marriage of time on the clock and the situation. He needed to learn how to impact the game even more without scoring. He had the tools. Next up was the mastery of how to wield them.

"I remember him coming back after that," Barnes said, "and he said to me, 'Coach whatever you have to do, I want you to teach me how to play this game from a mental standpoint.' All that stuff became really important to him. It became really, really important. I think he realized there was more to the game than just a physical side of it."

Durant was heavily invested. When the team broke for water, and his teammates scurried to their squirt bottles, Durant went to query his coaches. When practice ended and it was time to wind down, Durant was picking their brains. He was asking about his defense. He was asking how he could be better. He was asking about specific situations in games and moments, the basketball minutiae that separated the good from the great.

"He really wanted to learn the game and how it works," Barnes said, "as opposed to just playing. But that's again what made him special."

Stars with that kind of humility leave a mark. The juxtaposition of his stratospheric talent and grounded persona endeared him to

Texas. They ate it up like the flakiest biscuits covered in the smoothest gravy. There is a reason Springmann named his firstborn son Durant.

Barnes will never forget Durant's reluctance to take center stage during the Big 12 Media Day. He and A. J. Abrams were slated to go. Durant didn't want to because he thought all of his teammates should be there.

Lessons from home stayed cemented in Durant's mind. Shine, but not too much. Nobody likes a spotlight hog. Show up but stay humble. Doing too much invites issues.

It was all so new to Durant. He may have been six-foot-nine and growing, but he was freshly eighteen years old with a powerhouse program strapped to his back and NBA greatness at his fingertips.

Often people see talent and expect it to just manifest itself through osmosis. Expectations can be as much of an anvil as failure. The pressure of squandering a golden ticket has broken many young men, especially from Durant's neck of the woods. Durant's recourse was not to accept all of the added weight of attention and expectation. If you talk about it, you've got to be about it. Then you have to deal with the people who are mad that you were about it. So Durant chose to be low-key. He stayed out of the way. He wasn't at house parties thirsting for attention. He wasn't hustling to get the latest gear so he could be fly. No, Durant was a lanky tower, ducking low enough so his head didn't stick out. He deflected praise, shared accolades. He chose to creep up on success. He chose to keep his head down, get his work done, and end up on the other side victorious.

Where he grew up, the guys who did a lot of talking didn't always have the game to match. They also invited drama, taunting it into existence. Durant knew those rules and long ago chose to let his game speak for him. That was pressure enough anyway.

Durant was the marquee on the youngest starting five Barnes

has ever fielded. He was joined by Mason, D. J. Augustin, and Damion James, four freshmen starters alongside sophomore A. J. Abrams. When they went to Kansas in March 2007, the juggernaut that owned the Big 12 Conference, Barnes told Durant he needed to carry them.

"We all said to him, 'Hey, KD, you gotta take this game over,' " Barnes said.

Augustin had learned early how to prod Durant. The freshmen hit it off immediately, both gym rats who beneath their humble coatings had fiery cores. When he needed to, Augustin would say what he needed to make Durant mad. Angry KD, even at Texas, was unguardable. Augustin knew that, so he would needle Durant until he was furious.

"KD's real sensitive, so I could make him mad in a second," said Augustin, now running point guard for the Orlando Magic. "I love making him mad. When I see him getting mad, I just keep going and going. On the court, off the court. Whatever, it doesn't matter. But even now I tell guys all the time when we're playing against them, and guys are kind of going back and forth. I tell them, 'Hey, man, don't wake him up. When you start talking to him on the court, he turns into somebody else.' "

That somebody else was needed this game. The showdown with Kansas would be one of those games where the offense would boil down to giving Durant the ball and letting him make magic. The Jayhawks were one win from collecting their fifth straight Big 12 Championship. Few players get the Jayhawks shook as much as Durant did that night.

Augustin got Texas started with a 3-point play on a layup, then Durant made his first four shots to send a nervous panic through Allen Fieldhouse. He scored 12 straight points in a span of three minutes and seventeen seconds. The Jayhawks had to start double-teaming Durant. His teammates, riding the wave, knocked down the open looks created by Durant's dominance. At one point Texas made twelve straight shots.

Durant had 25 in the first half. Texas led by as much as 16. It was an electrifying performance against the No. 3–ranked team in the country. The crazy part about this performance was that Kansas was geared up for it. Durant came into the game leading the conference in scoring, rebounding, and blocked shots. If anyone could put Durant in his place, it was Kansas. And they couldn't.

"Durant was on fire the first half," Jayhawk Julian Wright, a six-foot-eight athletic forward from Chicago, told reporters after the game. "We just tried to keep playing defense the way we were taught to play it and tried to limit his easy points. But he was awesome."

Kansas went on a surge to start the second half and turned it into a close game. It wasn't until Texas was down 64–61 that Durant made his first shot since the break. Over the first five and a half minutes of the second half, he'd taken just two shots, a missed 3-pointer and a made pull-up that pulled the Longhorns within a point. He was playing smart, giving up the ball against Kansas's double teams. This was setting up for a big finish.

But then at around the eleven-minute mark, with Kansas ahead 71–65, Durant sprained his ankle. It was actually a reaggravation. He had sprained it initially the day before in practice. Durant received treatment and returned to the game, but he wasn't the same. Visibly hobbling, he became an easier guard for Wright, Brandon Rush, and Darrell Arthur, who took turns defending him when Kansas wasn't double-teaming him. The big finish Texas needed, Durant couldn't provide. He was just three for eight from the field in the second half, finishing with 32 points. But there was no doubting his dominance after his first-half display. It was his latest and largest dose of the weight of the world being on his shoulders, and he put together a performance that left everyone who watched him certain about his supremacy.

In his lone season at Texas, Durant averaged 25.8 points on 47.3 percent shooting to go with 11.1 rebounds, 1.9 steals, and 1.9 blocks. He shot 40.4 percent from 3-point range, feasting on the closer line in college.

He was named Player of the Year by the Associated Press, the Big 12 Conference, *Sporting News*, and the National Association of Basketball Coaches. He won the coveted Naismith College Player of the Year Award, the John R. Wooden Award, and the Adolph Rupp Trophy. Durant was also a Consensus All-America First Team selection.

He played his first NCAA tournament game against New Mexico State in Spokane, Washington. Texas was given a No. 4 seed, so they were heavy favorites. But Durant was nervous. His mother could hear it in his voice during interviews, so she called him.

He was eighteen. This was the biggest stage of his life. Everyone back home could watch him, not to mention the fact that every NBA team was watching. The pressure of the NCAA Tournament has swallowed up many NBA-bound talents.

Durant scored 27 points, his seventh straight game with at least 25. This one was different, though.

He only took thirteen shots, making six, just like Abrams. Augustin made half of his twelve shots. Normally, it was Durant doing most of the chucking. But he wasn't feeling it. He was zero for four on 3-pointers. So he did his damage at the free-throw line.

He made eleven of twelve in the second half, finishing fifteen of sixteen. Texas led by 12 in the second half. But New Mexico State rallied. They trailed by a point with seven minutes left. Durant was determined not to let his one tournament experience be a choke job. In a huddle with his teammates, he clapped his hands to get their attention and screamed, "Let's go!" Texas ripped off a 12–4 run. Durant made six consecutive free throws. He came up with a clutch steal, dashing the hopes of the underdog Aggies. Texas advanced.

Durant had 30 the next game against USC, led by junior guard

Nick Young, with whom Durant would later win an NBA championship. Durant's 3-pointer still wasn't falling, two for nine, but it didn't matter. Texas was overwhelmed by the No. 5 Trojans. They had more experience, more depth. The Longhorns got down by 17 and needed something spectacular from Durant. But he played right into the Trojans' hands by going one-on-one.

Durant couldn't dominate this game. Texas never really threatened USC. So his spectacular career at Texas ended with a relative thud. Four years earlier Carmelo Anthony, who preceded Durant at Oak Hill Academy, led Syracuse to the 2003 National Championship. Durant couldn't carry the Longhorns' youth past the second round.

All that was left was the question of whether Durant would go pro, which in hindsight wasn't really a question at all. If he stayed at Texas, they could've built a powerhouse. The youngsters got valuable experience their first year together. If they had had the chance to grow together, they could have been special. But Durant didn't come home from an AAU tournament years ago to declare to his mother he was going to be an NCAA champion. The goal had always been the NBA, ever since he was a PG Jaguar. Now it was right there. The only uncertainty regarding Durant's NBA status was whether he would be the No. 1 pick or if that honor would go to Ohio State big man Greg Oden.

But departing Texas on a second-round loss didn't define Durant's stay at Texas. Not in his mind and not in the school's. They'd accomplished so much in a year.

Barnes remembers more than just Kevin's growth on the court that season. His last semester, Barnes says like a proud parent, Durant made the dean's list. Assistant athletic director Scott McConnell and associate athletic director Randa Ryan, head of academic services for UT's student athletes, worked diligently with Durant. He famously couldn't bench-press 185 pounds during the NBA Draft Combine, but he was stronger in so many ways.

Todd Wright, the strength and conditioning coach, did have his work cut out with Durant's body. He came to Texas a stringy 205 pounds. How he matured physically was as important as getting him to mature. They didn't want to just load him with weight or get him to the point he could bench-press a certain number.

They worked on movement, agility, speed, strength. They worked on defense. He didn't need bulk as much as he needed skill development. He didn't need to bang in the paint. His specialness was in being basically a seven-foot guard. They needed to maximize that in the one year they had him. But they were building more than his body.

"I remember when he finally got his first car. It was like a black van," Barnes said, "and I asked him why he got it like that. He said, 'Well, I got to have a place to get my teammates where we can hang out.' It was all set up for them just to have fun."

That's what made Texas special—the same components that made PG special. He wore No. 35 to memorialize Big Chucky. He got a van because he learned about team and fellowship and bonding in Chucky's van, which his AAU teammates piled into for games and practices.

Texas became an extension of everything that was good about Durant's life. It was an intensified re-creation of the great times he had had with his teammates, the feeling of being cared for and caring, of getting through rough times as a group.

He never had much to call his own. When he did, he wanted to share. Sometimes each other is all you've got. That was what he learned from his own family, what was emphasized through AAU basketball. That was what had been embedded in him in DMV.

"I think Kevin is a very, I would say a quiet, very sensitive person in the fact that he really cares about people," Barnes said. "He is one of the kindest, [most] loyal people. I mean, if you can see his interaction with this college teammates, it would tell you how much people love him, and I think that's a real comfort zone for him. I think he respects team and his teammates so much."

Durant went on to be selected No. 2 in the 2007 NBA Draft. Oden was selected No. 1 overall. At the time, there was some sense to it, even if history should have warned the Portland Trail Blazers.

Oden was a seven-foot, 250-pound monster in the middle. He had good athleticism to go with his size. He was an intimidating defender and a capable offensive player. He had the intangibles of size, touch, and fluidity that NBA general managers would sacrifice their firstborn to get. In the NBA, size is everything. Height is a bankable skill that, combined with strength, becomes a force in pro basketball. Shaquille O'Neal epitomized the combination and was arguably the most dominant big man of all time. They don't come around that often. Oden had the tools that made him look as if he might be next in the lineage of Wilt Chamberlain, Kareem Abdul-Jabbar, and Hakeem Olajuwon. If he was, Portland's franchise was set for ten to fifteen years. That's quite a seductive option. High-risk, high-reward.

But another school of thought says to get the best player available. That wasn't as prevalent a thought as it is now, as centers have been marginalized by perimeter players. But many who had seen both, especially when you factor in Oden's health concerns, thought it was a no-brainer. Durant was easily and clearly the best player in the draft. He had the most talent, the most skill. And he wasn't just any random perimeter player. He measured out at above six-foot-eleven. So he was as much an anomaly as Oden.

But Portland went with the big man. They had been burned this way before. In 1984 they selected big man Sam Bowie with the No. 2 pick. Olajuwon had gone first and no one disputed that. He was, indeed, a future Hall of Fame big man. But the Blazers had the choice between Bowie, Charles Barkley, and Michael Jordan. They chose

Bowie. Chicago took Jordan at No. 3. And the rest was history. Jordan went on to be the greatest basketball player ever. Bowie's career was cut short by injury. Portland missed.

And now they missed again. They passed up the best player and chose the best big man. And Oden, whose career was cut short by injuries, never panned out like they had hoped. Seattle took Durant No. 2 overall and got a franchise cornerstone for nine seasons.

.   .   .

Standing at a podium, facing an audience of past and present Texas basketball players, as well as Barnes, the president of the University, and Durant himself, former teammate Justin Mason spoke what he knew to be true.

"Everyone calls him a superstar, but it's hard for me because he always wanted to be normal, to me he's always been a normal guy," he said. "Regardless of the fame, the celebrity, the money—none of that has ever changed when it came to his brothers, the relationships he's built here. He's always treated us like family."

It was January 5, 2018. They were there to celebrate Durant's massive donation of $3 million to his alma mater—$2.5 million to the Texas basketball program and $500,000 to the school's Center for Sports Leadership & Innovation, a center that launched in 2015 with the mission of cultivating character development and leadership skills. The main entrance to Denton A. Cooley Pavilion is now the Kevin Durant Texas Basketball Center. The men's basketball facilities are now the Kevin Durant Basketball Facility for Men.

Durant's donation was the largest ever by a former Texas basketball player. A ceremony was held to honor the gift. Scott McDonnell told Justin Mason that the gathering would be intimate. It would've been more accurate to call it infinite.

During his speech, Mason shared a personal moment from the summer of 2009, going into his senior year, when Durant had just averaged 25.3 in his first season in Oklahoma City. Still, he wanted to come back and hoop at Texas.

"I think we were on AOL Instant Messenger at that time," Mason said, prompting laughter from the audience.

"He was online and he hits me like, 'Yo, where are you staying this year?' And I was, like, 'I don't know, I think I'm going to get an apartment or something.' He goes, 'You mind if I room with you?' "

Durant pulled up outside of Mason's apartment a few weeks later in a custom minivan. It was a GMC Savana. It had his logo in the leather headrests on each seat. A moonroof. A twenty-six-inch liquid crystal TV that was set up to play his Xbox 360. It had a built-in ice cooler and the Texas Longhorns logo on the chrome rims. A backup camera. A motorized sofa bed. And second-row swing-out doors.

He stayed with Mason the whole summer, but they weren't alone. It was like Grand Central Station in that two-bedroom apartment. They worked out together and ate fast food from Sonic or Whataburger.

"Kevin didn't always pay," Mason deadpanned.

Mason's mic-drop moment brought Durant to his feet. They dapped each other. The time had come for Kevin to speak. At this ceremony, the last words were his. Nearly four minutes' worth of words out of the mouth of Durant, uninterrupted.

"Walking into this practice facility, it wasn't even about basketball, because I could've played basketball just about anywhere," Durant said to the audience. "It was about the culture that was set from T. J. Ford, the reason why I wanted to come to Texas. Well, the second reason. The first reason is because Coach Barnes told me I could shoot whenever I wanted to when I came."

This scene—it all starts making sense. At the core of Durant is something affectionate. The desire to love and be loved unconditionally. He gets it at Texas. He gives it to Texas. His leaving didn't change that. Perhaps there isn't anything he could do to change it.

"I'm always supporting Texas," Durant said, "the place that helped mold me into who I am today, so that's the least I can do is support. So no matter what sport it is, I'm always going to show my love and always support 'em no matter what."

5 | THUNDER UP

FOR TWO YEARS THE NEW ORLEANS Hornets called Oklahoma City home, and the city got to show it was more than just a small-market backwater town. Hurricane Katrina ripped through the Gulf South in 2005, leaving destruction and devastation in its wake. Katrina also left the Hornets homeless, forcing the franchise to temporarily relocate to Middle America. Many thought the NBA was nuts for planting a team, even temporarily, in the heartland. But the people on the prairie proved to have an unforeseen and unbelievable passion for hoops. They sold out games. They stood until the home team scored its first basket. They cheered and cheered. Then cheered some more. They raised the bar on rowdy. And Chris Paul, then a baby-faced NBA newcomer, became the state's favorite son. In those two seasons, Paul put on a show, turning college football country into a basketball-crazed state. He won Rookie of the Year, lifted the vagabond Hornets to the brink of the playoffs, and showed Oklahoma City what being big-league was all about.

But in the spring of 2007, the NBA broke up the love affair. Again, it was always a limited-time relationship. David Stern, the league's commissioner at the time, mandated then-owner George Shinn return to

New Orleans even though that meant leaving behind a cash cow in Oklahoma City. Ditching New Orleans, a city dealing with so much despair, would have been a horrible look for the NBA. For Stern, the NBA not returning to the Big Easy simply wasn't an option. When the Hornets left, the Okies were heartbroken. For them it was not better to have loved and lost. The toughest pill to swallow was losing Paul, a rising star who quickly went on to etch his name among the best point guards the game has ever seen.

It turned out Paul was foreshadowing what was to come. Durant would be the new prodigy who captured their hearts.

On July 18, 2006, while the Hornets were gearing up to play their final season in the Sooner State, an investment group led by Oklahoma City–based businessman Clay Bennett (who helped facilitate the Hornets' two-year stay in his town) purchased the Seattle Super-Sonics. The new ownership initially said it would keep Seattle's oldest professional franchise in the city and planned to secure the new arena the previous ownership group couldn't. But once the sale went through and Bennett was involved, the smart money was always on the Sonics moving to Oklahoma City.

Durant was just a freshman at the University of Texas but a basketball prodigy Oklahomans would keep a close eye on while picturing a dream scenario in which someday he might serve as a consolation prize for losing Paul. The Sonics were sinking fast. They went from 52 wins and losing in the second round to 25 wins in 2005–2006 and missing the playoffs. Coach Nate McMillan was fired and the franchise's future in Seattle was uncertain. A terrible season was in the offing. If the Sonics were indeed coming to Oklahoma, a top pick was possibly coming with them. Anyone reading the tea leaves had their eyes on the best players and colleges, and arguably no one was better than Durant.

Oklahoma's first glimpse of the future came midway through

Durant's lone season with the Longhorns when he made a cameo in Stillwater. In a triple-overtime thriller against Oklahoma State, only an hour north of Oklahoma City, Durant dazzled. He scored 37 points, grabbed twelve rebounds, and blocked four shots. Texas lost a 105–103 shoot-out, falling on a deep game-winning jumper with three seconds remaining. OSU fans stormed the court, euphorically celebrating their triumph in the battle of top twenty-five teams and over the fabulous freshman who would go on to be named Consensus National College Player of the Year. Durant labeled it his favorite college game and never forgot the intensity of that night's crowd. The locals weren't just rooting against the Longhorns; they were leaving an indelible impression on Durant. As much as it was their first taste of Durant's terrific talent, it also was Durant's first look at the passion Oklahoma could have for basketball.

The Sonics selected Durant with the No. 2 overall pick in the 2007 NBA Draft. A year later the Sonics relocated to Oklahoma City, with Durant arriving as the reluctant face of the franchise. He was flanked by Jeff Green, the No. 5 overall pick from Durant's same 2007 draft class and also a PG County product, and a little-known rookie point guard from UCLA named Russell Westbrook. The rest of the roster was dotted with castoffs, journeymen, and fringe NBA talents.

In those days Durant had a quiet, almost passive demeanor. About the only thing anyone knew about his personality was that he enjoyed playing with neighborhood children during his rookie year in Seattle, opening his upscale Mercer Island home and inviting a few to play video games with him. In that sense Durant was more like the kid next door than a superstar in the making.

Of course, Durant's reserved personality was present only when he wasn't on the court. On it he transformed into a terror. With his insatiable work ethic and fiery focus, Durant was determined to build upon his rookie season, a campaign that brought about his share of critics in spite of his individual success. Some labeled Durant too one-dimensional in Seattle, a high-volume and low-efficiency chucker. In his second season, his first in Oklahoma City, Durant was consumed with changing that narrative.

With the Thunder forced to expedite all operations in time for the 2008–2009 season, the franchise made a makeshift practice facility by purchasing and converting an old roller rink. It sat off a narrow two-lane side road, across from an empty field and down the street from a dog food plant. On windy days—essentially every day in OKC—the aroma of a fresh batch would waft its way right to the Thunder's front door. It didn't matter to Durant. It was home. He showed up to practice early, he stayed late, and he returned even later.

"We were always in there all hours of the night just hooping," Durant told the *San Francisco Chronicle*. "It was just, like, a pure basketball feel."

Practice was the fun part. Games were just painful.

The Thunder started the season 1-12, which included ten straight losses and a 13.3 average margin of defeat. It wasn't just that the Thunder were losing; it was how they were losing. The new team in town was getting embarrassed, and those first thirteen games ultimately cost head coach P. J. Carlesimo his job.

The Thunder turned to Scott Brooks, who served as an assistant under Carlesimo. Brooks had never been a head coach but had instant credibility due to his ten-year NBA career as a player and his contributions to the 1994 champion Houston Rockets. Brooks was much more of a player's coach, more mellow and forward-thinking than Carlesimo, who deployed the six-foot-nine Durant at shooting guard. It was Brooks who would soon shift Durant to his natural small forward position and insert Westbrook into the starting lineup.

"Not taking anything away from P. J., he wanted the best out of us," Durant told reporters after Brooks's debut game, "but Scott did a great job of giving us a little bit of room for error."

Brooks's tenure began the same way Carlesimo's had begun in Oklahoma City, with a 1-12 record. But there was a big difference. The Thunder became more competitive, slashing their average margin of defeat to 8.2 points in those 13 games. A ragtag roster, however, just wasn't good enough to collect wins, and the Thunder, after starting 1-16, limped to a 3-29 mark through late December, putting them on a pace for eight wins—on track for the worst record in NBA history. The 1972–73 Philadelphia 76ers won just 9 games.

Those were tough times for the Thunder. But they were necessary times. Durant and Westbrook especially were molded by the fire. They learned the hard way how to win, the kind of effort and dedication it took. They bonded through those tough lessons.

The NBA circles didn't know this about Durant yet, but he was good with grinding. He had never lost like he did with Oklahoma City. But as long as success was a matter of sweat equity, he was fine with that. As long as the franchise's fate rested on his desire to get better, the Thunder was in a good place. The willingness to work, along with his uncanny marriage of height and skill, has always been the constant in Durant's success.

The turnaround, and the Thunder's subsequent climb toward elite status, began in earnest on New Year's Eve of 2008. After that woeful 3-29 start, the Thunder toppled Golden State at home to kick-start an encouraging fifty-game stretch. They went 20-30 to finish the season, and the sudden spike in their winning percentage coincided with a spike in Durant's productivity. He got better month over month. In November he averaged 22.9 points on 46.1 percent shooting. For February: 30.6 points on 53.8 percent shooting.

Durant averaged 25.3 points, 6.5 rebounds, 2.8 assists, and 1.3

steals in his second season—an improvement in each category—
shedding the stigma as a one-dimensional chucker. He also shot a
higher percentage from the field and from the 3-point line. He finished
a distant third in voting for the 2009 Most Improved Player award, a
rarity for a reigning Rookie of the Year and a testament to how much
Durant had blossomed.

He also had help on the way. The Thunder's reward for going 23-59,
the fourth-worst record that season: James Harden, the third overall
pick in the 2009 draft and the third straight home-run selection made
by Thunder architect Sam Presti, the franchise's shrewd and long-
standing general manager.

Something else happened that summer. While at his annual youth
camp inside an Oklahoma City high school, Durant boldly predicted
that the Thunder would make the playoffs the following season. His
proclamation elicited mockery and laughter. But he knew the Thunder were on a mission and would soon be a team to be reckoned with.
Anyone could see the growing stable of talent in OKC, which was why
many labeled the Thunder a team on the rise. But with Harden as the
team's only significant offseason acquisition, few dared share Durant's playoff prognostication.

"If this were a 25-and-under league, you'd really like their
chances," NBA columnist Mark Heisler wrote in the *Los Angeles Times*.

By season's end, Durant looked like a psychic. The Thunder improved by 27 wins, one of the most dramatic turnarounds in league
history. Their 50-32 record landed them the eighth and final seed in
the Western Conference Playoffs.

On the final day of March 2010, the Thunder stormed into Boston
and upset the Celtics with an authoritative performance that left no
doubt Oklahoma City had arrived. These Celtics won the 2008 NBA
Championship and were contenders to get back to the NBA Finals
in 2010. Paul Pierce, Kevin Garnett, Ray Allen, and Rajon Rondo, the

band of "Ubuntu" brothers, were in their third year together. Boston put an 18-point beating on the Thunder in OKC back in December, when the Thunder were finding their way. Oklahoma City was just 10-9 after that loss. Three months later the tables had turned. This time the young Thunder stood toe-to-toe with the veteran-laden Celtics before delivering a surprising knockout punch. In a back-and-forth final twelve minutes with five ties and seven lead changes, OKC closed the game on a 9–3 spurt that flummoxed and frustrated the home team and its fans. Durant scored a game-high 37 points with eight rebounds that night. He made all fifteen of his free throws. That last bit left Kevin Garnett miffed.

"I thought we were playing Michael fucking Jordan the way he was getting the whistle," Garnett said after the game. "Durant damn near shot more free throws than our whole team."

The Celtics went thirteen for seventeen from the stripe. Garnett had a point, which cost him $25,000 when the league later levied a fine for his public criticism of game officials. But this was a watershed moment for Durant, for the Thunder. For the league, even. It was Oklahoma City's forty-sixth victory of the season, doubling its output from the previous year. It also gave the Thunder a win over every NBA franchise since relocating to Oklahoma City. And for Durant it was validation: a grumpy Garnett, then a thirteen-time All-Star, a former league MVP, and a future Hall of Famer, telling Durant in his own defiant way, "We can't stop you."

"We've grown up," Durant declared after the game.

Lost on Garnett was that Durant had been doing the same thing to defenses all season. It was the fourteenth time Durant had attempted at least fifteen foul shots. He would do it twice more before the end of the season and finish with an average of 10.2 foul shots per game, tied with LeBron James for most in the NBA. But Durant made 90 percent of his, while James made 76.7 percent.

"Kevin's really improved a lot in how he gets his points," Brooks said that season. "He's thinking the game more. But that just comes with maturity."

Manufacturing points at the free-throw line became a big part of Durant's scoring prowess. With the help of former teammate Desmond Mason, Durant took an old move Tim Duncan used, perfected it, and popularized it. While standing far out on the perimeter, Durant would swing his arms through a defender's extended hand using a low, swooping motion to initiate contact before powering through and giving the pretense he was shooting. Of course, he wasn't actually trying to shoot. He was trying to draw a foul. And, without fail, the referees would blow the whistle, deeming it a shooting foul and giving new meaning to the term "freebie." The move became known as the rip-through. It stumped opposing stoppers. It drove opposing coaches crazy. Durant got so good at it and spawned such a league-wide movement of players mimicking it, the league stepped in two years later and made it a point of emphasis for officials. Starting in 2011–12, the move would no longer be ruled a shooting foul but a common foul. Smart scorers still pulled it out when opponents were in the bonus.

Already a scoring machine, Durant moved a step toward unstoppable. He finished the 2009–10 season averaging 30.1 points to win his first scoring title. At twenty-one he became the youngest scoring champ in NBA history, breaking a sixty-two-year-old record held by Max Zaslofsky, who at twenty-two led the league in scoring while playing for the Chicago Stags in the 1947–48 season.

"It's something I really wasn't coming into the year saying I wanted to get, but it feels good to be a part of history, and it's something I'm going to always remember," Durant said. "It feels even better to get 50 wins."

He was named an All-Star for the first time, selected to the Western Conference reserves by the coaches. It would have been his second if not for the Thunder's shoddy record. But he got a greater honor at the end of the season when he was named All-NBA First Team. Only fifteen players make All-NBA and Durant was deemed one of the five best in the league.

The next phase of Durant's maturation process came in the 2010 playoffs. After a twenty-seven-game improvement and 50-win season, the Thunder's prize was a date with Kobe Bryant and the top-seeded defending champion Los Angeles Lakers in the first round. On paper it wasn't a fair fight. The Lakers were stacked with a star-studded lineup that featured Bryant, Pau Gasol, Lamar Odom, Andrew Bynum, and Ron Artest. The Thunder would have been happy to get a game. Oklahoma City had talent, but it was inexperienced. Durant, Westbrook, Jeff Green, James Harden, and a sensational shot-blocking rookie big man named Serge Ibaka made up a promising young core, but they hadn't been battle-tested. They were pups at the time with an average age of just 21 years old, compared with the Lakers' five-man group averaging 28.4 years old. Not to mention, on the Lakers' bench was Phil Jackson, already a ten-time champion as a coach. Brooks was a second year coach making his postseason debut.

Just before the start of the series, Durant downplayed the increased intensity of postseason basketball. He declared he had seen every defense and looked forward to whatever the Lakers threw at him.

Whoops.

Durant struggled mightily in his playoff debut, held in check by the Lakers' go-to defensive goon. Artest was a five-time All-NBA Defensive Team selection and the 2004 Defensive Player of the Year. In 2010, a year before legally changing his name to Metta World Peace, Artest could put anyone in handcuffs. Even Durant. In the six-game series, Durant's production plummeted. He averaged 25 points, five fewer than his league-leading average from the regular season, and he needed 20.5 shots per game to get those 25. He only needed 20.1 shots to average 30 during the season. Durant also turned the ball over twenty-two times in the six playoff games, compared with four-teen assists, and shot just 35 percent from the field.

Still, this series had one of those moments when Durant's special-ness shined through and it was clear the Thunder were headed in the right direction. In Oklahoma City's first home playoff game, Durant detonated for 29 points and nineteen rebounds. But this wasn't one of those times Durant got hot. He can be otherworldly when he's in a groove. In this game, however, he leaned on the intangibles that greatness requires. In this game he played worthy defense on Bryant, one of the greatest scorers of all time. And while Durant's shot wasn't falling—he missed his first seven shots and was eight for twenty-four—his aggressiveness remained high. This was gritty Durant, fueled by resilience when he didn't have much else. Bryant, who was regarded as the NBA's ultimate closer, went two for ten in the fourth quarter. Even Bryant tipped his cap to Durant.

"It was a matchup that caught me by surprise," Bryant said after the game. "I think he did a good job."

With Durant bottled up, Westbrook rose to the occasion and re-vealed on a national stage his star potential. With thirty-five-year-old Derek Fisher starting opposite him, the twenty-one-year-old West-brook was virtually unstoppable. He averaged 20.5 points, six re-bounds, and six assists in the series. What's more, his play mirrored the magnificent efficiency for which Durant would soon become known. Westbrook shot 47.3 percent from the field, 41.7 percent from the 3-point line, and played with patience, poise, and precision. He av-eraged just 2.3 turnovers, a sign of how in control he was. Durant was the chosen one, but the Thunder's maiden playoff voyage was West-brook's coming-out party. It was the series that kick-started one of the most dynamic duos in NBA history, the series that set the stage for what would become an anything-you-can-do-I-can-do-better relationship between the two teammates.

Meanwhile, the Thunder was turning heads as a team that would soon make its own history. After stubbornly pushing the Lakers to six games and coming within seconds of forcing a Game 7, Oklahoma City had officially arrived. No longer were they a team of the future. They had become a problem for opponents in the present.

"It's all a process," Durant said after the series. "It's all about going through ups and downs. The better days are ahead of us. If we continue with that mindset, coming in, working hard, playing basketball the right way, respecting everybody we play, then the sky is the limit for us."

That summer Durant took another leap, morphing into the magnificent player many predicted he'd become. It happened with Team USA at the 2010 FIBA World Championship, after losing the final spot with Team USA at the 2008 Olympics in Beijing to Tayshaun Prince, due solely to experience. The entire 2008 edition was dubbed the Redeem Team, because they were charged with making up for USA's disappointing bronze-medal performance in the 2004 Athens Games.

Durant returned to the USA Basketball program two years later as an undeniably dominant force. Jerry Colangelo, the managing director of the men's national team, had already pegged Durant as a future leader of Team USA following the Beijing Olympics. If he was unstoppable in the NBA, the world had no hope of defending him. The plan was to build around Durant beginning in 2010.

The 2010 squad had Chauncey Billups, thirty-three at the time, serving as the elder statesman. Lamar Odom was the only player with Olympic experience, his coming in the 2004 Games. Six players on the squad were twenty-two years of age or younger. Stephen Curry, then a second-year guard for the Warriors, and Andre Iguodala, the player charged with replacing Allen Iverson in Philadelphia, were also on the 2010 squad. Tyson Chandler was the team's lone true center. And so Durant emerged as the team's premier player. Curry, Westbrook, Kevin Love, and the following season's eventual NBA MVP, Derrick Rose, all took a back seat as Durant led Team USA to a 9-0 record and a gold-medal finish in Turkey. He earned tournament MVP honors after averaging a team-best 22.8 points and 6.1 rebounds. No other player averaged double figures in scoring. Durant's 38 points in a semifinal win over Lithuania set a USA World Championship record for most points in a single game.

He was simply sensational, and he brought back countless lessons. His Team USA coach, Duke's Mike Krzyzewski, taught him some motivational tactics that stuck with him. Durant picked Billups's brain about leadership and adapted to physical play, the same kind Artest used to handcuff him in the playoffs four months earlier. Opponents pushed him around a bit.

"Those guys in international play, those guys are strong," Durant said upon his return to the Thunder. "It's just natural for them. They pushed me around a lot the first couple of games. But I was able to kind of use some of that against them and also learn how to play against it. So it's helping me a lot."

Before he embarked on his fourth season, Durant had some business to tend to. He signed a five-year, $89 million extension to remain with the Thunder. Despite emerging as one of the game's biggest names, Durant stunned everyone when he quietly announced the deal with a short post on his Twitter account in July 2010. He did so one day prior to LeBron James's live and highly publicized sit-down interview with ESPN to announce his intentions to leave Cleveland for Miami. The stark contrast between how the two stars handled their respective matters endeared Durant even more to the public, further building his brand as a humble superstar.

Industry insiders and hard-core fans, meanwhile, were in awe of Durant's unique decision to turn down a wildly popular opt-out clause. Most stars on his level would make sure to have an Early Termination Option before the last year on the contract. It would have reduced Durant's commitment and enabled him to explore his options as a free agent one year earlier. Instead, the deal Durant signed kept him under contract through 2015–16. Durant had spent the previous two years declaring his love for OKC and his desire to remain in place for as long as possible. Declining the option to get out of his contract sooner was his way of standing behind his words.

"He told everyone from day one that he's committed to five years and doesn't care about an out," Durant's agent at the time, Aaron Goodwin, told the *Oklahoman*. "And that shows you the magnitude of the person Kevin Durant is."

There were so many other examples. Three months later Durant was chosen to grace the cover of *Sports Illustrated* for the magazine's annual NBA preview issue. Durant would agree only if the magazine included the Thunder's entire starting lineup. The two sides met in the middle, and Durant selected unheralded guard Thabo Sefolosha and center Nenad Krstić to join him. Sefolosha and Krstić never would have come close to sniffing the cover of the prestigious magazine without Durant.

"A good experience. What can I say?" Krstić told the *Oklahoman*. "Thanks, Kevin."

Westbrook, on the other hand, was well on his way to star status. Following his eye-opening playoff series a year earlier, Westbrook boosted his scoring average to 21.9 points per game and was named to his first All-Star team.

Four days after the festivities, though, the Thunder sent shock waves through the NBA when they acquired Kendrick Perkins and Nate Robinson from Boston in exchange for Green, Krstić, and a first-round pick. Fans in both cities were heartbroken. Perkins was a beloved figure who had helped the Celtics win the championship in 2008. The Celtics nearly had a second title in 2010 but lost Game 7 after Perkins tore his MCL and PCL in Game 6. To this day those Celtics swear they would have won had Perkins been available. Green, meanwhile, was a fan favorite in OKC, ranking second in the eyes of the people behind Durant.

The trade gave the Thunder the bruising defensive anchor they needed at center. Krstić was a shooter, all finesse. Perkins was an enforcer who could help the Thunder survive against Tim Duncan and the Spurs, Gasol and Bynum with the Lakers, and Marc Gasol and Zach Randolph in Memphis. But the deal had two other far-reaching tentacles: it turned Westbrook into Durant's undisputed costar, supplanting Green, and it opened Durant's eyes to the business of the NBA. Green was a longtime friend dating back to high school. Durant could only watch as the Thunder traded him away. There were also financial considerations involved. Durant had already signed his extension and his huge salary was about to kick in. Westbrook was clearly headed for a big chunk of the salary cap, too. Second-year guard James Harden and second-year big man Serge Ibaka were already looking like high-ceiling players. With Green, that made five players who could eventually command a sizable second contract. A small-market team like Oklahoma City doesn't have the money for that kind of bill and had to start preparing to make tough choices. It was the first time Durant would have a close teammate snatched from him. But it wouldn't be the last.

On the court, however, the pieces suddenly fit much better. Instead of Green, a natural small forward who was playing out of position at power forward, the Thunder could now trot out Westbrook, Sefolosha, Durant, Ibaka, and Perkins. Suddenly they were a terror. They had size, length, athleticism, shot blocking, and two All-Stars.

Durant and the Thunder cruised through the 2010–11 regular

season, hitting their stride at Christmas and going 35-17 from that point on. They finished with 55 wins, earning the No. 4 seed. They had successfully lived up to raised expectations. Durant led the league in scoring for second straight season, averaging 27.7 points while beginning to dial back his offensive game to accommodate a more assertive Westbrook.

OKC annihilated Denver in the opening round of the 2011 playoffs, with Durant torching Wilson Chandler, Danilo Gallinari, and Kenyon Martin. Durant averaged 32.4 points, 5.6 rebounds, and 3.6 assists in the five-game series, which he bookended with a pair of 41-point performances. In the decisive Game 5, Durant scored 16 in the fourth quarter, turning a 9-point deficit with 3:30 left in the game into an improbable 3-point win. He scored 14 of the Thunder's final 18 points.

"You don't see it often, and you don't see it often in that setting," Brooks said. "You might see it during the regular season and you might see it occasionally in glimpses. But down nine with three to go doesn't happen often. Those are moments that only special players can create."

It was Durant's first signature playoff series, atoning for the subpar showing he had made against the Lakers one year earlier.

The series was not without its share of controversy. Midway through the Thunder's Game 4 loss at Denver, TNT sideline reporter Pam Oliver reported Durant and Westbrook got into a verbal dispute. It was their first major sideline spat. It also wouldn't be the last between the All-Star duo. It is normal for NBA teammates to clash, especially stars. Shaquille O'Neal and Kobe Bryant famously spent their years beefing with each other while winning championships. The Bad Boys Pistons from the late '80s would literally fight each other. It's natural for players as great as Durant and Westbrook to butt heads, especially as they were both still coming into their own as players, figuring out how to reach the pinnacle of the league. Westbrook infamously took thirty shots to score 30 points, missing all seven of his 3-point attempts, eliciting nationwide criticism. Durant was the proven scorer, but he took just eighteen shots that game to get his 31 thanks to five 3-pointers and ten free throws. But he steadfastly supported his point guard.

"He wants to do so well all the time," Durant said. "He's so hard on himself. He's his biggest critic. He might miss a shot or get a turnover and sometimes he lets that affect him a little bit. But he's getting past it. He's been working on that. And as teammates, we got to do a great job of helping him out and encouraging him. That's all we've been trying to do."

The Thunder moved on to dispatch Memphis in the conference semifinals, winning on their home court in Game 7. With two stout defenders thrown at him in Tayshaun Prince and Tony Allen, Durant wasn't as dominant as he was in the first round, but he still did his thing. In Game 4 at Memphis, Durant delivered a 35-point, thirteen-rebound, four-steal performance in a crucial triple-overtime classic.

Although the Thunder survived, the series saw OKC turn in its first of many playoff clunkers. With a chance to steal a road win in Game 3 and reclaim home-court advantage after dropping Game 1, the Thunder blew a 13-point lead at the start of the fourth quarter. They led by 11 with 7:30 remaining, only to watch the Grizzlies close the fourth quarter on a 15–4 run before outscoring them 15–7 in overtime. Similar collapses, marked by stagnant offense and suspect defense, ultimately defined the Thunder's postseasons during the Durant era. Some blamed poor coaching. Some pointed to a flawed roster. Some targeted Durant and Westbrook. The truth is it was all of the above, and no one in OKC could concoct a formula to keep it from happening again and again.

.   .   .

Near the conclusion of that Grizzlies series, just before the Thunder punched their ticket to its first Western Conference finals, fans near and far had a growing interest in how and why Durant wore a backpack. After games, he'd strap on a black or light-gray backpack and make his way to the interview room, where, without fail, he'd wear it on the podium while answering reporter's questions. Because the postgame interviews were broadcast live on NBA TV and sometimes TNT, the world grew more curious by the game. It became a thing. People wanted to know about it. While Durant and Westbrook sat side by side on the podium, one intrepid reporter finally asked Durant if he was aware of the growing interest in the backpack and whether he'd share what was inside. Even the notoriously cantankerous Westbrook laughed lightheartedly at the question.

"Yeah, that's why I wore it today," Durant said. "I've got my iPad. I've got my Bible. I've got my headphones. And my phone chargers."

With that, the press conference concluded, Durant and Westbrook stood and exited the interview room, and the basketball world could rest easier knowing one of the game's greatest mysteries had been solved. Left unsaid was how Durant began daily Bible reading earlier that season. His black leather Bible with his name engraved on the front cover became his source of inspiration. He'd even digest passages at his locker before games. The practice began in early March, when a visit to chapel just before the start of a road game in Memphis moved Durant and altered his mind-set. A team chaplain for the Grizzlies, a fellow Maryland native, told Durant how daily reading could change his life. Durant began his devotion the next day.

"I just want to grow spiritually with the Lord," Durant said. "It's something I always talked about, but I never really got into it. I'm keeping strong at it, just trying to make my walk with faith a little better. That's making me a better person, opening my eyes to things, and I'm maturing as a person. I'm just trying to grow."

Durant's image skyrocketed once again. No longer was he simply a humble superstar. He was now a humble superstar who was a backpack-wearing, Bible-reading baller. Oklahomans ate it up, as if he had been dropped down from heaven just for them. And here he was, leading their Thunder to the 2011 Western Conference Finals in only the franchise's third season in town. But it wouldn't be a happy ending this season.

Led by Dirk Nowitzki and Jason Kidd, Dallas manhandled the young Thunder. The Mavs took the series in five games, outclassing OKC and exposing the Thunder's numerous flaws and insurmountable inexperience. In Game 1, Nowitzki scored 48 points with six rebounds, four assists, and four blocked shots. He made ten of his first eleven shots, finished twelve for fifteen from the floor, and set an NBA playoff record with twenty-four consecutive made free throws. Durant dumped in 40 points with eight rebounds, five assists, and two blocks while going eighteen for nineteen from the foul line. But with the length, strength, and savvy of Shawn Marion assigned to him, Durant couldn't keep up with Nowitzki's level of play. Nowitzki averaged 32.2 points on 55.7 percent shooting in the series. Durant was held to 28 points per game on 42.9 percent shooting.

The Thunder had a chance to tie the series at two games apiece but blew it when they suffered one of their patented late-game meltdowns. Durant hit a 3 to put the Thunder ahead by 15 with 5:06 remaining. He looked to his bench, put his hands to his waist, and spread them apart as if fitting himself with a WWE-style championship belt. Brash move, but it was premature. The Mavs mounted an epic comeback, outscoring the Thunder 28–6 the rest of the way and winning in overtime. OKC missed eight of its final nine shots and turned it over twice. Durant and Westbrook combined to shoot zero for five in overtime and had both of the team's turnovers.

"I let the city down," Durant said after the game.

The Mavs closed out the Thunder in Game 5 in Dallas with a similar run, this time a 17–6 spurt over the final five-plus minutes. Dallas went on to defeat LeBron James and the Miami Heat in the NBA Finals. But the Thunder would be back. Durant was too determined, and now he had some playoff stripes. He increased his points, rebounds, assists, steals, field goal percentage, and 3-point percentage in the 2011 postseason. He also cut down his turnovers. And, thanks to battles against Kenyon Martin and Tony Allen, he learned to play through physicality while overcoming length used by Tayshaun Prince.

"I'm just working harder, trying to push myself," Durant said midway through his 2011 postseason. "Last year I was disappointed in how I played and how I didn't help my team as much as I wanted to. I just want to leave all the chips on the table and just go out there and play."

. . .

An impasse between the National Basketball Players Association and the NBA owners led to the players being locked out, the opposite of an employee strike. Owners were still smarting over LeBron James orchestrating a super-team with the Miami Heat, leaving one of their own, Dan Gilbert, with a crumbling franchise minus its star. They were also tired of players taking home a lion's share of the basketball-related income (BRI) and no longer wanted to get locked into incredibly long lucrative deals. The players were receiving 57 percent of the BRI and could sign for as long as six years. So when teams made a mistake on a big contract, they were trapped. Obviously, the players did not want to give up the larger share of the BRI and wanted the long-term security, so the two sides hit a wall that shut down the season. Other issues were on the table, including the age limit. The result was NBA stars who had a lot of time on their hands.

Durant, perhaps unknowingly, seized the opportunity. He let the nation see the boy inside of him that grew up in PG County. And with no games to dominate people's attention, he had the eyes of a hoop-thirsty nation on him.

That summer, with the NBA in the midst of a 161-day lockout, Durant became a pied piper of blacktop. He was practically a traveling show as he took part in streetball games and pro-am leagues across the nation. Durant crisscrossed the country to appear at parks and gymnasiums in Atlanta, Baltimore, Dallas, Los Angeles, Miami, New York, Portland, and Washington, D.C., among other places. But it was what Durant did on August 1, 2011, that made him an instant playground legend and internet sensation. That was the day Durant dropped 66 points inside New York City's famed Rucker Park.

Playing in an Entertainer's Basketball Classic game before an over-sized crowd standing shoulder to shoulder, lining the perimeter as if they were waiting to storm the court, Durant scored 43 second-half points, electrifying fans with a flurry of 3-pointers. At one point in the game, a moment immortalized forever on YouTube, Durant unleashed a 3-point barrage that set off pandemonium. He made two straight to get the frenzy started. He dribbled downcourt in transition, with the energy peaking, and drained a third 3-pointer. The crowd went ballistic as he stared into the sea of cheering fans, a few jumping on him before he turned to head back on defense. The next time down, everybody at Rucker Park expected another one. They rose to their feet and yelled as he dribbled the ball up court. The defense picked up at half-court this time, so Durant launched from deeper. When it splashed the net, the crowd couldn't contain itself anymore. They stormed the court, swarming him where he stood. They bounced and screamed around him, hugged on him, patted his chest, and rubbed his head. The game had to be stopped. He stood with a straight face as he soaked it all in. The NBA was shut down but basketball was alive and well, creating the memories that make it addictive, because of Durant.

"That much love from the crowd at one time was a lot," Durant told *GQ*. "It was like a quick burst of joy like I haven't felt on a basketball court before. It was amazing."

It was also in line with the image of Durant. He was reachable. They actually touched him. He was among them because he was one of theirs. It bolstered his humble superstar persona. Plus, there was something about the purity of his love for the game. It was undeniable. It was magnetic. In the 1998 lockout, players took a PR hit by complaining about how tough it was to feed their families during the work stoppage. Millionaires uttering the cries of the working class didn't go over well. But Durant embodied the spirit of something players often say as hyperbole: that they love the game so much, they would play it for free. Now Durant was actually doing it, playing for free, playing for love. And he did it at the grassroots level. It was part of what made Durant so endearing, the anti-diva superstar who valued the things emphasized in the development stages.

That magical night at Rucker Park—which has been viewed more than 13 million times through the five most popular videos on YouTube—saw Durant finish with 66 points, 2 points shy of tying the EBC scoring record and 12 shy of tying what at that time was the Rucker Park scoring record of 78. One night later Durant scored 41 in a Nike Pro City League game in New York, silencing hecklers by hitting the game-tying 3 to force overtime before knocking down the bucket that put the game away in the extra period. Still in New York two days after that, Durant scored 29 in a head-to-head matchup against longtime friend Michael Beasley in a Dyckman Park battle.

The basketball world went berserk over Durant's streetball appearances. As the lockout lingered, he led a movement among fellow

NBA players. Parks, playgrounds, and pro-ams became their stomping grounds. Players played for pride rather than obligation, defending their reputations and representing their respective cities and coasts. The Washington, D.C.–based Goodman League became Durant's de facto home team. Durant had competed in the league's legendary events in the southeast Washington, D.C., neighborhood of Barry Farm since he was sixteen, back when he was just a high school hotshot. Now he was the headliner, the main attraction. The lockout just shined a light on what Durant always did in the off-season: hit the high-level blacktop and pickup scene.

"We really hoop though," Durant said. "Wasn't no cameras. No show. That's how I was working out. I broke my foot in 2013 because all I was doing was hoop in the mornings, then I would do my thing, go through my shit, work on my game. Then I would go practice at Barry Farm by just cooking these (cats). I would do that every day. After a while, it was so much wear and tear on my foot that it just broke. My thing was, I wanted to let these cats know where I grew up at. This ain't no joke. I'm in the league now but you cannot fuck with me. So I wanted to show all them that grew up with me, who thought they were as nice as me, them muthafuckas ain't as nice as me. Nah, I'm a real animal out here. So I had to go back. And they loved it."

He took his local-legend status to new heights in a 2008 Goodman League game when he scored 60 points in a nail-biter against a playground star they called P-Shitty. In 2011, during the NBA lockout, Durant shined as several stars played organized pickup at Morgan State University in Baltimore. LeBron James, Chris Paul, and host Carmelo Anthony played for the Melo League out of Baltimore in a showdown versus the Goodman League, which featured Durant, Jarrett Jack, and Jeff Green. Durant scored 59. This was ten days after he scored a game-high 44 points at Trinity University in the Goodman League's heart-stopping win over the James Harden, Brandon Jennings, and the Drew League squad from Los Angeles.

Durant also dedicated significant time to supporting charity games: rapper/actor Ludacris's in Atlanta, Josh Howard's in Dallas, LaMarcus Aldridge's in Portland, and one of his own, which featured a who's who of All-Stars, in Oklahoma City. Durant traveled to the Philippines for a charity game and even played in a star-studded exhibition game dubbed the Obama Classic, hosted by President Barack Obama.

"Durant's gone on a rampage," Carmelo Anthony told the *Washington Post* that summer. "I told him to slow down. Because every other night I see him in a different city playing. But that's just the love of the game that he's got, and I respect that."

Fans who were hungry for hoops ate it up, accepting basketball however they could get it. Nike quickly capitalized on the summer circuit, coining the phrase "Basketball Never Stops" and making Durant one of the prominent faces of the campaign.

For Durant, the hectic summer of streetball was about so much more than simply playing or working on his craft. It also was a way for him to connect with people, to give back to underserved and overlooked communities, to put on a show for so many who might not otherwise have an opportunity to watch him live. Durant saw the barrier between NBA players and the everyday people who admire their craft. He wanted to tear it down, show people he is tangible.

Durant's dominant summer substantiated what was quickly becoming clear: he was blossoming into one of the most lethal players in the world, on the trajectory to becoming one of the best of all time.

By late September, however, Durant had grown tired of barnstorming, saying the games were becoming "played out." Four days before his comment, the NBA had canceled training camp and the first week of preseason games. Durant began seriously contemplating signing a contract to play internationally, which many NBA players did, although none were the caliber of Durant. His representatives were in talks with basketball clubs in Turkey, Russia, and Spain. Durant, like other players who chose to sign internationally, would have had an opt-out clause allowing him to return to the NBA whenever the lockout concluded.

Instead, Durant played flag football. Really.

Bored on Halloween, Durant posted a message to his Twitter account asking if there was a game anywhere. He found one at Oklahoma State University, getting an invitation from a senior fraternity member whose squad had won the intramural championship each of the past three years. Durant made the drive to Stillwater, drew an impromptu crowd of more than five hundred, tossed four touchdowns, and intercepted three passes. One month later Durant hooked up with LeBron James in Akron, Ohio, to play a friendly game of flag football with his good friend and biggest rival. Team LeBron defeated Team KD 70–63.

That was also the off-season Durant filmed the bulk of *Thunderstruck*, a family-friendly film produced by Warner Bros. in which Durant plays himself but mysteriously swaps basketball skills with an unathletic high school kid.

"My agent at the time brought it to me and I said no at first," Durant told the *Oklahoman*. "I didn't want to be a part of something like that because it takes so long. But then I thought about it and said, 'It will be cool, and it will be something for the kids to watch.' I've got a lot of little cousins, so I thought it'd be nice for them to see their big cousin in a movie. So I thought, 'Let's do it.' "

The summer of 2011 was also when the world learned Durant, the clean-cut superstar who was seen by many as a choir boy, had tattoos. Lots and lots of tattoos. While in China for a promotional tour, Durant was photographed without a shirt, revealing tats all over his torso.

Many were stunned to learn the rising star with the squeaky-clean image had so much ink. The tattoos had been strategically placed, stopping just before they would protrude from his No. 35 jersey when he was on the court. They were labeled "business tats," a measure Durant took to refrain from possibly jeopardizing his marketability by marking up his limbs. Durant's response to those shocked at his tattoos: "So what?"

But the revelation rubbed some the wrong way, representing the first blemish in Durant's image and serving as a sign he wasn't the choir boy he had been portrayed. Durant had only two tattoos when he arrived in Oklahoma City: his mother's name, Wanda, on his left pec and his grandmother's name, Barbara, on his right pec. He had drawn fanfare for strolling over to their courtside seats after games to kiss them before walking off the court. However, a segment of fans took umbrage at the new form of expression Durant chose. Never mind that most of Durant's new tats were inspirational sayings in the form of scripture or names and images that paid homage to his family and hometown.

Inscribed at the bottom of the right side of his stomach, Durant has "Walk by faith not by sight," from 2 Corinthians 5:7. Immediately above that is a cross. Directly above the cross is another scripture, Proverbs 15:33, which reads: "The fear of the Lord teaches a man wisdom, and humility comes before honor." On the left side of his stomach, Durant has an image of the house he grew up in. In front of the house is a boy wearing a No. 35 jersey and dribbling a basketball. And above his belly button Durant has the Washington Nationals' cursive *W* insignia. The top half of his back is covered with a tattoo. "Maryland" is spelled out across the width of his back, from shoulder to shoulder, in an outlined script font. Underneath, in the center, is an angel with an Afro holding a basketball. On either side of the angel is a hand. One is holding up the No. 3 under the *M*, the index finger and the thumb connected to form a circle. The other hand his holding up the No. 5 under the *D*.

To some in Oklahoma, the meaning behind the tattoos didn't matter. And the condemnation coming from certain corners perhaps should have been expected, considering that Oklahoma became the last state to legalize tattooing when it passed legislation in 2006. Five years later, here was the face of the state's only professional franchise covered in the ink many locals still frowned upon. But it was only a prelude to what became one of Durant's biggest forms of expression as he evolved as a personality off the court.

The 2011 lockout proved to be a revelation about Durant. The curtain to the soul behind the sweet jumper was opened more, enough to see inside. He was getting more comfortable in his own skin, more willing to let fans see the parts of him they might not like.

On November 26, 2011, the NBA and the players' union reached a tentative agreement. On December 8 the lockout officially ended. The players got 51 percent of the BRI. Part of the new agreement also included shorter deals. The longest contracts were for five years, reserved only for certain players. The rest maxed out at four years. And the ability to sign a player to a five-year extension a year before he became a free agent was eliminated.

The new collective bargaining agreement came with more punitive luxury taxes, too. All of these would conspire against the relationship between OKC and Durant.

The 2011–12 season finally began on Christmas Day. For the Thunder, the year began with controversy. In just the third game, a road contest at Memphis, Durant and Westbrook got into another heated verbal altercation on the sideline during a timeout. What began as a quarrel between Westbrook and then Thunder forward Thabo Sefolosha spilled over to the two All-Stars and quickly escalated after Durant initially tried to play peacemaker. Teammates and coaches stepped in to separate the two, preventing the spat from turning physical. As the two retook the floor following the timeout, Durant patted Westbrook on the head and the two finished the game without further incident. Back in OKC a day later to play a nationally televised game against Dallas, the Thunder downplayed the tense moment, chalking it up as typical of competitive athletes. But it was yet another moment in which Durant and Westbrook clashed, fueling speculation about how long the pairing could last.

The Thunder cruised through the shortened sixty-six-game season, going 47-19 and earning the No. 2 seed. Durant led the league in scoring for the third straight season, averaging 28 points along with career highs of 8 rebounds, 3.5 assists, and 1.2 blocked shots. Most notable from the regular season was how Durant and Westbrook devised a workable offensive solution that would satisfy both All-Stars' need for touches and shots. Westbrook would dominate the ball, dictate the tempo, and search for his shots in the first and third quarters. Durant then would do the same and get his in the second and fourth quarters, with Durant always being the go-to guy down the stretch and in last-second situations. Durant also began his march toward becoming tremendously efficient, which allowed Westbrook to be better while doing more as Durant mastered doing more with less.

Midway through the season, Durant was again named an All-Star, his third straight selection. This time his Thunder coach, Scott Brooks, earned the honor of coaching the Western Conference All-Stars. With the game being held in Orlando, Durant won All-Star Game MVP honors, scoring 36 points in the West's 152–149 victory.

"It's just exciting to be named [an] All-Star, but to step it up another level and become MVP, it's only something as a kid you dream about," Durant said after the game. "Coming from where I come from, I didn't think I would be here. Everything is just a blessing to me."

In the 2012 postseason, the Thunder disposed of Dallas in the opening round, getting revenge of sorts on an aging Mavs team that had retooled and could no longer keep up with the young legs from OKC. In Game 1, Durant scored or assisted on 10 of the Thunder's final 12 points and drained the game winner on an off-balanced fifteen-footer over Shawn Marion with 1.5 seconds remaining. The Thunder then dispatched the Lakers from the Western Conference semifinals in five games, demonstrating how much had changed since they were on the wrong end of a five-game series in 2010. In Game 2, Durant made the go-ahead shot on a baseline runner over Pau Gasol with 18.7 seconds remaining, and in Game 4 at Staples Center he hit the go-ahead 3 over Metta World Peace with 13.7 seconds remaining. This time Durant averaged 26.8 points on 51.6 percent shooting and 39.1 percent from 3-point range.

The Thunder then knocked off San Antonio in six in the West finals, winning four straight after dropping the first two. It was only the fifteenth time a team had come back to win a series after trailing 0–2 and just the eighth time a team had won a best-of-seven series with four consecutive victories after trailing 0–2. In Game 4 he put up 36 points and eight rebounds. In Game 6, he ended the series with a 34-point, fourteen-rebound masterpiece. In the clincher, the Thunder erased an 18-point first half deficit and outscored the Spurs 59–36 in the second half. Durant played all forty-eight minutes of Game 6, ensuring the Thunder would not go back to San Antonio for Game 7 and would instead move on to the NBA Finals.

"As sad and disappointed as we are, you really have to think about it almost like a Hollywood script for OKC in a sense," Spurs coach Gregg Popovich said after the game. "They went through Dallas, last year's NBA champion, then they went through the Lakers, then they went through us. Those three teams represent 10 of the last 13 championships, and now they're going to go to the Finals and play either Boston or Miami, and that'll be 11 of the last 13 championships.

I don't know if anybody has ever had a run or gone through a playoff playing those kinds of teams. It's just incredible, and I think it's pretty cool for them."

The Hollywood script wouldn't have a storybook ending.

. . .

Miami clawed back from a 3–2 hole against Boston in the East finals to set up a highly anticipated showdown between Durant and James, by consensus the two best players in basketball. It was James's third Finals appearance, with his previous two trips ending in defeat to San Antonio in 2007 and Dallas in 2011. The Heat, with Dwyane Wade and Chris Bosh by James's side, were battle-hardened veterans. The Thunder, despite all their talent, were still a year or two ahead of their time. And the gulf showed in the series.

The Thunder won Game 1 in OKC by 11 points, getting a game-high 36 points, eight rebounds, and four assists from Durant. It was the second-most points scored by a player in his Finals debut since the NBA merged with the ABA. Allen Iverson had scored 48 in his Finals debut in 1996. Durant scored 17 points in the decisive fourth quarter, helping the Thunder erase a 13-point second-quarter deficit and outscore the Heat 31–21 in the final frame. Durant also took the challenge of defending James for the first three quarters, hounding the league's MVP into 23 points on eighteen shots entering the final period. James defended Kendrick Perkins.

In Game 2, the Thunder trailed 18–2 in the first eight minutes, missing eleven of twelve shots and turning the ball over four times. They tried to rally once again, using a 27–16 spurt to storm back from a 13-point deficit with nine minutes left. Durant scored 16 points during the run, but it was his last attempt that will forever hang over the Thunder. On a short-corner jumper from seven feet out with 9.9 seconds remaining and the Thunder trailing by 2, Durant appeared to be fouled by James as he gathered and went up for the shot. The shot missed. A foul wasn't called. James corralled the rebound and sank two free throws for the final margin, a 100–96 Heat victory.

"I think I shot a good shot," Durant said. "That's a shot I shoot all the time. I just missed."

Durant was asked if there was contact.

"I was just worrying about the shot," he said. "I really couldn't tell you. I've got to watch the film, I guess."

Asked once more, Durant refused to blame the officials.

"I missed the shot, man," he said.

The Heat went on to win the next three games and take the series in five. James had his first championship. The wait would continue for the Thunder.

But at just twenty-three, Durant had stood toe-to-toe with James, by then a three-time MVP and the game's unquestioned best player. In the five-game series, Durant averaged 30.6 points, 6 rebounds, 2.2 assists, and 1.4 steals, shooting 54.8 percent from the field, 39.4 percent from the 3-point line, and 83.9 percent from the foul line. James was just a shade better and had more help. The Thunder had no answer for a new era of small ball ushered in by Heat coach Erik Spolestra, and it didn't help that Harden, who had been named that season's Sixth Man of the Year, was a disappointment, averaging only 12.4 points on 37.5 percent shooting in the series.

A forgotten footnote from that year's Finals is how the Thunder, despite owning home-court advantage, never got more than two games on their home floor. It was the last year of the 2-3-2 Finals format, leaving the Thunder without another chance to face the Heat in OKC after losing all three games in Miami.

Getting back to the Finals was going to be tricky. The summer of 2012 featured some major business to handle. Both Harden and Ibaka were eligible for contract extensions, and Brooks was up for a new contract as well.

"This is something special here," Harden told Oklahoma City reporters a day after the Finals loss. "A dynasty could be—is being—built here. So we're winning, we're having fun, and we're brothers. The other stuff, you can't buy it."

Four months later Harden was traded to Houston. He and the Thunder couldn't come to terms on a contract extension. It was a deal that rocked the Thunder and their fans and would alter the landscape of the NBA for the next decade. First Jeff Green was traded. Now a second major piece was ripped from underneath Durant, who initially took the high road and voiced support for management's decision but in time would rue the fateful trade when reflecting on the deal.

Thanks to stellar drafting, the Thunder had a five-man lineup that had the makings of a serious contender: Durant, Westbrook, Harden, Green, and Ibaka. But, especially in hindsight, keeping all five wasn't even remotely possible. Keeping three was acceptable, as the NBA trend had stars traveling in threes. But Oklahoma City couldn't keep the best three, which was clearly Durant, Westbrook, and Harden. They would each eventually become MVPs. But the price tag was too high, and Houston gave Harden the money he wanted.

"It's not until four or five years later, and you start to see the impact of that trade that you realize, 'Fuck, we really miss this guy,'" Durant would tell the *San Francisco Chronicle* years later. "We tried to plug in different pieces each year to fill his role, and it never happened. Guys weren't good enough. You can't replace him."

It didn't stop Durant from continuing his dominance. He won gold at the 2012 Olympics in London. Playing alongside more established stars in James, Kobe Bryant, Chris Paul, and Carmelo Anthony, Durant averaged a team-leading 19.5 points with 5.8 rebounds and 2.6

assists. Led by Durant, Team USA went undefeated. In a 7-point win against Spain in the gold-medal game, Durant scored 30 points, the first 30-point game in an Olympic final in U.S. history.

That summer Durant took heat for off-season workouts with James, who hosted Durant in Akron, Ohio, for the second consecutive summer. Many were critical of Durant's decision to buddy up to James. They were the game's undisputed two best players, who happened to play the same position, who happened to have just met in the NBA Finals. No one knew it at the time, but it was an early glimpse into how clearly Durant saw what so many others consider blurred lines between camaraderie and competition.

Durant's stance was that his competitiveness led him to the workout. He is so committed to progress, he'll cross enemy lines. "I would have worked out with Kobe Bryant," he explained. No one can argue with the results.

Durant led the Thunder to a 60-22 record and a league-leading 9.2-point differential in 2012–13, their best season in the franchise's Oklahoma City era. Durant became the epitome of efficiency, going down as only the sixth player in NBA history to shoot at least 50 percent from the field, 40 percent from the 3-point line, and 90 percent from the free-throw line. At the time, Durant joined Larry Bird as the only players to pull that feat while averaging at least 28 points.

That season also marked the first time Westbrook averaged more field-goal attempts than Durant, finishing with 18.7 per game to Durant's 17.7 average. Durant's 28.1-point average ranked second that season behind Carmelo Anthony. But no longer did Durant need scoring titles as validation. He was now starving for the NBA title.

A palpable shift in Durant's demeanor became evident. He began racking up technical fouls, amassing twelve alone in 2012–13 after being slapped with that same amount in his first five seasons combined. Durant's new on-court temper coincided with Nike's "KD is not nice" campaign, which launched in December 2012. It was a confusing concept, all things considered. Here was Nike seemingly sabotaging a golden-boy image and refuting Durant's reputation as the nicest, humblest superstar in sports. But the campaign was intended as a double entendre. A full-page ad in *Sports Illustrated* that season contained explanations for why "KD is not nice." Replete with images of a howling, scowling Durant, Nike's campaign played with the phrase: "Leading the league in scoring is not nice" and "Making defenders famous in all the wrong ways is not nice" and "Dropping 30 points before anyone realizes what hit them is not nice."

Of course, off the court he was still winning over the community. He was on Twitter in January 2013 before the Thunder hosted the Minnesota Timberwolves. That's how he learned about Ramarcus Ervin.

He was a kid at the Children's Center Rehabilitation Hospital in Bethany, Oklahoma, suffering from muscular dystrophy. His particular case, nemaline myopathy, attacked the fibers in his muscles, even the ones he used to breathe. Ramarcus would need a ventilator all of his life and twenty-four-hour care to remain alive. When he was born, doctors put his life expectancy at three months. But Ramarcus blew that away. For his fifteenth birthday, he wanted to meet Durant. He was a huge fan of the Thunder star.

The Children's Center posted a picture of Ramarcus and requested Durant come visit him for his birthday, including Durant's Twitter handle in the post. Scrolling through his mentions before the game. Durant saw Ramarcus in his hospital bed at TCC wearing an Oklahoma City Thunder shirt underneath the ventilator connected to his neck. Durant saw the plastic basketball court next to his bed, a pennant featuring his likeness on the wall, a DVD of the movie *Thunderstruck*, starring Durant, in Ramarcus's hand. A handmade sign on his bed read "Make My Birthday Wish Come True." Others retweeted the post, asking Durant to grant the wish. Durant put his people on it. He scored 26 points that night as the Thunder blasted Minnesota. The next day he was at the hospital, a special guest at a birthday celebration for Ramarcus:

Ervin couldn't speak well but he learned to communicate better than had ever been expected. Still, the noise he exuded when he saw Durant was unmistakable: shock and joy. Ramarcus's mother, Rafael, hugged Durant as tears streamed down her face. The fact Durant had showed up for her son—she couldn't even try to hide how much that meant. And the All-Star came bearing gifts. He gave Ramarcus a pair of autographed KD 5 shoes, a signed jersey from his first All-Star game, a signed Oklahoma City Thunder Jersey, and a signed copy of the *Thunderstruck* DVD.

After Ramarcus's party, Durant stayed longer and toured the hospital, meeting with other patients and thanking employees for working with the children.

"So many kids go through different things every day," Durant said. "And to have the love and care, and the support here, is all they really need." Ramarcus died on September 1, 2017.

Moments like these meant Durant was still the good guy. But the layers of his personality were starting to show. At the start of the 2013 postseason, *Sports Illustrated* plastered on its cover a candid quote from Durant in which he, for the first time, openly discussed his desire to reach the pinnacle of success. The crack in his shell widened.

"I've been second my whole life," Durant told the magazine. "I was the second-best player in high school. I was the second pick in the draft. I've been second in the MVP voting three times. I came in second in the Finals. I'm tired of being second. I'm not going to settle for that. I'm done with it."

Two weeks later Durant officially finished second in MVP voting for the third time—and for the third time in four years he was the runner-up to LeBron James.

But he wouldn't get another crack at James on the biggest stage. A fluke injury to Westbrook in the opening round of the playoffs derailed the Thunder, crushing their championship hopes and setting off a three-year run of awful and franchise-altering injuries. Patrick Beverley was the culprit. A rookie backup with the Rockets at the time, Beverley crashed into Westbrook's right knee while lunging at the ball as Westbrook attempted to call timeout near the sideline just past half-court. Westbrook ended up with a torn lateral meniscus that sidelined him for the rest of the postseason. The Thunder survived the Rockets but flamed out in the semifinals against Memphis in five.

An offense that had been criticized for years as being nothing more than a glorified your-turn, my-turn system starring Durant and Westbrook predictably crumbled when Westbrook went down. Without him, the Grizzlies loaded up on Durant and made his life hell.

Durant played all but sixteen minutes and forty-one seconds of the series. He played every second of Game 5. He paid a price for the lack of rest, coupled with the Grizzlies' defense. Durant made just 42.1 percent of his shots and averaged 4.4 turnovers. In Game 4 he was two for thirteen in the fourth quarter and overtime. He took five of the Thunder's eight shots in the extra period and missed all of them. Then, in Game 5, in Oklahoma City, Durant scored 21 points while missing sixteen of his twenty-one attempts.

He was spent. His tank was empty physically, mentally, and emotionally. That he still managed to average 28.8 points, 10.4 rebounds, and 6.6 assists was perhaps a testament to his greatness. Watching him doubled over, it was clear the burden of carrying the Thunder weighed on him. With the season on the line, and Oklahoma City down two in the final seconds and needing a score to keep the season alive, it was obvious that Durant was going to get the ball. With Westbrook watching from a luxury suite, the game was solely on Durant to save despite his struggles, despite his obvious fatigue. But Durant's mid-range jumper with 4.9 seconds left clanked. And the season was done.

"I gave it all I had for my team. I left it all out there on the floor. I missed 16 shots but I kept fighting, I kept being aggressive. That's all I can ask for," Durant said in his postgame interview. He wore black-rimmed glasses with a black leather jacket. The fatigue that dripped off him seemed to have disappeared. The exasperation had morphed into inspiration. Durant the leader had emerged.

"Some nights it was good, some nights it was bad. But I can live with myself knowing that I gave it all I had. . . . Down the line, we're going to look back at this and really appreciate it. Sometimes, you've got to ride out them storms to get to the sunshine."

Durant's sixth season in the NBA was complete. He was a few months from his twenty-fifth birthday and change was in the air. The off-season of 2013 turned out to be monumental in several ways.

In May 2013, a massive, mile-wide tornado with winds up to two hundred miles per hour devastated Moore, Oklahoma. The storm lasted forty minutes, leveling the small town. Two schools were damaged and three hundred homes destroyed. Dozens of people were killed. It was the most devastating tornado in Oklahoma since 1999. Seeing that kind of devastation prompted many to act. The nation felt for Oklahoma as the images of devastation flooded the media. Durant lived just twenty minutes away. He was especially touched.

Durant, towering over everybody, walked through the rubble in Moore. What were once homes had become piles of debris. Smiling, tired faces of workers and residents greeted the local star. Durant passed out fruit punch and lemon-lime Gatorade. He signed basketballs and shirts, and took pictures with victims of the tornado. Fittingly, he wore a bright red shirt, as his heart was on display. He just wanted to be with the people. Whatever joy they might feel from meeting a celebrity, from shaking hands with the player they'd cheered for, Durant wanted to provide it.

"This is my home," Durant said in an interview with Rachel Nichols for ESPN. "I just wanted to give back. I wanted to do something that was bigger than normal. Natural disasters are something that we really can't control. But we can control how we come together and how we bounce back."

He also donated $1 million of his own money. Nike matched the donation from the sale of Durant's signature shoe. Because of the care he showed, Durant became the face of all that is right with professional athletes. He became the example of their power and how impactful it can be when wielded properly. He had no haters. He became a local hero, a national hero. His concern and warmth bolstered his reputation as one of the NBA's good guys and endeared him to the community.

In early June, Durant parted ways with his agent, Rob Pelinka, then head of Landmark Sports Agency. The rumors had Durant teaming up with Jay-Z, who had launched the sports wing of his entertainment company in April with the signing of then Yankees second baseman Robinson Cano. Durant made it official June 24, joining WNBA star Skylar Diggins and NFL players Victor Cruz and Geno Smith on the Roc Nation client list. Durant instantly became the headline star, the coup that made Jay-Z's venture legitimate. But the move also legitimized Durant's maturation into a celebrity figure. Hindsight reveals this as a turning point for KD, when he decided to become more than a basketball player. He was universally regarded as one of the best players in the NBA and now he was taking his status and career in his own hands. And part of this arrangement with Roc Nation landed him a new agent named Rich Kleiman.

Kleiman was managing the music component of ESPN's docu-

series *The Life* when he met Jay-Z. The renowned rapper brought Kleiman on as one the producers for his movie *Fade to Black*, a cinematic
display of the concert accompanying what was then said to be Jay-Z's
final work, *The Black Album*. When Jay-Z created Roc Nation in 2008,
Kleiman was on the label as an artist manager, representing, among
others, singer Solange, sister of Beyoncé; rapper Meek Mill; and rapper Wale, a D.C. native whom Durant deemed a big brother. Kleiman
helped Jay-Z start Roc Nation Sports and was named VP, switching
over to exclusively athlete clients. As Durant's agent, he would become a central figure in Durant's life and unleash the mogul that was
starting to surface that summer.

Then, a couple of weeks after announcing his Roc Nation signing
on Instagram, Durant made another big move: he proposed to his
girlfriend. A couple of days after Independence Day, he got engaged
to Monica Wright, a WNBA star from PG County whom Durant had
known since he was a teenager. The oversized kid who used to invite
fans to his house to play video games and get in the mind-set for
games by dancing, showing off his Dougie moves on the sidelines,
was now making grown-man moves. He was trying to take control
of his life off the court, seizing the opportunities basketball delivered him.

It bled over into his on-court persona, too. Durant entered the
2013–14 season with bold declarations. He owned his inward desires
by having the moxie to share them outwardly. In a preseason interview with the *Oklahoman*, Durant again made his desire clear.

"I want to be the greatest," Durant told the newspaper. "I want to
be remembered as one of the greatest. When they redo that top 50
players [of all time], I want to be a part of that. This whole thing is a
fraternity. But it's a different fraternity when you're staring at a group
of guys that won championships, MVPs, and you can say you're on
that level with them in your career. It's only a handful of guys, maybe

15, 20 guys, that you can get in that conversation with. And I'm no-where near there yet. So that's where I want to be."

With Westbrook bouncing in and out of the lineup and missing thirty-six games that season due to complications and subsequent procedures on his surgically repaired knee, Durant unleashed his full arsenal on the game. He led the league in scoring for the fourth time in five years, averaging a career-high 32 points. He made slightly more than half his shots and connected on 39.1 percent from 3-point range. And that was with an average 7.4 rebounds and a career-high 5.5 assists.

His best basketball came during a three-month stretch from early January through early April. That was when Durant scored 25 points or more in forty-one consecutive games. His fame grew with each game as the nation tracked his scoring exploits. Only Oscar Robertson, with forty-six straight games in 1963–64, and Wilt Chamberlain, with eighty straight games in 1961–62, owned longer streaks. Durant's streak started with him scoring at least 30 points in twelve straight games, giving rise to an apt nickname: the Slim Reaper.

Incredible monikers are rare in sports. The best ones, they just ring. It fits the player's game and person. It packs the right tone and feel. It's just cool to say. The best ones are so perfect, they can't even apply to anyone else. And they are almost always given, not contrived self-brandings but organically applied. Magic Johnson, who smiles like one who knows how to put on a show and plays with a flair, passes with a wizardry that produces the awe of a magician. Air Jordan—anyone who saw him play witnessed the way he seemed to fly, just hang in the air, gliding. Air was so simple yet so perfect. King James—he seemed born for it. He was not only the king of high school basketball when he was given the name but he had already been deemed the rightful heir to basketball's throne. And he fulfilled his purpose. There are more. Vinny "the Microwave" Johnson. Gary Payton as "the

Glove" and Jason Williams as "White Chocolate." George "Iceman" Gervin and Julius "the Doctor" Irving. Watching them play, their nicknames just fit. And now Durant had one that was sticking perfectly. He'd been called other things: KD; Durantula: he named himself "the Servant" before. But the Slim Reaper was the drop-the-mic nickname. It embodied one of his most defining traits as a person, the thinness that always stood out, and his game on the court, which just killed defenses, took the life right out of them.

The only problem was, Durant didn't like it. The moniker didn't fit his faith-based sensibilities.

"I'm here to shine a bright light," Durant said. "I'm not here to be a guy of, I guess, death."

He was nonetheless deadly on the court. His forty-one-game streak included seventeen 30-point games, nine 40-point games, and two 50-point explosions, including a career-high 54 points in a home win against Golden State on January 17, 2014. Durant averaged 34.8 points on just 22.2 shots over that span. The Thunder went 27-14 over that stretch, including a 17-7 mark when Westbrook was out of the lineup. They would finish 59-23, the second-best record behind the 62-win Spurs.

Durant's momentum carried into the postseason as the Thunder faced their nemesis in Memphis. He scored 33 points in the Game 1 win, getting Oklahoma City out of the blocks. But his next four games were rough. The Grizzlies and Thunder set an NBA record with four consecutive overtime games. Durant missed his last two 3-pointers in overtime of Game 2. He missed the game-tying 3-pointer with 22 seconds left in overtime of Game 3 as the Thunder lost in Memphis. In Game 4, Durant had just 15 points on twenty-one shots. Oklahoma City survived, but it was guard Reggie Jackson who provided the overtime offense, scoring 8 of the Thunder's 12 points.

But the series was tied 2–2. Oklahoma City was headed back home with a chance to take control of the series. But Durant struggled again. He had 26 points on twenty-four shots with six turnovers. In another overtime game he scored the first two baskets but failed to come through in the clutch. He stepped to the free-throw line with the Thunder down 100–98, but he missed the second free throw. Then, after an Oklahoma City stop, he missed the game-winning 3-pointer attempt at the buzzer, curling off a pin-down screen with 2.5 seconds left in the game, catching and firing from the left wing. The Thunder trailed 3-2 in the series and was headed back to Memphis.

The next day the April 30, 2014, edition of the *Oklahoman*, the primary newspaper in Oklahoma City, ran a headline in big, bold letters spanning the width of the front page of the sports section: "Mr. Unreliable."

"I'm unreliable? Me, Mr. Unreliable?" Durant said to reporters the next morning.

"They're going to build you up, they're going to break you down. You just have to stay even-keeled, and that's what I am. It's all about what have you done for me lately, and I understand that."

The headline caused such a stir, the newspaper ended up apologizing.

Durant was indeed underperforming, shooting 40 percent from the field and 28.6 percent from 3. He was even down to 71.8 percent from the foul line while averaging four turnovers. The Grizzlies had two excellent defenders in Tony Allen and Tayshaun Prince haunting Durant. Plus, Durant had put a lot of miles on those wiry legs of his. He led the league in minutes during the regular season. He had played 49 minutes or more in three straight games and was averaging 47.6 minutes through five games.

But he did just carry the Thunder to 59 wins. Even though the Thunder faced elimination, and Durant hadn't come through in four straight close games, there were still games to play.

On the night the headline appeared in the city's newspaper, Durant erupted for 36 points and ten rebounds in a 20-point road win in Game 6. He followed that by scoring 33 points in the clinching Game 7 to get the Thunder to the next round. The Oklahoman went with another bold headline: "Kevin Up," a play on the team's slogan Thunder Up.

Durant was back to scuffling to start the second-round series against the Los Angeles Clippers. Oklahoma City was outscored by 25 points when Durant was on the court. He had 25 points but they weren't as impactful, as the Clippers took the opener by 17.

The next day, though, on the off day between games, Durant got the validation his game had been warranting. He was named NBA MVP. He received 119 of 125 first-place votes. The runner-up: LeBron James.

At his award ceremony, which the Thunder turned into a community event inside the team's original practice facility, Durant delivered one of the signature moments of his career: his MVP speech. It was every bit as spectacular as it was surprising. He laughed. He cried. He reflected. He cried some more. He thanked everyone he could think of: God, his family, the Thunder owners and the team's management, his teammates, the fans, the media. But his final forty-eight words to his mother marked the speech's defining moment.

"We wasn't supposed to be here. You made us believe," Durant said as his voice cracked. "You kept us off the street. You put clothes on our backs, food on the table. When you didn't eat, you made sure we ate. You went to sleep hungry. You sacrificed for us.

"You the real MVP."

This was the heart of Durant showing up again. The man who felt to his core. He didn't fight the tears; he let them roll. He didn't play it cool at this landmark moment in his life; he soaked it in. And what defines him became the signature moment that defined him.

Durant went on to average 33.2 points to fuel the Thunder to a six-game series win over the Los Angeles Clippers in the Western Conference semifinals. But a calf injury to Ibaka in that clinching Game 6 knocked him out of the first two games of the West finals against San Antonio, greatly altering the Thunder's makeup. OKC lost Games 1 and 2 in San Antonio by a combined 52 points. Ibaka returned for the final four games, but the Thunder couldn't replicate their 2012 magic. They won Games 3 and 4 at home but lost Game 5 in San Antonio before losing Game 6 in overtime at home.

The next season, injuries hit hard from the start, ruining any chance the Thunder had of competing for a championship in 2014–15. Durant, who had just turned twenty-six, went down in mid-October with a Jones fracture, a broken bone at the base of his right small toe, the fifth metatarsal. Surgery would sideline him for six to eight weeks. It rocked the Thunder to the core and triggered a harsh new reality for Durant, who had appeared in 542 of a possible 558 regular season games prior to that point.

The injury was said to be a stress injury, one that occurs over time. Hindsight painted a clear picture that perhaps led Durant to this point. Durant had averaged 38.2 regular season minutes for his career and 42.3 minutes in 73 postseason games. Durant's 20,717 minutes since entering the NBA in 2007 were more than any other player over that span. LeBron James ranked second at 20,215 minutes, and only three other players had reached 19,000 total minutes over those seven seasons. Combine that hefty NBA workload with Durant's Team USA commitments and his penchant for playing pickup ball in the summers, and it's a toll that likely led to his injury.

Durant missed the season's first seventeen games, and the Thunder went 5-12 without him and a host of other players. He made his season debut on December 2, 2014, scoring 27 points while on a thirty-minute restriction. Nine games later, however, Durant rolled his right ankle at Golden State when Warriors center Marreese Speights slid underneath him to take a charge. Durant was cooking, having poured in 30 points in nineteen first-half minutes, showing signs he was back and as good, if not better, than ever. He missed the next six games, including a marquee Christmas game at San Antonio.

Durant rejoined the lineup on New Year's Eve, torching the Phoenix Suns for 44 points, ten rebounds, and seven assists in a home win. He played twelve straight games before spraining his left big toe and missing four of the next five games. He returned on February 6 and played four consecutive games before the All-Star break but appeared to be in obvious discomfort, limping and wincing as he attempted to play through it that fourth game, a home date with Memphis.

He was determined to travel to New York and participate in that year's All-Star festivities. But he played a career-low ten minutes in the 2015 All-Star Game. Meanwhile, Durant's disposition changed. He grew surly and became increasingly and uncharacteristically combative. It started at his media availability on the Friday before the All-Star Game, when questions began to fly about the MVP award. Durant, the reigning MVP, strangely began downplaying the award's validity because of what he deemed media-driven narrative.

"I think the media and guys get too much power to vote on stuff that, quite frankly, I don't think you really know a lot about [or] as much as we [players] know about it," Durant said. "We play against these guys every single night. We battle against these guys. We know what they say on the court. We know how they handle their teammates. We know how they approach the game, and our vote should count. Our opinions should count. Like I said, I don't think you guys know as much as we do, and I don't see why you have more power than we do."

A day later, in his final media session before Sunday's All-Star Game, Durant took exception to a question about rampant speculation about Brooks's job security as Thunder coach.

"You guys really don't know shit," Durant told the assembled media. His public swearing was another deviation. Durant made a habit of watching his mouth publicly. He cursed in private but in the eyes and ears of fans he put forth less provocative language. He wanted to be a good example, a model for kids and embraceable by the populace. But even that restraint was withering away.

In that same session, Durant was asked what the media was not paying attention to that he would like them to talk about more.

"To be honest, man, I'm only here talking to y'all because I have to," Durant responded. "So I really don't care. Y'all not my friends. You're going to write what you want to write. You're going to love us one day and hate us the next. That's a part of it. So I just learn how to deal with y'all."

Durant later apologized for his comments. Most had already given him a pass, chalking it up to frustration. Durant was in the midst of his most injury-plagued season, his team sat only three games over .500 at the break, a half-game out of the playoff picture, and his coach was facing questions about his future. But the truth was, that was the start of Durant doing things his way, something he first broached in an interview with *USA Today* the previous September. The topic was raised when Durant was asked about criticism of his eleventh-hour decision to withdraw from the Team USA roster that was preparing to compete in the 2014 FIBA World Cup.

"Seriously, to be honest, I was like fuck 'em. You can write that, too," Durant told *USA Today*. "Seriously, though, I'm just going to be me, man, and that's how I felt."

At that All-Star media session Friday, Durant expounded on his new direction when asked which life lesson he was carrying most at the time.

"I'm 26 years old so I'm in my mid-20s, almost to 30," Durant said. "My first few years in the league I was just finding myself. I think most of the time I reacted based off of what everybody else wanted and how they viewed me as a person. And I'm just learning to be myself and not worry about what anybody says. I'm going to make mistakes. I just want to show kids out here that athletes, entertainers, whoever, so-called celebrities, we aren't robots. We go through emotions. We go through feelings. And I'm just trying to express mine and trying to help people along the way.

"But I'm not going to sit here and tell you that I'm just this guy that got programmed to say the right stuff all the time and politically correct answers. I'm done with that. I'm just trying to be me and continue to grow as a man."

Durant returned to OKC following the All-Star break and appeared in one more game before undergoing a second surgery on his foot to alleviate lingering soreness. He was expected to be evaluated in one week. But one month later, further consultation revealed regression. On March 31, 2015, Durant underwent a third surgery, this time a bone graft. He needed four to six months just to return to basketball-related activities. His season was done. So was the Thunder's. OKC missed the playoffs for the first time since 2009. Durant missed fifty-five games.

It was the last of three straight significant injuries that dashed the Thunder's championship dreams in three straight seasons.

Brooks ultimately was fired after the 2014–15 season. Two-time national championship coach Billy Donovan was brought in from the University of Florida in hopes that he would revamp the Thunder's offense. It worked.

Oklahoma City vaulted back to No. 3 in the Western Conference. Durant got over the foot injuries that had plagued him the previous season and was back to his normal dominant ways: averaging 28.2 points and a career-high 8.2 rebounds.

The Thunder played at a faster pace under Donovan. The insertion of André Roberson into the starting lineup raised the defensive potential. But they had one Achilles' heel: they struggled in the clutch. Despite having Durant and Westbrook, two bona fide stars, the Thunder made a habit of falling apart down the stretches of games.

Oklahoma City played forty-four games that were within 5 points with five minutes or fewer left in the game. They only won half of those games, tied for seventeenth most clutch losses in the league. Both Durant and Westbrook struggled with efficiency in the clutch. Westbrook shot 38.9 percent in those games, Durant 41.2.

The Golden State Warriors took the league by storm that season. After winning the 2015 NBA Championship, they started the 2015–16 season with 24 straight wins and went on to set the NBA record with 73 wins, breaking the previous mark set by the 1995–96 Chicago Bulls. In what turned out to be one of the greatest regular season games in recent memory, the Thunder and the Warriors had an epic clash in Oklahoma City that illustrated the narrative of both seasons.

It was a riveting clash of titans. It revealed how the Warriors and Thunder were on par from a talent perspective, but the Warriors had a special something Oklahoma City didn't have and had been struggling to find. That was first clear in their February 27, 2016, matchup.

The Warriors came in an astounding 52-5, way ahead of the Thunder (41-17) in the standings. But through three quarters, the Thunder had led by as much as 14 and held an 83–78 lead entering the fourth quarter. Durant was nothing short of dominant: 30 points on eleven of nineteen shooting, outdueling Stephen Curry, who was feeling it from 3-point range and had 26 points.

The Thunder led by as much as 12 in the fourth quarter. They were up 96–85 with 4:51 left in the game after a Westbrook layup. This was Oklahoma City's game to win—and it would have been a huge one, too. But the collapse came fast and was astonishing.

The home team missed nine of its last eleven shots. Westbrook was zero for four. Durant was one for four. Ibaka was one for three. The Thunder's three best players took all the shots and their offense sputtered. Still, Durant buried a 3-pointer with 14.5 seconds left, putting his team up 103–99. It felt like Oklahoma City had survived. But Klay Thompson answered with a layup and Durant, who got trapped near the baseline, threw the ball errantly and the Warriors picked it off. Andre Iguodala ended up fouled while shooting a jumper with seven-tenths of a second left. He made both free throws, sending the game into overtime. Another clutch failure by Oklahoma City.

The Thunder were much better in overtime, scoring the first 5 points of the extra period, then after the Warriors tied it going back up by 4. Oklahoma City led 118–115 with 33.9 seconds. One stop away from knocking off the champions on national television. But Westbrook fouled Thompson on a layup. The 3-point play tied the game. Oklahoma City burned twenty-one seconds before Westbrook missed a bank shot under duress. The Warriors got the rebound and Curry drilled the game winner from thirty-seven feet.

It was an epic ending for the ages. The Warriors stars had outplayed the Thunder's in crunch time and punctuated their supremacy. It wasn't that long ago Durant and Westbrook had the Thunder atop the Western Conference, a perennial power. And now they were clearly looking up at the Warriors. But all that changed when they met in the Western Conference Finals three months later.

The Thunder stole Game 1 despite Durant struggling mightily in the second half, going three for twelve from the field. The series shifted to Oklahoma City for Game 3, the series tied at 1. That's when the Thunder sent an emphatic message.

It was a slaughter.

The Thunder led by as much as 41. Durant scored 33 points on ten shots in three quarters. Westbrook had 30 in the same span. None of the six All-Stars from both teams played the fourth quarter. The Warriors wrote it off as an aberration. A formidable foe had everything go right and the Warriors had everything go wrong. They excused it as one of those things. Then it happened again.

The avalanche came in the second quarter of Game 4, this time led by Westbrook's 16. The lead grew to 25 in the fourth quarter. It wasn't a fluke. The Thunder had the Warriors' number. Golden State had blitzed the league with what was dubbed the Death Lineup. They moved the power forward, Draymond Green, to center and added a guard, Iguodala, to the lineup. They were long, athletic, and skilled. They used this lineup to pick up the pace. They ran circles around teams with big men. And the teams who could also pull the center just didn't have the talent they had. But the Warriors had never faced a foe like Oklahoma City. Steven Adams was a center mobile enough to keep up, but he also punished the Warriors inside like few others could. But the Thunder also had the pieces to go centerless as well.

Ibaka at center was taller and more athletic than Green, and Ibaka could shoot the 3. Durant moved over to power forward, giving the Thunder an advantage at that position. Roberson played the defensive specialist like Iguodala. Dion Waiters was the extra guard who added to the scoring punch. Oklahoma City was just as potent offensively, even more swarming defensively and even better in transition. They had the Warriors rattled. The defending champions, who set a record for regular season wins, trailed 3 games to 1 and looked inferior to the Thunder.

But the Warriors still had something Oklahoma City didn't have. They'd won a championship. They had resolve, pedigree. They'd become acquainted with pressure and mastered it. They had another gear. They had a miracle game from Thompson and some dominance from Curry. Most important, the Warriors had a system, a philosophy, they believed would outlast the Thunder's style of leaning heavily on their two All-Stars.

In the end, the Warriors were right. Oklahoma City fell apart.

The Thunder led by 13 points in the second quarter of Game 7 in Oakland. But that was erased by a Warriors' surge in the third. Thompson caught fire. Curry scored 15 points in the fourth quarter. The Thunder were finished.

That night, Durant was at 724 Hookah, a lounge in the Tenderloin District of San Francisco. He came in with his own party. Draymond Green arrived with his crew later. Eventually the two combatants who had just finished an epic seven-game series were at the same booth. That's where the conversation began. They chatted well into the night.

Twenty days later they were chatting again. This time via text message. The Warriors had just lost Game 7 of the 2016 NBA Finals. Like the Thunder, the Warriors also blew a 3–1 lead. So Green enacted the plan he and Durant had already talked about.

"We need you," Green told *Sports Illustrated* he texted Durant. "Make it happen."

This was Green's closing pitch. They had talked about it. They had imagined the possibilities. Green had put in the time recruiting Durant. In his mind, doing so after Game 7 would let Durant know he was serious. Per the *Sports Illustrated* piece, Oklahoma City officials noticed the change in Durant after the Warriors lost the Finals. Durant's responses were more distant. Green's recruiting was working. As Lee Jenkins wrote:

The Warriors would have to endure a summer's worth of mortifying memes—punishment for squandering a 3–1 Finals lead—but by the time Green peeled off his home whites and hit the showers, he could sense that his squad would laugh last. Durant's response flashed across the screen: "I'm ready. Let's do this."

6 | OK—SEE YA

IT'S A FUN GAME TO TRY TO PINPOINT when Durant first thought about coming to Oakland. There were certainly hints before his hangout with Green or his free agency meetings held at a mansion in the Hamptons. An interesting conversation between Durant, then still with the Thunder, and a Warriors public relations rep suggests he might have been eyeing the Warriors even earlier.

Randomly, before a game, Durant had a question for the Warriors' staffer, who was available in the visitors' locker room to provide the opponents with what they needed: tickets, statistical packets, answers. This request, though, was a bit of a curveball.

"When does the new arena open?" Durant asked. This was February 6, 2016. Durant was still the face of the Thunder.

The Bay Area was buzzing at the time. The Warriors were well into a historic season. They had captivated the nation and frenzied the region with a 24-0 start to the season and were still rolling at 45-4 when Oklahoma City came to town. The Super Bowl, set for the next day at the 49ers' Levi's Stadium, had brought its own mania to the Bay. Durant remained in town after the game and went to the Super Bowl as a photographer for the *Players' Tribune*, an online magazine (of which Durant was part owner) dedicated to players' perspectives.

A week earlier the Warriors had announced a naming rights deal with JPMorgan Chase. Their new home, scheduled to open in 2019, would be called the Chase Center, a billion-dollar arena on San Francisco Bay, a quick jog from baseball's famed Oracle Park. The Warriors celebrated the twenty-year naming rights deal with a big production at the Masonic Center in San Francisco, featuring a performance by the Glide Memorial United Methodist Church's popular choir and a Q and A with MVP Stephen Curry. The naming rights deal was considered the largest of its kind.

Durant's curiosity was itching. After a couple of questions, the PR rep asked Durant if he would like to speak with someone who could tell him about the arena. Durant said yes. Moments later he was getting the entire Chase Center breakdown from a high-up Warriors official.

Durant was known to give a random interrogation. He was curious like that. But was this *that*? Or was this a sign of interest from Durant? Was this a pending free agent vetting his options in advance?

Of course, Durant's line of questioning was juicy enough to report to Warriors management. The moment in this dank locker room was immediately relayed to Warriors owner Joe Lacob, and it was music to his ears. Golden State's brain trust had been plotting to acquire Durant for some time. After failing to get a meeting with LeBron James in 2010 and missing out on Dwight Howard in 2013, the Warriors set their sights on the free agency class of 2016, which was headlined by Durant.

Back in 2013 they signed free agent Andre Iguodala to a four-year deal in which the salary descended each year of the deal, such that the final year of the deal (2016–17) was the lowest. They did the same thing with the extension of center Andrew Bogut. This made both players more tradeable if they needed to get rid of their contracts to make room for Durant. Every player the Warriors signed after Iguodala was inked to either a contract that would be off the books by the summer of 2016 (when Durant was scheduled to be a free agent) or an expiring contract that would be valuable on the trade market.

Lacob coveted a splashy free agent move since he bought the team in 2010. Not even a championship trophy curbed his appetite for such a move. For Lacob, there was great validation in landing the top free agent on the market. It represented legitimacy. Especially after purchasing a veritable laughingstock of a franchise, having a superstar to choose the Warriors was the ultimate vindication. Even with Stephen Curry ascending to superstar status after becoming an MVP and leading the Warriors to a championship, management still wanted Durant. And this was an early sign that he might listen.

. . .

The genesis of Durant's eventual departure may have actually begun in Oakland on December 18, 2014, when he sprained his right ankle at Oracle Arena and eventually missed the last fifty-five games of the year. It was the first time in his career Durant had missed significant time in the NBA.

"It was the first time basketball had been stripped from his life for an extended stretch," said reporter Anthony Slater, who covered Durant for three years in Oklahoma City before moving to the Bay Area to cover the Warriors.

"He was kind of depressed about it, but it also sparked a little curiosity. He started thinking more about the world and his place within it, exploring different hobbies, discovering new interests. He became an amateur photographer. There's that story of him going to a Drake concert in Montreal and being shocked that the primary language there was French. Those months away from the game just kind of took his brain to a different, more awoken place. Basketball could've kept him in OKC. Nearly did. If they'd won it all in 2016, and they very nearly did, I very much doubt he leaves. But I also don't think he leaves if he doesn't spend those sidelined hours, sometimes in a wheelchair or walking boot, finally searching for a deeper understanding of who he really is and what he really wants."

Durant had a ball in his hands since he was nine years old. Basketball had been his life. It was his peace in a tumultuous childhood. It was his fun undeterred by limited resources. It was his adjunct for some valuable life lessons, filling the blanks left by a wanting public school system and a broken family. Basketball was his conduit to friendship, where he got his confidence despite his awkwardly tall and skinny frame, acne, and empty pockets. Basketball was his method for escaping the struggle that had embedded in him. It gave him permission to dream.

But it was also his burden. It was his identity and his worth. He had lived for years under the pressure his excellence at basketball brought him. He had been indoctrinated with his place in the world, his contribution to society, what was expected of him and what his limitations were, by the politics and boundaries of basketball. What's more, this relationship was non-negotiable. It was all or nothing. The promises and spoils of basketball came only with wholehearted commitment. Surrounding him were plenty examples of how flagging devotion destroyed potential. So Durant remained faithful to basketball.

He was a natural at it, but he also devoted himself with the fervor of an addict. He gave the game a hard decade of his life in pursuit of the NBA. He played all year. Untold hours. Innumerable shots. Many basketball players pick up the sport out of obligation. Their physical gifts, witnessed and lauded by others, serve as a shove in the back toward hoop. Many have played the game in their youth but don't take it seriously until late in their teenage years, when it becomes a viable asset. But Durant was an early convert who pledged his love in pre-adolescence. The smoothness in his game was the result of basketball being second nature, a perk of being so talented and dedicated to basketball so early.

Durant initially hurt his foot because of this devotion to basketball. When the NBA season ended, he was returning to his old stomping grounds and hooping. He was making millions of dollars. He was adored by fans across the nation—the world, even. He had a contractual obligation to his franchise, to this multibillion-dollar professional league, to be at his maximum when the season began, which required monitored and scripted off-season work. Teams would love to have their trainers and strength and conditioning coaches work with their stars all year round. But the collective bargaining agreement prevents such off-season oversight. A code of conduct policy in contracts specifically rules out certain dangerous activities, such as skydiving and motorcycles. But beyond that there is an understanding between the employer and the player that he preserve himself and be prepared for the season.

But the blacktop was magnetic for Durant. His affinity for basketball didn't subside with the off-season. And he was doing what would make all professional trainers cringe: playing basketball regularly on concrete surfaces with unpolished players.

Durant was twenty-six years old when his foot caused him to miss fifty-five games. He had already made more than $80 million on the court and still had $20 million coming in the final year of the five-year, $89 million extension he signed back in 2010. Back then, at twenty-one years of age, free agency didn't entice Durant. He signed his contract extension matter-of-factly, never even testing the waters, choosing loyalty over the experience of being courted. Just over a week later, after LeBron James made his controversial decision to leave Cleveland and join the Miami Heat, Durant sent out a tweet criticizing players for joining basketball powerhouses.

"Now everybody wanna play for the Heat and the Lakers? Let's go back to being competitive and going at these peoples!"

Back then, he thought exclusively in basketball terms, by the laws of the world in which he existed. Most of his success and adoration came from basketball. Most of the perks he enjoyed came from basketball. Most of his understanding came from basketball.

When he launched the Kevin Durant Charity Foundation, officializing his desire to give back, one of his most passionate works was his "Build It and They Will Ball" initiative. Announced in 2015, it refurbished and built basketball courts in low-income neighborhoods around the world, giving youth high-quality courts on which to play. He built courts in Seat Pleasant, Oklahoma City, Oakland, Austin, Seattle, D.C., San Francisco, New York City, Germany, China, India, and Taiwan.

Durant found peace on the court. It was a space of fun in a childhood marked by hardship. He wanted to share that escape with children who needed one. Playing basketball kept him out of trouble. It was on courts that he learned about growth and maturity. Durant once thought he would spend his adulthood working at a recreation center, as Taras Brown and Charles Craig had done at Seat Pleasant. He found honor in that, being a coach and molder of young men. Making the NBA changed that career path. But these courts were a version of that. He couldn't be there with them, to shuttle them around in a van, to make sure hungry children got something to eat, to drop life gems in their formative minds. But he could give them a place to play. A fresh court with colors that inspired, painted lines and glass backboards to match the luster of their dreams.

Basketball has always been sanctuary for KD. And in this realm of life, the real credibility, came from beating the best with your guys. You went to the courts with a crew; the truest sense of victory was to win with them. Losing and wanting to switch teams was an infraction of the code. Underdogs were supposed to keep trying until they eventually won. So all the players going to join LeBron James in Miami or Kobe Bryant with the Lakers were violating the spirit of hoop.

Durant was loyal to the game. And therefore the code. And therefore to Oklahoma City. It made perfect sense, too, that Durant so loved Oklahoma City. It was the capital of his hoops paradigm. It was the Emerald City he'd worked toward all those years, the place where the payoff was realized and the bounty came in. He made that abundantly clear by signing his contract extension without even allowing another team to whisper in his ear. The Thunder was the crew he had come to the park with, and that meant he wasn't going to entertain playing with someone else. Basketball—sports, for that matter—really taps into the tribalistic nature of humanity. Durant, being from the inner city of D.C., knew well the rules of loyalty and respect. He took pride in his adherence to them. It made him real.

On top of that, Durant and Oklahoma City shared a bond as underdogs. Despite being a prodigy, life and its adversities made sure he always had a chip on his shoulder. At his core was an affinity for the grind. Being a nice guy mattered to Oklahomans, for whom hospitality and kindness are woven into the social construct. He could wear his heart on his sleeve and fit right in. His mother and grandmother were big on Jesus and so were Oklahomans, which made it feel like home. In many ways, Durant and Oklahoma City were a match made in heaven: a small town with big-city dreams for the big-city guy with small-town values.

ESPN's Royce Young, an Oklahoman, wrote about Durant's departure from the perspective of Thunder fans, of local citizens, trying to decode what had happened. Durant and the Thunder had a bond. It was obvious to outside parties. Most NBA players, gleaned from inner cities across America after their dreams and expectations had been shaped, were trying to get to the hottest spots. They typically want big cities rife with off-the-court opportunities, a bustling nightlife, millions of eyes, and luxury with which to enjoy their bounty.

Durant was a megastar, a surefire Hall of Famer and unquestionably one of the five best players in the NBA. But he sounded just fine in a place that seemed like the opposite of luxurious.

"Where I grew up, we were 30 minutes outside of Washington, D.C., but there was never anything new," Durant said in a *Sports Illustrated* article that dropped in May 2016. "In Oklahoma City everything is new. We've got a new Aloft Hotel up the street. There's a new arcade, Brickopolis, I want to try. Behind my house all these new townhomes are going in, and along the highway out to our facility, they tore down the old car wash and are putting up more new condos. I know that's not a championship. But the championships, the records, the who's the best player—there will always be new champions and new records and new players. What we're talking about, these are jobs, these are lives, these are things that will matter for 40 years, and that is very cool to me."

And the locals loved Durant because of his willingness to bond with them. He was an outsider who wasn't ashamed to be among them, never purported to be longing for something else bigger and fancier. They put him—the Prince George's County product—into their state Hall of Fame. He had expressed his affinity and love for Oklahoma and they loved him for it.

So what changed? Young asked this pivotal question at the end of his piece.

The obvious answer, Young concluded, was that Durant did. Something major in him had changed. Or perhaps it was a series of minor changes that produced this major outcome. But the Durant that decided to leave Oklahoma City was a different person.

Durant's time off from basketball because of his injury happened at a unique time in his life.

Perhaps a central element was Durant's age. Twenty-six is inside an interesting window of growth and maturity for men. NBA players, especially those like Durant who enter the league as teenagers, are kids in a candy store with a gift card. Especially the superstars, who get celebrity along with millions of dollars. Nothing is withheld from them. They get to scratch every itch. They live out a relative fantasy with access and perks. But then they get past twenty-five and start wanting more. Their values change.

Perhaps it's because a male adult's brain isn't fully developed until around age twenty-five (a few years later than women). Adulthood can't even truly begin until the frontal and temporal lobes—which regulate emotion, vision, judgment, comprehension, problem-solving, and even sexual behavior—are fully developed. The march from twenty-five to thirty is an awakening period. Some studies suggest men don't reach full maturity until their early forties. Despite their enlarged wallets, giant stature, and full-blown statuses, these professional athletes are still just young adult men who at some point transition into adulthood. Their emotions and desires and rationales change. The nightlife becomes less appealing. They begin to see more value in a strong relationship with one woman than superficial relationships with many. Money takes a back seat to "happiness." They start thinking about investments and entrepreneurship instead of splurging. They start thinking about how to make a bigger impact and how to use their voices. And after having already won in life, their urge to win on the court grows stronger.

It's not a coincidence that LeBron James made his decision to leave

Cleveland for Miami at twenty-five, then to go back home at twenty-nine. Kyrie Irving forced his way out of Cleveland, a move that symbolized being his own man, at age twenty-five. Kawhi Leonard, who was quiet and seemingly lacking in emotion, was suddenly fed up at age twenty-six and demanded a trade out of San Antonio. Michael Jordan walked away from basketball at twenty-nine.

None of that meant Durant was going to leave or should have left. But it would make sense if his time off due to his foot injury sparked a change. Probably for the first time since he was a preteen he thought about life outside of the context of basketball.

Durant probably felt like actress Bryce Dallas Howard in the M. Night Shyamalan movie *The Village*. She was just twenty-three at the time—well before her role in *The Help* catapulted her career into blockbusters like *Jurassic World*—and played Ivy Walker, the blind resident of a nineteenth-century village encircled by woods. She braved the dangerous woods and its deadly beasts in search of medicine for her fiancé. Eventually it was revealed that the setting wasn't the nineteenth century but the present day. The Village was a crafted existence to keep its residents from corruption. The blind girl got outside the perimeter of their society and learned there was an entirely new world beyond it, with new ways of doing things, new understandings, new beliefs.

Durant, too, stepped outside of his existence and learned there was more to life than basketball. *He* was more than basketball. He even discovered that there were levels at which he understood the game and its politics, and what he wanted out of the sport.

Who created the rule that required loyalty to the team and the fan base? What if everybody who came to the park was part of the crew, even if they ended up on different teams? Could location, off-the-court opportunities, and other relationships factor into where a player wanted to play? Why were the best players not allowed to do what lower-tier players were free to do without criticism? When was it okay to prioritize the heart over the code?

Additionally, a new era in player free agency was being ushered in. James's decision to leave Cleveland started a trend of NBA players putting their own interests over their teams' and the fan base—even over their own salaries. After losing some of their cut of revenue during the 2011 lockout, in an effort to control salaries, superstars made up for it by wielding their power on the free agent and trade markets. James demolished Cleveland when he left for Miami and resurrected the franchise when he returned. After being crucified in the court of public opinion, he turned out to be a pioneer of a new era. Players would no longer be pawns in the business of basketball but would dictate their own terms. They also began using their influence off the court, which required examining what mattered to them beyond basketball. LeBron James, Dwyane Wade, and Carmelo Anthony became voices against police brutality. Anthony, then thirty-one, even marched with protesters in Baltimore. Stephen Curry, at twenty-seven, broke out of his vanilla blanket and criticized President Trump.

Were there other factors that helped nudge Durant out the door?

Cole Cashwell, a high school junior from Cary, North Carolina, sent this to Durant on Twitter in September of 2017:

"Man I respect the hell outta you but give me one legitimate reason for leaving OKC other than getting a championship."

Durant has been known to engage with fans on social media his whole career. But this time he responded in the third person from his verified Twitter account.

"He didn't like the organization or playing for Billy Donovan. His roster wasn't that good, it was just him and Russ (Westbrook). Imagine taking Russ off that team, see how bad they were. KD can't win a championship with those cats."

Social media was abuzz with the implication. Durant had given the most honest and disparaging explanation in the third person. Why would Durant speak so freely and as if he were someone else? The public concluded it must mean Durant thought he was tweeting from a secret account but actually hadn't switched over and was still on his main account with more than 15 million followers. Which meant Durant had a secret account and, if this reply was any indication, he used it to defend his honor. Of course, it could have been a friend or someone who with access to Durant's account who was conversing with fans and went too far. But Durant didn't go with the my-friend-did-it excuse. He didn't proclaim he was hacked. At a tech conference in San Francisco, he confessed.

"I use Twitter to engage with fans," he said at TechCrunch Disrupt San Francisco 2017. "I think it's a great way to engage with basketball fans. I happened to take it a little too far."

That idea, that Durant was taking to Twitter anonymously to fire back at critics, was the dominant narrative. But did he reveal more about his decision to leave Oklahoma City?

This was more than a year after he left the Thunder. Was he using his former teammates and coach as scapegoats, or was he being honest about his real reasons? The third person suggested the latter: that Durant thought he was writing under the cover of anonymity, which emboldened him to speak freely.

What if the 2016 Western Conference Finals were the nudge he needed?

The common narrative about the epic seven-game series between Durant's Thunder and Stephen Curry's Warriors is how Oklahoma City was so close to dethroning Golden State. After a Durant 3-pointer, Oklahoma City was down five points with just over four minutes remaining in Game 5. They were up 101–99 with 2:22 left in the fourth quarter of Game 6. At home. They led by eight in the second half in Game 7 in Oakland, trailed by four with 1:40 left. Incredibly close.

But that series also crystallized Durant's can't-win-with-those-cats conclusion. For as close as the Thunder were to winning that series, losing perhaps revealed the flaws that made him believe winning there wasn't possible. If they couldn't win with that loaded team after being up 3–1, with Games 3 and 4 being a rout, then when could they win? What Durant witnessed was a team that had reached its utter maximum and still couldn't beat the Warriors. Even the Warriors openly admitted that the Thunder were a more talented team. The Warriors won a championship and then a record seventy-three regular season games with their vaunted small lineup with Draymond Green at center and Harrison Barnes at power forward—and Oklahoma City's version was better. They could put Serge Ibaka at center and Durant at power forward, and it was bigger and more explosive than the Warriors' version. They also had a legitimate center in Steven Adams, who gave the Warriors fits. How did the Thunder *not* win that series?

The 2015–16 Thunder struggled in close games all season. The NBA defines "clutch time" as the final five minutes of the game when the score is within 5 points. Oklahoma City had forty-four of those games in 2015–16. They won half of them, a percentage that tied them for seventeenth in the NBA. The Thunder had just twenty-seven losses all season. Winning close games is usually the mark of the NBA's best teams. Of the six teams with at least fifty wins that season, Oklahoma City was the only one that didn't have a winning record in clutch games.

In fact, one of their most gut-wrenching losses came at the hands of the Warriors: an overtime thriller on February 27, 2016, in Oklahoma City that was punctuated by Stephen Curry's half-court buzzer beater.

Then, in the 2016 Western Conference Finals, they couldn't close again. In Game 5, Durant and Westbrook combined for 71 points. But they needed fifty-nine shots and twenty-two free throws to get those points. They had to carry such a large load because the Thunder used basically only six players. The one reserve who got significant playing time, Dion Waiters, went scoreless in twenty-six minutes. A hot shooting night from Anthony Morrow, who scored 10 points on four shots in seven minutes, saved the Thunder bench from a virtual shutout.

The Thunder led 83–75 to start the fourth quarter in Game 6. They were twelve minutes from upsetting the top-seeded Warriors. The fourth quarter of Game 3 in OKC didn't matter. The Warriors were down 37 points after three quarters and waved the white flag early. In Game 4, the Thunder led by 12 entering the fourth quarter and put the game away by holding the Warriors to 12 points while scoring twice as many. But in Game 6 the collapse resurfaced. Thompson caught fire and prevented the Warriors from getting blown out again. He made an NBA playoff record eleven 3-pointers, shooting the Warriors into a close game. That meant the Thunder would have to beat the Warriors in a dogfight. They would have to muster the gumption to take down the champions. And they couldn't do it. Undoubtedly, a chunk of that failure rested on Durant, but the adjustments were also absent. His support proved minimal. The Thunder's scheme was exploited. They came unglued again. The Warriors banked on the flaws of the Thunder to come through and they were right on cue.

At halftime of Game 6 the Warriors made an adjustment. They started Iguodala in the second half, brought usual starter Harrison Barnes off the bench. The reason was Durant. He was six for nineteen in the first half—a lot of shots in twenty-one minutes. The Warriors wanted to bait him into shooting more. They inserted Iguodala in the starting lineup because they could be comfortable leaving him one-on-one with Durant and he would at least make Durant work hard. But the key was for Durant to notice the one-on-one defense. It was bait to get him to keep shooting. The Warriors knew the Thunder's offense was centered on the isolation abilities of Durant and Russell Westbrook. Part of their end-of-game struggle was when the defense turned it up a notch and focused on them, and the shots they were getting are suddenly less likely to go in. Durant was also known for falling in love with his jumper. The Warriors were hoping he would just take midrange pull-ups over Iguodala's outstretched arms the rest of the game. They could live with the results. Durant was one for seven shooting in the fourth quarter. And leaving Iguodala on an island against Durant meant the Warriors could funnel the help toward Westbrook. So when he attacked off the dribble, he ran into a crowd of defenders. Westbrook had a tendency to force his way to the rim, and when he did so in a crowd, his turnover rate went way up. Westbrook was two for seven shooting in the fourth quarter with four turnovers. Limiting Durant and Westbrook, more times than not, meant defeating the Thunder.

When the final horn sounded, the Warriors were celebrating, the Oklahoma City crowd was stunned, and the Thunder stars looked bewildered and defeated. The Warriors outscored them 33–18 in the fourth quarter. Durant and Westbrook totaled 12 points. The rest of the Thunder managed six. This wasn't so much a collapse of the Thunder as it was deconstruction. At times during the series, Oklahoma City looked invincible. They rocked the Warriors like no one ever had. But their core flaws doomed them.

"Now that we got KD, I can say it," Iguodala said on the popular radio show *The Breakfast Club*. "They were better than us. They were better than Cleveland. They were the best team in the playoffs. They should've won a championship."

7 | THE HAMPTONS

DOWN THE ROAD FROM TWO MILE HOLLOW BEACH in East Hampton, just on the other side of Further Lane, sits a gated mansion with manicured lawns and artistic hedges on a sprawling 3.2 acres looking out on the ocean. It has a rustic old-money vibe, like much of the real estate in the Hamptons portion of Long Island, New York.

Durant rented it for ten days at $10,000 a day in the summer of 2016 from Peter Wilson, a big-time lawyer in New York.

Wilson is not an NBA fan, so he probably had no idea who Kevin Durant was before his home became linked with basketball lore. His real estate agents who brokered the deal didn't even know who they were renting to initially. But Wilson is now part of NBA history. It was in his house that Durant decided to pull the trigger and create a dynasty. It was in Wilson's renovated old Mafia mansion, highlighted by gardens with vibrant flowers, underneath a shaded cabana, that five superstars met and talked about changing the course of basketball history.

The NBA would never be the same.

"That was my first meeting," Durant told *The Athletic* in a defini-

141

tive oral history of the Hamptons meeting, "and the whole time I was like, 'I need to finish the process, but I know where I want to be.' "

The NBA has been built on superiority. It is a league centered on greatness. Parity works well for the NFL, the king of American professional sports. The number of players on a team, the propensity for injury, the limited number of games, the hard salary cap—it all works together to produce a balance of power. At a minimum, it creates an environment where success is attainable in a short span. Hope floats for thirty teams, and that is of great appeal.

The Pittsburgh Steelers and the New England Patriots have six Super Bowl wins. The San Francisco 49ers and Dallas Cowboys have five. Throw in the four by the Green Bay Packers and New York Giants, and the six winningest franchises in NFL history have accounted for thirty championships, 56.6 percent. The NFL hasn't had a team repeat as champions since the Patriots did it in 2004 and 2005. The next thirteen Super Bowls saw ten teams win. The Steelers, Patriots, and Giants were the only teams with multiple championships during that stretch, none repeating.

In the NBA, the five winningest franchises have won 69 percent of the titles in the league's history. The Los Angeles Lakers and Boston Celtics have combined for thirty-three of the seventy-two titles.

In the last thirteen years the NBA had seven teams win a title. The Miami Heat, San Antonio Spurs, Los Angeles Lakers, and Golden State Warriors each won multiple titles, with the Spurs being the only team that didn't repeat.

Over a twelve-year stretch from 1957 to 1969, the Celtics won eleven titles. With apologies to coach Red Auerbach, the pioneering architect, Bill Russell was the face of twelve people from that era inducted into the Hall of Fame. The Celtics had another dominant window in the 1980s, led by Larry Bird. They won three championships and went to five NBA Finals in seven years. Kevin McHale, Robert Parish, and Dennis Scott all made the Hall of Fame with Bird.

The Los Angeles Lakers won five titles during an eleven-year stretch (1980–91), led by Magic Johnson. They were as legendary for their style of play, which came to be known as Showtime because of its fast pace and wealth of highlights. James Worthy, Pat Riley, and Jamaal "Silk" Wilkes became household names as well as Hall of Famers. The Lakers had a second dominant window with Kobe Bryant and Shaquille O'Neal. They won three straight titles and made it to four NBA Finals in five seasons.

The Spurs were a different kind of dominant. Theirs was defined by longevity. Over a fifteen-year span, they won five championships. They never won back-to-back championships but spread their success out over three decades.

Most would say the greatest run was led by Michael Jordan. He took the Chicago Bulls to six championships in eight years. The only two years those Bulls didn't win was when Jordan retired from basketball for a spell to play baseball. Their dominance lifted the NBA to a new level. The greatness of Jordan and the invincibility of those Bulls transitioned the NBA into mainstream culture in the '90s after Magic and Bird put the league on the map in the '80s. Jordan was doing such fascinating things, no team could beat them, and it was magnetic.

This was the lure of the Warriors, the element OKC simply could not match. Dynasties are part of the NBA's genetic code. The showcasing of its best at their best has always been the league's greatest draw. That was why the meeting that went on in the Hamptons is now etched into NBA lore. It was the host site for the summit that would form the NBA's latest dynasty and potentially the greatest the league has ever known. It was where Durant, with one decision, would transform the Warriors from a great team that had a good stretch, à la the

Bad Boy Detroit Pistons, into a superpower for the ages. Presumably. Peter Wilson had finalized many major deals on these confines. Perhaps he even hosted some major figures for some private meetings that would produce major impact. He represented Shell in its acquisition of Pennzoil and Quaker State, IBM in its acquisitions of Sterling Commerce from AT&T. He helped the Westinghouse Electric and CBS conglomeration expand its reach by consuming Infinity Broadcasting Corporation (which grew into a radio giant by buying up successful stations and moves like signing Howard Stern to a five-year deal in the '80s). In the days leading up to the Fourth of July 2016, another major merger was happening. Actually, it was an acquisition, as the Warriors would recruit and land a rare breed of superstar.

.   .   .

Since then, the national discussion has been centered on why Durant joined the Warriors and what it says about him. The union of KD and the Warriors took the drama away from the court, where their dominance has gone without great challenge, and transferred it into the storyline. He has become a lightning rod, a now-historic figure of an era that is currently both despised and revered.

The common refrain is Durant took the easy way out. He joined with a team that had one championship already, won an NBA-record seventy-three games, and were two possessions from winning back-to-back championships. Even worse, optically, he joined the team that knocked him out of the playoffs. Durant and the Oklahoma City Thunder were one strong quarter from dethroning the NBA champion Warriors. They took a 3–1 lead in the best-of-seven series and were ahead in the fourth quarter of Game 6 on their home court. Durant and Russell Westbrook had them on the ropes before LeBron James and Kyrie Irving did. But after losing to the Warriors, he joined them. The old adage "If you can't beat 'em, join 'em" fit perfectly.

But more was at play here. In the arc of Durant's career, of his life, that much was obvious. His decision was revelatory.

"So as soon as I sat down, had the first conversation," Durant continued in *The Athletic* piece. "No small talk. Straight to it. I'm like, 'This is where I need to go.' And everything else was the cherry on top. I was already sold when they walked in."

Durant had his manager, Rich Kleiman, and his dad, Wayne Pratt, with him for his free agent meetings, including the one in the Hamptons. The Warriors' contingent showed up eight deep. Owner Joe Lacob, general manager Bob Myers, assistant general manager Kirk Lacob, and head coach Steve Kerr represented the Warriors' front office. But the highlight was the Warriors four best players: Draymond Green, Klay Thompson, Andre Iguodala, and reigning two-time MVP Stephen Curry.

The impression was immediate. To Durant it probably looked like a movie scene as they all got out of the same car and walked to the entrance of the Hamptons house. The Warriors had arrived. It was probably worthy of super–slow motion and a background instrumental, like the astronauts in the movie *Armageddon* sauntering to the rocket so they could go save the world (Curry of course playing Bruce Willis' character).

Individually they walked in, accomplished in their own right. But collectively they were a team in much more than name only. Durant noticed the vibe immediately. The Warriors were a clique in that way. They interacted with each other as if no hierarchy existed. They each fought incredibly hard to prove they were exceptional and went to even greater lengths to remain tethered to their pack. They each had a unique refusal to be put in a box, to be bound by the standards and expectations of others, and yet they thrived by existing within the boundaries of their bond. The Warriors were a pack of cool kids made popular by their disregard for what was typically cool. Their chemistry was forged by the freedom they gave each other to be individuals. It popped in a league driven by superstars and their egos. Somehow the Warriors managed to have fun in an existence where fun was sucked out by business, politics, and pressure. Players around the league for years have whispered comments to Warriors players about how they'd love to exist in Golden State's environment. It has caught the eye of free agents and irritated the hell out of other stars. But watching it live definitely attracted Durant.

The initial Q and A happened in the Hamptons house. Kerr showed Durant some sets and how he would be used. Kirk Lacob had a VR presentation prepared. They answered questions from Kleiman, Pratt, and Durant. But the real meeting happened when the five stars ditched the formalities and held a players-only meeting outside. Durant's mind was close to being made up. He hadn't even met yet with other teams, but he knew he wanted to go to the Warriors. This private meeting with the player was reconnaissance. This moment was where he was sold. This was where he became one of the guys.

"To see them together, they all walked in and it looked like they were holding hands," Durant said. "It was just a family. I could tell they enjoyed being around each other. When I met these guys. I felt as comfortable as I've ever felt. It was organic. It was authentic. It was real. I just saw a bunch of real guys. Simple as that. It felt like they weren't in the NBA. It felt like those guys just play pickup every single day and they just really enjoy pure basketball. That's the kind of feel that I wanted."

One could argue, and some behind the scenes have speculated, that Durant was eyeing the Warriors all along. Maybe since 2015, when the Warriors leapfrogged the Thunder and won a championship. Meanwhile, the Big Three of the Thunder that was supposed to grow into a super-team was broken up because of money. In 2012

OKC traded Harden to Houston to avoid paying his massive salary demands. Durant, Harden, and Westbrook were the future, a trio of exceptional talents that only needed more experience to take over the league. They went to the NBA Finals in 2012 and it was just the start. But a small-market team paying big contracts for three players was untenable, so they made the tough choice to trade Harden and get a bounty for him. Three seasons after that, the Warriors beat the Thunder to a championship with a collection of players who were allowed to grow together. Up until the Warriors' title, the Thunder were considered next in line.

In 2012, when the Thunder made the Finals, the Warriors were coming off just twenty-six wins and still an NBA doormat. The next season the Warriors became darlings with a postseason run to the second round. Steph Curry became a star. Two years later they were champions. They made the right moves, spent the money, and used a scheme that helped usher the league into a new era of space and shooting. They had the coaching staff, front office, and roster talent. They had the buzz, the locale, the future. Durant, like several others in the league, saw this transformation happen. Iguodala jumped on early. Zaza Pachulia and David West did, too. Maybe Durant had his eye on what was happening with the Warriors and was comparing it to the Thunder's situation. But before he could consider making the leap, there was one thing he had to know.

"I just knew he was going to ask that question," Curry said.

Days before free agency began, Durant was already doing his homework on Curry. He sent a text to Jarrett Jack, one of his friends from the D.C. area, at about 3:00 a.m. Durant wanted some info from Jack about Curry.

"He texted," Jack said in an interview with Fox Sports, "and he was like, 'Man, can I speak to you for a minute?' I'm like, 'Yeah.' So, he called me and he was like, 'Yo, um, what's Steph Curry like? . . . Is he like how they portray him on TV or is he, like, a totally different dude behind closed doors?' And I said, 'Ahhhhh shit.' "

Durant's primary concern was how he would be received by Curry, the face of the franchise. It was the most pressing question at the Hamptons meeting, since Curry had the most to lose.

When Curry burst onto the national scene in 2013, Jack was his backup point guard. The two shared the court a lot, as coach Mark Jackson ran a three-guard offense quite a bit, putting Jack at point guard and Curry at shooting guard with Klay Thompson at small forward. Jack played only a season with the Warriors but they went to the postseason, upsetting Denver and putting a scare into San Antonio. Durant knew Jack, a straight shooter, would tell the truth about Curry.

And Jack knew this call meant Durant was considering joining the Warriors. And he knew his answer would probably help Durant make the leap to Golden State.

"So I was like, 'Look, bro, I'mma tell you like this. Steph [is] one of the best people I've ever met in my life, you know what I'm saying. Male. Female. Basketball. Not. Like, he's one of them great dudes.' Then he kept asking me questions about them and this and Bob Myers and Mr. Lacob and the fans. I said, 'Ahhhhh. This ain't good here.' . . . Before that phone call, I never thought the Golden State thing would happen."

This seems to point directly to Durant's relationship with Westbrook. For years NBA fans who followed closely heard about their clashes and saw their run-ins on the court. Westbrook was a headstrong guy who had grown from Durant's sidekick into a dominant player with foaming-at-the-mouth aggressiveness. Westbrook often dominated the ball at the expense of Durant. The rumor mill told of more dysfunction.

The two always said the right things about each other publicly and came across as competitive brothers more than anything. But was Durant shopping for Curry as a replacement costar?

Durant and Curry had history. In about 1998, Durant's AAU team traveled to Charlotte for a game. Durant's team entered the gym and saw some kid draining deep 3-pointers.

"I thought he was white," Durant famously said about the kid.

Durant didn't realize until years later Curry was the kid he saw stroking threes. At the time, Curry was unknown. In 2010 they were both on the U.S. men's national team that competed in the FIBA World Championships in Turkey. Durant was the star of the team—he won MVP of the tournament—and Curry was a scrappy reserve. But both were youngsters surrounded by veterans like Chauncey Billups and Lamar Odom. They were both All-Stars from 2014 to 2016. They seemed to have a lot in common: down-to-earth, faith-based dudes with a genuine appreciation for the privilege of being in the NBA. Their connection, however peripheral it was at the time, was evident at the end of the Game 7 in the 2016 Western Conference Finals. While Westbrook wanted no part of an embrace with the Warriors, Curry and Durant shared a moment in front of the cameras. They shared with each other their mutual awe at being part of such an incredible series, for creating the kind of legendary battle they grew up watching as kids.

Still, in the Hamptons, Durant needed to hear it from Curry. He wanted to look him in the eyes, read his body language, absorb his vibe.

Having spent most of his career as an elite star, Durant knew all-too-well how sought after status is in the NBA. Major endorsements are scarce. Signature shoes only go to a select few. The branding of an athlete requires an investment: the backing of a marketing arm, access to premier platforms, connections to other industries. Those don't go to every athlete. And when a player gets that, he has a coveted spot.

That's what Curry had, and it took him a while to get it. Curry left Nike because, among other things, they didn't have a path for him to get prime placement in the company. Nike already had a point guard under contract—Kyrie Irving was on track for marquee status in the company. Nike told Curry back in 2013, before he became a global icon, that if he made All-Star, they would talk about getting him a shoe. Meanwhile, Under Armour was offering to feature Curry. An All-Star appearance guaranteed him a shoe. They chose him to build their basketball wing around. And it worked. Curry became an All-Star, an MVP, a champion. His miraculous rise took the Warriors and Under Armour with him. He became a coveted pitch man for several companies—Kaiser, Infiniti, Brita—and a king in the Bay Area. In the No. 6 market in the country, in Silicon Valley, Curry was the undisputed tops. He was the face of the national, even global, phenomenon the Warriors had become. If anyone anywhere in the world was going to get a Warriors jersey, the first choice was Curry's No. 30. He went from No. 2 in jersey sales in 2015 to No. 1 in 2016. In March 2016, Morgan Stanley analyst Jay Sole told *Business Insider* that Curry's signature shoe—the Curry 2—was "already bigger than those of LeBron, Kobe and every other player except Michael Jordan."

Durant knew what Curry had going because Durant had been in that spot for years. He was the face of college basketball while at Texas. He had long been a premier player in the NBA, extremely well compensated by shoe giant Nike. He also knew how NBA players coveted the position. He could probably run off a list of players who would give up a kidney to be among that superstar ilk. Curry had made it. Was he *really* going to give that up? Was he really going to want Durant, a superstar whose star was bright enough to potentially outshine his? Would he really be content if Durant came in and dominated, assumed the unofficial status as the team's best player? Durant had dealt for years with the conversation about whether the team belonged to him or Westbrook. Could Curry deal with that being in question on the Warriors? Because it was for sure coming.

That was why Durant had to look Curry in the eye and find out.

Because the truth is, too, that the Warriors presented off-the-court opportunity for Durant as well. He'd spent eight years in Oklahoma City, which was comfortably outside the top forty markets in the country. There stood to be great gain if Durant became A1 in the Bay Area market. If nothing else, he would be undercutting a Nike competitor by potentially grabbing some of Curry's market share. Depending on who you ask behind the scenes, Nike was either pushing for Durant to make the move or encouraging him to follow his heart while secretly wishing he would make the move. Also, depending on who you ask behind the scenes, Under Armour either hated the move or was talking themselves into believing it was not a big deal.

What's more, Durant has long had designs on building an empire. Kevin Durant is not just a basketball player, he is the head of a multifaceted company. The Durant Company is his investment arm, which has poured money into companies like Postmates, the Players' Tribune, LimeBike, and Pieology. The Kevin Durant Charity Foundation is how he gives back to the community and flexes his heart for the underrepresented. Thirty Five Media is his foray into content production, including the YouTube channel he created in 2017. This was also possibly part of the plan for Durant coming to the Bay Area, to expand his reach.

But this was Curry's territory he was expanding into. Was he really okay with that? Curry had a reputation for being humble off the court. His game was flashy, even exuded arrogance. But it stood out in a league full of such bravado because it didn't match his off-the-court persona. Durant knew this about Curry. They both had memberships in the sports good-guy club.

"Steph and I played together in 2010 in Turkey, and after practice we would come back to the gym at night when we were overseas and just [get] some shots up," Andre Iguodala said at his introductory press conference after signing with the Warriors in July 2013. "I believe Kevin Durant was with us a lot of the time. So it was us three, maybe one or two other guys, but us three were always together. Kinda got a chance to see him work. Knew how in love he was with the game, so we built a pretty good relationship. We had chapels together before every game so we definitely got to know each other. Us three were always together."

But was Curry really *that* unselfish? Did he have enough humility to scoot over and share the big chair with Durant knowing he could potentially be unseated? Does anybody?

Durant had to see Curry, talk to him, hear it from his mouth. He had to get a read on whether they might run into issues later, because Curry really didn't want to share. So Durant asked him.

"Why do you want me here?"

Curry told Durant he fit well with the culture and chemistry the Warriors had developed. He told Durant he wasn't concerned with having a pissing contest. It didn't matter to him who took the most shots, scored the most points, or got the most hardware. He told him the Warriors would be a great place for him if he wanted to win and play with fellow good guys, have fun, and win.

Just in case that wasn't enough, Curry reiterated his stance. After leaving the Hamptons, he stopped off in the Bay Area on his way to Hawaii for a family vacation and the Warriors' fantasy camp. But he fired off a text message to Durant first.

He reiterated that he didn't care about accolades. He didn't care about who sold the most shoes or who was being pushed as the face of the franchise. He told Durant he wanted him on the team, on the journey with him.

Durant had looked into Curry's eyes in person. Now he looked into Curry's heart through a text. He saw all he needed to see.

8 | KEVIN WAYNE

DURANT BOUGHT A PLACE IN THE hills when he moved to Oakland. He has since bought a place in San Francisco, where the team is moving to play in the Chase Center for the 2019–2020 season. But one of the small, enjoyable benefits of his place in Oakland was the drive to Oracle Arena.

His home was positioned so he could almost drive a straight line to the arena. He didn't have to take the freeway because the streets got him there efficiently. He would cruise down the winding streets in the hills, underneath the MacArthur Freeway, and onto Edwards Avenue, which descended to the flatlands, turning into Sunkist Drive before becoming Seventy-Third Avenue. Once he crossed MacArthur Boulevard, that was when the ride got good. Ironically, that was when the scenery became decidedly urban.

A retro McDonald's—including the logo with Speedee from the 1960s—was the first landmark that let Durant know he'd reached the flatlands. It was part of Eastmont Mall, a former shopping and entertainment hub that over the years had become a home for social services and discount stories. The sidewalks started looking grimier. The greenery decreased and became less manicured, less green. The litter in the crevices had become part of the ambiance. Fast-food joints and gas stations. Elementary schools on busy streets. Loud music blaring from cars. People outside, walking, loitering. Churches seemingly on every other corner. Yeah, Durant liked this drive. It felt like home. He saw the resemblance to his childhood. The ride down Seventy-Third Avenue to International Boulevard was a window into how the crack epidemic ravaged another neighborhood. It was still visible how this had once been a vibrant community. East Oakland, like much like PG County, was full of owned homes and hardworking people. The remnants of a generation that migrated west to create a life was still evident underneath the coat of struggle.

"It reminds me so much of Chocolate City, man," Durant said, using a nickname for the Washington, D.C., area. "I be missing home a lot. So when I ride down through East Oakland to go to the game, I get my fix. I definitely feel like I'm riding around in my own neighborhood."

Durant was in the Bay now. The journey had begun. But in Durant you don't just get a basketball player. His package includes a unique figure among NBA celebrity concoctions.

· · ·

Durant was talking.

In the bowels of AT&T Center in San Antonio, after the Warriors won Game 3 of the 2018 Western Conference first round series over the Spurs, he was at his locker. He was fully dressed; his gray Nike tech sweatsuit had a pink tint, as if it had been washed with a load of red. He grabbed the wrinkled black dad hat with a small white gallon jug logo on the front, a gift from the JaVale McGee Juglife Foundation, and slapped it on his head.

The Warriors locker room was buzzing about the stunning result out of Portland the same night. The No. 3–seeded Blazers had just lost to No. 6–seeded New Orleans. In Portland. The Pelicans led the series 3–0 after handling the Blazers easily. What was wrong with Portland, how good was New Orleans really, and who did and didn't see this coming was much of the chatter, mixed in with some dialogue about the Warriors' own 110–97 win over San Antonio. They were paying attention to that Blazers-Pelicans series because they would face the winner. They'd just gone up 3 games to 0 over the Spurs, so a Golden State–New Orleans showdown was all but officially in the offing.

"I'll tell you what's wrong with Portland," Durant said, grabbing his phone from the locker and putting it in his pocket.

A breakdown was coming. When Durant got into this mode, it usually meant he was about to pull back some layers and reveal the reality he believed everyone else was missing. Or was about to share the real backstory, provide another context that he usually followed with, "But nobody wants to talk about that." He became the sweetest shooting adjunct lecturer of all time, and part conspiracy theorist, taking the listeners to school.

Durant was in no rush to leave the locker room. He stood, comfortable, relaxed, reporters huddled around him, all looking up at him and waiting for the goods. Recorders were turned off and notebooks dropped to sides. Durant surveyed his surroundings. He was about to say something poignant and off the record. He focused his attention on one reporter not in the huddle but still within earshot.

"You recording this? Don't be recording this," Durant told the beat writer, who was waiting on another player. The reporter took exception to the implication.

"You know how the media be. You muthafuckas can't be trusted."

Before or after any game in Oakland, Durant could be found in a familiar position: slumped in his chair, his eyes pointed downward at his phone, revealing the hair gradually deserting the crown of his head. Before the game, this was his position while he was fully dressed. Eventually, he tossed his phone in his locker and got up to get undressed and change into his uniform. After the game, this was his position with his uniform on, his feet in a bucket of ice. Invariably, in either case, someone would approach Durant and steal his attention, prompting him to lift his head and reveal widened eyes that suggested he was all ears.

Durant often held court at his locker. He could be found chatting with reporters and teammates about nearly everything. Sometimes the chats were private. You know the ones that were because his hand gestures were louder than his words. But usually Durant spoke with the volume and emphasis that invited unintended ears and curious types. He might break down the Redskins struggles or reveal truths about the inner workings of the NBA. He was known to sound off on everything from battle rap to Silicon Valley start-ups to NBA gossip. He could carry his part in a conversation while getting naked, methodically disrobing without revealing his private areas, and then stand with only a towel on and finish the conversation. Eventually, he would take off to the shower, come back, and talk more while he got dressed.

And Durant laughed a lot. At a reporter's fashion choices. At an inside joke with a teammate. At a funny line he shot off to the media. He shot the breeze with the same ease he pulled up for a jumper. There was a down-to-earth–ness about him. He was seven feet tall but an expert at getting eye-to-eye with people. Talking was his pastime. It was a manifestation of his ideology, which was that everyone, at the core, is equal. You know he believed that when you watched him talk to everyone with the same fervor, including people he didn't even like.

He was an NBA superstar but he'd spark a dialogue faster than a bagger at Whole Foods. Part of it was a by-product of how he viewed himself in relation to everyone else. The off-the-court Durant, the one fans got to meet and people got to interact with, believed in being approachable. It was a significant component of his self-evaluation, knowing he kept his feet on the ground no matter how high he rose. Part of it, though, was also because he had so much to say, so much going on in his head, so much he wanted to know. He chewed on the world, on life, via conversation.

.   .   .

On May 1, 2018, in an appearance at TMZ, hip-hop mogul Kanye West stirred up social media and prompted a national reaction. During his sit-down interview with Harvey Levin and Charles Latibeaudiere, West's rant included a controversial sound bite.

"When you hear about slavery for 400 years. For 400 years?" he said, perking up in his chair to add emphasis. "That sounds like a choice."

West immediately followed with a smile and a pause. It seemed as if his inflammatory statement was intended to be more an irreverent punch line than an epiphanic stance. He seemed rattled when met with the awkward silence it produced. He doubled down on the line, raising his voice and adding hand gestures.

"Like, you was there for 400 years and it's all of y'all?"

Still no reaction. West started scrambling.

"You know, like"—he looked down and quickly pinched his nose—"it's like we're mentally in prison. I like the word 'prison' because, because 'slavery' goes too direct to the idea of Blacks. It's like slavery, Holocaust. Holocaust, Jews. Slavery is Blacks. So prison is something that unites us as one race. Blacks and whites being one race . . ."

Most of what West said before and after his "slavery is a choice" line was drowned out by the ensuing flabbergast. A week earlier he had caused a stir with a celebratory tweet about getting his Make America Great Again hat signed by Donald Trump. In a Twitter rant, he called Trump his brother. Of course that angered just about every Black celebrity in America and many others in the African-American community.

Whatever else West was saying after this recent bomb fell on many a deaf ear. That was a final straw for West fans who once loved him for the pro-Black, antiestablishment rhetoric in his lyrics. For so many, he had become a caricature of himself, no longer the voice of the community but a deranged casualty of celebrity. He went from declaring on network TV that President George W. Bush "doesn't care about Black people" to declaring his love for President Trump. Few bothered to parse through the salacious bits for the essence of what West was saying, or intending to say, too fed up with his sharp deviation from the empowering voice that produced *The College Dropout* and *Late Registration* and *My Beautiful Dark Twisted Fantasy*.

Durant was asked about West's rant before Game 2 of the second-round series against New Orleans at Oracle.

"Nobody wants to hear what I think about it," Durant said as he pulled down his slate jersey until "The Town" and the "No. 35" were unveiled on his torso. "They won't like what I have to say."

By the time Durant got in the locker room that night, he already knew what the general reaction would be. He got a dose on the ride to Game 2 with Cassandra Anderson, whom he was dating at the time. She ended up tuning him out for much of the drive to Oracle. He had parsed out West's intentions and wanted to discuss his understanding of it. But like many she was too irritated to listen. Anderson was a volleyball star at Florida, a six-foot-one middle blocker whose game was at the net. She had no problem erecting a wall between them. Durant's explanations bounced right off the invisible shield. She was impenetrable.

After the game, Durant decided to engage the reporters even

though he knew his wouldn't be a popular opinion. It began with Durant brushing off the most offensive interpretation of Kanye's statement. The idea that the longevity of slavery in America and its ensuing systems of oppression was a product of acceptance by the enslaved, and not the relentlessness of the oppressor, violated recorded history. The 1739 Stono Rebellion in South Carolina. The Haitian Revolution–inspired 1811 German Coast Uprising in Louisiana. The Nat Turner–led Southampton Insurrection in Virginia. Many slaves died trying to fight for their freedom. Frederick Douglass rolled over in his grave at the accusation of compliance. Durant knew that was an argument he couldn't win.

"I obviously don't agree with the slavery part," Durant said before launching into his explanation.

"But if you think about it, many people are in prison. People chose to be imprisoned in their minds. People don't want to be free. They accept the limitations. They accept what they're told. I'm telling you. When you really think about it, it is a prison. The prison of your mind."

Durant's first attempt at explaining his telepathy with West was more proverbial than profound. The concept of mental incarceration has been an analogy used by revolutionaries for centuries.

Then he turned to the Socratic method.

"Can you do anything you put your mind to?"

Responded one reporter, diving headfirst down the rabbit hole of Durant, "No. Actually, I can't do anything I put my mind to. I can't be a mother."

Durant suddenly stopped, dropping his arms to his side while flashing a smirk and tilting his head just enough to underscore the "C'mon, man" expression on his face. Durant was backstroking into the depths of defiance, willingly venturing out into absurdity. Yet, here he was, shifting to lifeguard and chiding the reporter for going too far. The irony of the rabble-rouser playing conversational referee is lost on him.

"Obviously you can't be a mother, but you know what I'm saying. If you devoted yourself to something, put in the work, couldn't you do anything?"

Do this dance enough with Durant and it becomes clear his intentions are not purely to say the outlandish thing but to use the outlandish to draw ears to his process, and usually at the core of what he is trying to say is a simple truth, sometimes even a simple request.

"No. I can't do anything," the reporter responded. "I have my own gifts and talents and if I operate outside of them, it probably won't work out. And that's fine."

"See," Durant responded. "You're in prison. You're not free. I believe in you. You can do whatever you put your mind to."

Durant went on to put up 29 points, seven assists, six rebounds, and three blocks in the Warriors Game 2 win over the Pelicans. It flew under the radar as Stephen Curry's much-anticipated return from injury, and his 28 points were a spectacle that overshadowed everything.

After the game, Durant finished his deep dive.

"People believe the lie they're being told and put these limitations on themselves. The media tells you what you can be and who you should be and that's what you end up being. And people end up in prison in their own mind because they aren't living up to their full potential."

The reporter responded. "But what if the freedom is in understanding the gifts and strengths I have, and the weaknesses and limitations I have? I'm free to be who I am supposed to be because I understand my gifts."

"But what is weakness except something you haven't worked on?" Durant retorted. "And who told you what is a weakness is actually a weakness? If you put your mind to the shit, you make it a strength. That's what I'm saying. It's a prison. People just accept what they are told and limit themselves."

The locker room had thinned out. Players and reporters were mostly gone, either to the media workroom or the interview room where the NBA set up a mini–press conference for the game's biggest names and most impactful players. While most conversations were about the Warriors taking a commanding 2–0 lead in the series, reminding the basketball world that the hot Pelicans weren't ready to contend with the champs, Durant was engulfed in a completely unrelated topic. And he was into it. He was waving his hands, fluctuating his voice.

But the interview room was calling. So Durant started making his way toward the exit of the locker room, but he stopped in his tracks before escaping into the hallway. He heard a statement that took the conversation further, perhaps to the intended destination.

"But even if that is true," the reporter pressed, "the circumstances that broke so many down to that point was not a choice. Losing the fight does not mean they chose those circumstances. And the ones who do make it do so because they get breaks many others don't. You didn't choose to be six-foot-eleven."

"I didn't make it to the NBA because of that," Durant said. "Yes, I was blessed to be seven feet or whatever. But I made it here because of discipline. The NBA was something I set my mind to and I worked my ass off. There is so many things that can knock you off course. But you've got to really believe it and put in the work. You have to choose this. And I feel like if I did something else, or if I want to do something else, if I put my mind to it and work hard, I can do that, too. It's a mentality. People don't have that mentality. I believe I can do anything I put my mind to."

Durant had drifted far from Kanye West and into Tony Gaskins

territory. And he landed on what was a talking point for him. If nothing else, Durant wanted it to be clear that his basketball greatness
was not handed to him. If you asked any credible basketball mind to
analyze Durant's game, it wouldn't take long before they were awed
at his combination of height and skill. The qualities that stood out
were the ones that seemed divinely planted in his DNA. He had the
height to tower over most players, the intangibles of touch and feel
and fluidity of motion usually reserved for smaller men. These were
all gifts unique to Durant and completely out of his control. But to
give those elements too much credit was disrespectful in his eyes, because even the rarest of gifts need to be maximized. That requires
work ethic, investing countless hours of intensive effort. Basketball
talents are gold refined by fire. The silkiness of Durant's game, how
easy he made it look, was more a symbol of the diligence he had put in
than it was proof Durant won some sort of genetic lottery. Both were
true, but Durant boldfaced, italicized, and underlined the former and
downplayed the latter. That was probably why he had always rejected
being labeled as seven feet tall. He was always listed at six-foot-nine
on NBA documents but he admitted on Bay Area radio station KNBR
that he is six-foot-ten-and-three-quarters barefoot, so with shoes on
he became a seven footer. Even before his admission, he was imputed
that rare status.

To say he was seven feet is to put him with the likes of NBA centers, which came with it an understanding of strengths and weaknesses. And contrasting that standard with Durant's skill set, which
was much more like a guard's, only made what Durant did so jaw-
dropping. It was the easiest and best way to verbalize the ridiculous-
ness of his game. But Durant preferred to stiff-arm the seven-foot
accreditation because he would rather awe people with his insatiable grind, the mental toughness it took to remain focused and disci-

plined. The great victory was in overcoming his background and not falling prey to the traps set for him. It wasn't in being tall.

It was partly why the criticism from his decision to play for the Warriors bothered him so much.

"It's like, man, you worked your whole life to get to this point and sometimes you don't even enjoy it because you're worried about what other people have to say," Durant said in *Still KD*, a documentary produced by his media team for YouTube. "That's the struggle some days, especially when you're playing in the NBA where all you hear is the noise. It's hard to tune that shit out. As much as people want us to, like, be tough-minded and have thick skin, sometimes it's hard to, like, not take up for yourself, like, 'Yo. I work hard as hell. You not in the gym after shoot-around and after practices. You don't know what's going on through my head the day before the game. You don't know.' It's just a game to some people but this shit be real life to us."

Spend enough time around Durant and you got the sense he purposely shrouded the simplicity of what he was trying to say. Jesus taught in parables as a way of reserving the nuggets he delivered for those who truly wanted to understand. The wisdom was the reward for whoever wrestled with the layers and complexities of his analogies and did the work to make it relevant to their lives. Many of the Galilean's rivals thought he was possessed because of some of the wild things he said. Even his own disciples were often left scratching their heads, trying to comprehend the meanings. Unwittingly, Durant operated similarly. He packaged his dialogue in a way to solicit reaction, to jar the sensibilities of his intended target. He would talk in circles, weaving you through the obstacle course that was his logic.

"If you heard half the stuff he says," Draymond Green said with a smile.

You had to care enough to get to the core of what Durant means.

You had to want to understand him enough to wade through his verbiage and incitement. At the end of the winding, trippy road was a treat you just don't get from superstars: it was Durant. The real him. Not the superstar. Not the millionaire mogul. But Kevin Wayne Durant. The person who would be there if the money wasn't, if the fame never came.

Durant was not the vanilla appeaser superstar, made popular by Michael Jordan. Durant was not the commercialized presentation pro athletes became when they reached the upper echelon of celebrity, a packaging LeBron James has mastered. Durant was not even the carefully sculpted rebel, the kind of choreographed "real" that Kobe Bryant assumed as an elder statesman. Durant was unique among NBA superheroes because he refused to wear the glasses and the suit to disguise his true identity. He had grown increasingly comfortable with your seeing who he was.

Not only did Durant offer this treat of his true self, he wanted you to find it. His eccentricity was a trail of bread crumbs leading you to him. That was the admirable beneath the absurd. To be vulnerable was courageous. Durant had the resources to erect a great facade, to hide his warts from the world. And yet he didn't.

"I think it is one of his great qualities," Steve Kerr said on the *Lowe Post* podcast. "He's a real human being. He's not like a machine. He's vulnerable like we all are."

. . .

Durant was talking.

The hood on his dark blue Nike sweatshirt was pulled over his head. He was sitting on the railing of a walkway that led down a level to the Houston Rockets' practice facility, both hands gripping the rails like a gymnast on the uneven bars. At the bottom of the walkway, which descended like a ramp, was organized chaos. The throng of media was crammed on the borders of the practice courts, waiting for players to finish their workouts. When players came off the court, heading to their seats along the baseline or an open space against a wall, they got swarmed by media, enclosed in a huddle of interrogation. The questions and answers blended with the rest of the chatter happening, creating an ambient sound that rivaled a bar.

Much of the questions and the talk was connected to the Warriors' convincing Game 1 win over the host Rockets. Nearly a year earlier, in June of 2017, Houston made a blockbuster trade to get Hall of Fame–bound point guard Chris Paul to pair with face-of-the-franchise James Harden—the Rockets rebuttal to the Warriors' collection of All-Stars. Houston emerged as the top seed in the 2018 Western Conference playoffs, and Harden put together a spectacular MVP season, feeding the notion the Rockets might be primed to knock off the Warriors. But after Durant got finished in Game 1, any notion of Houston's superiority felt more like a pipe dream. He just destroyed the Rockets in isolation situations, finishing with 37 points on twenty-seven shots as the Warriors controlled the game in the second half. After a season of Rockets hype, of prognosticators pegging them as king slayers, the Warriors made it all feel irrelevant. They took back home-court advantage, foiled the talk of their demise, and seemed to make life itself futile for many NBA diehards. So every sports journalist on the globe converged onto the Rockets practice facility to query the Warriors about world domination.

Durant, having endured his swarming, was doing more interviews in a quieter setting, up the ramp, literally above the fray. The scene behind him, visible through glass windows, matched his tone. The manicured trees surrounding the Toyota Center painted the foreground of this backdrop. The downtown skyscrapers sparkled in the distance against the clear blue skies of a warm afternoon. People shooting hoops on the sunken outside court across the street from the arena helped make this Tuesday look more like a chill Saturday. And Durant was chilling, too, waxing poetic about the Warriors' rising to the occasion and circumventing the obstacles that looked to derail them.

"Ego is the downfall of every human," Durant said. "When you're comparing yourself, that's a part of your ego trying to boost yourself up. When you care about getting praise, that's just you wanting to be bigger and better than everybody else and have more power. Do you just want people to say you look good? So it's just like so much that goes into your ego. When you release that shit, you kind of humble yourself and you look at life as a student. Everybody wants to be a teacher before they learn the whole lesson. That's your ego. I feel like everybody here kind of went through their lumps and learned the game and now they can give their input. That's the proper way to do shit."

This sounded like Durant on a high horse, sneering at those still on the leash of their id. He came off as if he were a master discerner who had conquered the baser yearnings of humanity. But really he was speaking as a survivor of those yearnings. The "everybody" he mentioned included him and he knows it. This wasn't him bandying about highfalutin psychology. This was wisdom talking, understanding gleaned from experience.

This was Durant's center, the home base of his value system. At the core of Durant was still the PG Jaguar who liked playing basketball with his friends and hanging out afterward. He relished being one of the guys. He found something special in the bond of team sports. There was a noted reciprocity. Investing emotionally in a team more often than not produced returns. Unselfishness recouped support. Commitment produced loyalty. These bonds lasted a lifetime. Even now, as a seasoned professional, Durant's engagement with his team is obvious. He fist-pumps the feats of his teammates, explodes off the

Durant—here playing in the 2006 McDonald's All-American game—
played for three high schools. He started at National Christian
Academy, switched to Oak Hill Academy for his junior season, and
played his senior year at Montrose Christian. (*AP Photo/Denis Poroy*)

Durant—seen here dunking in a 2007 Big 12 tournament game in Oklahoma City—led Texas in minutes (35.9), scoring (25.8), rebounding (11.1), steals (1.9), and blocks (1.9) as a freshman. (*AP Photo/Ty Russell*)

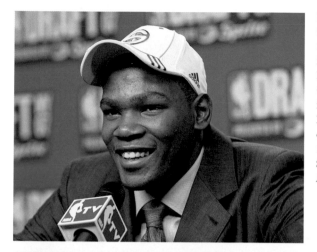

It was pretty clear Durant was the most talented player in the 2007 NBA Draft. (He was the first freshman to win the John R. Wooden Award.) But Greg Oden looked to be a once-in-a-generation center, and Durant was the only player out of 80 who could not bench 185 pounds. So Durant fell to Seattle at No. 2. (*AP Photo/Jason DeCrow*)

Durant standing with his parents, Wanda Durant (right) and Wayne Pratt (far right); his grandmother Barbara Davis (far left); and friend Cliff Dixon (left) after he was named Rookie of the Year. (*AP Photo/Ted S. Warren*)

(Above) There was a time when the next NBA power team was in Oklahoma City. The Thunder had Durant, Russell Westbrook (left), and James Harden (right)— all young and dynamic perimeter talents. They made the 2011 NBA Finals. But in 2012, Harden was traded to Houston. All three would become NBA MVPs. (*AP Photo/Sue Ogrocki*)

Wanda Durant (right) with her son after a 2012 playoff game in OKC. Wanda had a Lifetime movie made about her: *The Real MVP*. (*AP Photo/ Eric Gay*)

Durant averaged a career-high 32 points per game on 50.3 percent shooting during the 2013–14 season. Despite his highest-scoring season, Durant was the most efficient of his career. He also created a moment with his speech, tearing up when talking about his mother and calling her "the real MVP." (*AP Photo/Sue Ogrocki*)

Durant hits an epic shot over LeBron to clinch Game 3 of the 2017 NBA Finals. (*AP Photo/Tony Dejak*)

At a special 2018 preseason game against the Kings in Seattle, Durant took off his warm-up top to reveal to the crowd the jersey of SuperSonics legend Shawn Kemp. (*AP Photo/ Ted S. Warren*)

Curry and Durant have found that together they are practically unstoppable. (*AP Photo/Tony Dejak*)

An NBA MVP, two
championships, and two
Finals MVPs so far. Will
he add to his collection in
Brooklyn? (*Trillicon Valley/
Khristopher "Squint" Sandifer*)

bench in celebration of their success, builds rapport up and down the roster. Some of his best friends are former teammates, like Royal Ivey, whom he played with at Texas, and Michael Beasley from his neighborhood and Spencer Hawes from the AAU circuit. He takes seriously his role as mentor and elder statesman in basketball. His forays into social media exchanges have gone public for him doing battle with online adversaries. But Durant's DMs are also a space for private counseling and mentoring. He doles out advice and offers encouragement, even builds online friendships.

But Durant doesn't always exist at his center. He gets pulled away from it.

As communal as he can be, Durant is also a bit of a loner. He has friends all over the league. He's connected in New York, Los Angeles, D.C., and now the Bay Area. He has celebrity friends from other industries on speed dial. While he isn't opposed to going out, Durant is more likely to find himself holed up in some low-key environment. He often prefers privacy. He is an open book in a glass case, visible and inviting yet still guarded.

Some of it can be credited to his eccentricity. In many ways, he is atypical from his peers. He clashes against the expectations of an NBA star. For the longest time, his desire to blend in was his most defining characteristic off court. He was marked by his humility, a superstar with the look of a sixth man. He did his part feeding that persona, too. He hid his cursing and tattoos from the larger public.

You still won't find Durant in gaudy jewelry. He hasn't been swept up by the fashion wave in the NBA. While players are pushing the boundaries of luxury attire, Durant is loyal to his sweatsuits. He occasionally steps his game up with a pair of jeans and maybe an expensive T-shirt that resembles a thrift-store find more than high fashion. But as Durant has grown older, more comfortable in his own skin, his full personality is being revealed. He no longer clings to the persona of a humble antitype. Instead, Durant chooses to reveal more of himself as a way of destroying the box professional athletes are supposed to fit in. He aggressively questions the why of what he formerly just accepted, sometimes solely because it is accepted. He no longer filters his language for the masses, choosing not to carry the burden of being a pristine example for kids, while at the same time constantly giving to young people. He's been spotted on stage at an Ultimate Rap League event and a Drake Concert, and also Hillsong Church in New York and at a tech convention in San Francisco. His peers describe him as a different dude, a colloquialism for people who ride their own wave and break social mores.

Perhaps the most telling example of Durant being a different dude is his hair. It's been a running joke for years how Durant doesn't brush his hair, a grassroots dialogue that intensified in the spotlight of the dynastic Warriors. Several professional athletes have barbers on their payroll. Some even travel with them. Properly groomed hair is a passion for many of them, an attribute ingrained by the communities that reared them. There is long, storied history with Black people in America and hair. It has been a symbol of success, of refinement, of assimilation, even of rebellion. History includes stories, many passed down by grandparents and great-grandparents, of hair being a barometer of acceptance. Establishments and organizations, including churches, would use a comb test to determine entry. If the comb couldn't pass through the Black person's hair unimpeded, he or she couldn't get in. The demonization of coarse, curly hair has impacted Black culture for centuries, leading many to straighten their hair. It was a Black woman, Madam C. J. Walker, who was credited with inventing the hot comb to help press out the kinks without the use of chemicals. The '60s and '70s saw the rise of the Afro, a rejection of hegemonic standards of hair. It became a hairstyle of pride and culture. While this counterculture existed, permanent relaxers were still the rage, popularized by the likes of James Brown and Little Richard. The '80s brought in the processed curls, which became trendy in the inner city thanks to the likes of Michael Jackson and Ice Cube. The 2000s saw locks—which, like Afros, were a celebration of natural hair and a rebellion against societal standards—filter into mainstream culture.

All of this undergirds the meaning of hair in Black culture and the consistent dialogue about it. Even Chris Rock made a movie decoding the meaning of "good hair," a label ascribed in the Black community to people whose hair is not kinky. But no matter the hairstyle or the hair grade, the one nearly universal understanding, passed down from generation to generation, is that it must be presentable. Most Black men have stories from their childhood of visiting barbershops, of getting lotion or Vaseline slathered on their faces and their hair brushed real quick by their moms before being sent off to school. Durant was indeed raised in a culture that dictates getting regular haircuts and brushing his hair as maintenance, especially for important life events such as school pictures, job interviews, and dressy gatherings. The common perception is that anyone who is on television is involved in an important life event, hence the dismay that Durant routinely enters the public space with ungroomed hair. But his unkemptness isn't a calculated resistance against the culture. He will get lined up when he needs to. Some occasions have prompted even Durant to treat his mane. He was crispy when he guest appeared on the Showtime series *Billions*. But, outside of special occasions, Durant just doesn't care that much. Even his teammates rib him for it, specifically Draymond Green, who has a personal barber and is usually meticulous with his haircuts. Durant is fine with just throwing a hat on and won't think twice. Or go hatless and not be bothered at all. He's heard all the jokes. He's seen the memes. He's had barbers implore him to try a little brush maintenance. But, by and large, Durant is blasé about a time-honored tradition of his culture.

He'd much rather create new culture, like one that emphasizes scholarship. He opened the first College Track center in his hometown. It's called the Durant Center.

College Track is a college completion program that helps students from lower-class communities graduate from college. A month after announcing a $3 million donation to the University of Texas, Durant's foundation announced a $10 million commitment to the College Track program in Prince George's County, the first College Track program on the East Coast.

"This is the realization of a dream of mine," said Durant, who won the Muhammad Ali Sports Humanitarian Award for what was perhaps his most impactful gift: the Durant Center.

"To come back home and positively impact the lives of kids—who share the ambitions I've always had—with world-class educational opportunities and resources that can completely change the game in our community for generations to come."

Durant doesn't seem to have much problem existing in his own space, running counter to expectations or raising the standards.

Few things illustrate the different-dudeness of Durant than the tattoo covering his left thigh. It's ink of a rock star portrait taken by Lynn Goldsmith. She has captured thousands of celebrities, including Michael Jackson, Bruce Springsteen, Bob Marley, Prince, Sting, Miles Davis, and Steely Dan. On New Year's Day, 1981, she took a portrait of one megastar that Durant would convert into body art: Rick James.

The close-up shot captures James in a pair of dark aviator glasses, with the reflection artfully added in white to make the tattoo pop. The full lips that crooned jams like "You and I" and "Mary Jane" were shaded in great detail and topped with a mustache. His braided bob fell to either side of his face. This was thirty-two-year-old Rick James, still young and spry before drugs, weight, and age altered the shape of his face. The picture was taken months before his fifth album, *Street*

Songs, was released, featuring some of his biggest hits in "Give It to Me Baby" and "Super Freak" and "Fire and Desire."

Rick James was heavy in the rotation on the soundtrack for Durant's Saturday morning cleaning sessions. He would get distracted from sweeping, pretending the broom handle was a microphone as he sang along. *Cold. . . . Cold-blooded.* In many Black households, weekend cleaning was accompanied by music. The era of the adults determined what tunes would be blasted while the dishes were washed and carpets were vacuumed and furniture was dusted. It's how many children raised on hip-hop kept connected to the R&B, Motown, and the jazz music their parents loved.

Rick James's freedom spoke to Durant. Already with odes to 2Pac and Wu Tang Clan, it would have been more expected for the Notorious B.I.G. to follow, or even Michael Jackson. But Durant went with one of the most eccentric choices in the music lexicon.

James died in 2004 a cultural icon, revived for Generation Xers by a skit on Dave Chappelle's hit show. But in his heyday James was eccentricity on steroids. He resurrected Motown Records, a label famous for soul music, doo-wop, and R&B. But Rick James injected new life with his funky music, semi-androgynous style, and rambunctiousness. Rick James was unapologetically flamboyant. He was what they called a freakazoid, a Black man fully engrossed in the '80s era of neon colors, orgies, and drugs. He was talented and liberated. It makes sense Durant would appreciate Rick James's spirit.

The question hovering over Durant, though, is whether his comfort with seclusion is a symptom of a larger void. So many people who know Durant and want the best for him sometimes wonder about him.

Is there really peace behind that warm grin of his? Durant oozes a smoothness on the court. His basketball feats are pulled off seemingly without effort. That's why one of his favorite nicknames is Easy Money. His Instagram handle is @easymoneysniper. He makes scoring look like a weekend job test driving luxury cars. That smoothness dribbles over into his off-the-court vibe. He moves with a relaxed pace, talks with a cadence to match a rhythmic handshake. He is an expert at small talk, chopping himself down to size with a friendliness that allows him to fit into any environment. But it's hard not to wonder if Durant has just mastered the art of hiding. Is he so good at surface relationships as a way of avoiding the deeper ones?

The trauma Durant has endured in his life doesn't fade away. The scars are still there. The drama that comes with being a professional athlete ordinarily makes players keep their circle small. Durant underwent a bit of a purge over the last few years. He formerly was surrounded by family and childhood friends. But many of them have been pushed to the periphery. His agent-turned-business partner, Rich Kleiman, is now his right hand. They spend a lot of time together. Durant calls him a brother. His father—the general manager of his AAU program, Team Durant—is also a staple in his circle. For the 2018 postseason, not even his mother and brother were around, a first in Durant's career.

Some have suspected Durant's lonerism is loneliness. The fluctuation of what he prioritizes, the swings of his mood, the relative isolation—it sometimes feels like Durant is coping as much as he is comfortable. Behind the scenes, his biggest supporters and advocates are hoping he gets married and starts a family—at least have a child. Durant told *GQ* he broke off his engagement to WNBA star Monica Wright because "he didn't love her right." He was again single when the 2018–19 season kicked off, as his relationship with Cassandra Anderson didn't survive the 2018 off-season. So those hopes are still on hold.

Becoming a father has anchored many men. Having a child changes a man's perspective. It can provide focus and give a greater purpose to one's life. Having a spouse to share life with has a way of trivializing what was once germaine. They want that for Durant, a new epicenter for his life.

But happiness can seem elusive for Durant. He contends no one, especially the media, knows the real him. It's hard not to wonder if that's just him hiding from not knowing what would actually make him happy. He doesn't seem to be truly close with his teammates, save for Quinn Cook, who is more like a little brother. Part of that is the makeup of the Warriors' locker room—none of them are especially tight. And part of it is Durant flows differently—a seven-footer who can vanish into thin air at a gathering.

No one knows what makes him happy. Of course, that makes it hard for the people who want to.

"He's such a great guy," Steve Kerr said. "All everyone really wants is for KD to be happy. He deserves to be happy."

. . .

Durant was talking.

He was also snacking at the same time. He was in New York with Portland Trail Blazers guard C. J. McCollum. Durant was a guest on McCollum's podcast, *Pull Up*. McCollum flew out to New York for this conversation with Durant. Some forty minutes in, the conversation shifted to the Warriors' acquisition of DeMarcus Cousins, the All-Star big man who shocked the league by signing for a super-bargain $5.3 million.

McCollum confessed to being mad about Cousins's signing, setting off incredible banter between two professionals.

"Why are you mad about this stuff?" Durant asked.

"Bruh, I'm in the league," McCollum responded. "What do you mean, 'Why am I mad about this stuff?'? I'm in the Western Conference. I gotta play you MFers all the time anyway as it is. Over and over again. We done got eliminated by y'all a few times in the first round."

Durant assumes the role of big brother. He's three years older than McCollum but has six years more experience. He's also several levels above McCollum in the hierarchy of NBA stardom.

"I mean, you know," Durant said, shifting to a more serious tone. "You know you guys aren't going to win a championship."

"Bruh, we have the team," McCollum said, sounding more as if he were convincing himself as Durant laughs tauntingly. "We have the capabilities. Anything is possible. We can win a championship."

Durant continued the real talk, dishing it straight to his little brother in this NBA fraternity. He shared how he liked Portland's guards, the high-scoring duo of McCollum and All-Star Damian Lillard, but the Blazers didn't have enough to be serious contenders.

McCollum's contention: Portland could've been a serious contender if Cousins had signed with them. The combination of Cousins and Jusuf Nurkić was the one-two punch the Blazers needed, McCollum said. But Durant wasn't buying it.

"What about y'all two?" he asked about McCollum and Lillard. "Y'all gon' be pissed you can't shoot them deep-ass threes and dribble eight times before you get your shot off. No way it's happening. Gotta have a nice yin and yang, bro. It's going to be too much of one thing with y'all. So we stopped that."

McCollum relented, conceded to the expertise of the two-time Finals MVP. Durant didn't miss the opening.

"I suggest you just keep playing, man, and don't worry about what goes on at the top of things."

"We right there at the top of things," McCollum shot back. "We was a third seed last year. Bro, we was right there, just slightly below one and two."

"But how'd you play?" Durant asked.

"Some unfortunate situations happened in the first round," McCollum continued, ignoring the question. Durant asked again.

"How'd you play?"

"Some unfortunate circumstances," McCollum repeated.

"Like a eight seed," Durant jabbed, followed by laughter.

Like all superstar athletes, Durant has an arrogance about him, too. It can be masked by his nice-guy persona, but he got this far by believing he is better. In 2013 he famously told *Sports Illustrated* he was tired of being second. In a league dominated by LeBron James, he openly declared his intentions for a coup of NBA supremacy. And Durant doesn't just fight for titles and trophies. He fights for No. 1 in the court of public opinion. He loves debating basketball, but often at the crux of his stance is a thirst for his superiority to be recognized. There is something distinctly down-to-earth about Durant hearing criticism and being willing to engage. He's been told by so many to not give the opinions of others so much credence. But he does. Because he wants you to recognize—needs you to recognize—the depths of his greatness. Stacked on top of his core of humility and selflessness is a supreme desire for reverence. Maybe they are next to each other, arrogance and humility, warring for the right to control his thoughts. Arrogance leads him to read every article and if necessary approach the reporter to counter a conclusion or two. Arrogance has him spending hours in his mentions, absorbing often uneducated commentary and firing back at will.

Being unselfish and arrogant seems contradictory, but Durant's existence is a microcosm of the human experience. Humility is not the absence of desires to be on top and be revered, just the ability not to be governed by those desires. In a culture where it's cliché to pretend to not care about what people think, Durant is unabashed in his care for such and not above giving into its temptation. It's not governing him in the sense that outside opinions inform his view of himself. He isn't losing self-esteem because someone on Twitter calls him soft. He's painted as sensitive because of it, but the part of him being hurt is his ego. It's tapping into the same competitive spirit that makes him want to take down LeBron James. How could anybody have a disparaging view of Durant? That's a wrong that must be set right.

Durant is a guy who will text a reporter at 2:00 a.m. to complain about a line in an article or confront an analyst to his face about something he said on television. He is also the same guy who will go out of his way to tell a media member how much he notices and likes his expertise or text a writer about how inspired he was by his piece. The same person who coined the term "Blog Boys"—a moniker criticizing bloggers who pay more attention to the drama of basketball than the game itself—is the superstar most likely to talk to them in depth. These two spirits coexist in Durant, and he is just genuine enough to reveal both.

The lofty ideals in him have always had a way of winning out. It is his default. But the Durant the world now knows has grown much more comfortable stepping outside of that core mode. Perhaps it's not even really straying, as his core is always tethered to him. Perhaps the sacrifices of blending in, of exalting others perennially, feels like being taken advantage of, and Durant is done allowing that. There was a time when he wouldn't say things because his core told him it wasn't right. But that also means what needed to be said went unsaid.

Now he's calling his shot. He's claiming his value. He's saying the uncomfortable thing.

"I look at it like this," Durant said, flashing that easy-money smile before he drops an NBA hot take, the calm before the hyperbolic. "This is a Black culture and we built this shit up so good that you got people from ghettos of America making $40 [million], $43 [million], $44 million dollars playing this shit. This is like the greatest group of people in the history of man, in my opinion. We created a monopoly on sports, basically. We got everybody in the world wanting to be basketball players."

9 | THE VILLAIN

TRAILING 95–94 WITH JUST OVER FOUR minutes remaining in Game 3 of the 2018 NBA Finals, Durant had the ball at the top, well past the 3-point line near half-court, with LeBron James defending him. He signaled for a screen from Andre Iguodala, who was being defended by Kevin Love, perhaps the worst defender on the floor.

Now isolated on Love, Durant leaned right and crossed over to start his drive. His move didn't lose Love, who rode alongside Durant as he dribbled down the left side of the paint. So Durant rose up, drifting left in the air before releasing over Love's outstretched hand. After he saw the shot go in, Love threw his hands up, both landing on his head in disbelief. He played great defense and it didn't even matter. The Warriors led 96–95.

The next time down, Curry rebounded J. R. Smith's missed 3-pointer. Before Curry could get going, Durant was demanding the ball. Clap. Clap. Clap. Curry dropped the ball off without looking. It was Durant's time. He was looking for the kill shot. But after running the same action to get Love on him again, Durant drove left and spun back to the middle, his fadeaway missing the rim. The second trip didn't net any points, but it revealed a pattern. When Durant called for the screen, James was all too willing to oblige. Iguodala didn't even have to set a meaningful screen and the switch was made. James was not committed to fighting through the screen and making sure he stayed connected to Durant. That meant the Cavaliers' best perimeter defender would not be an impediment.

After a pair of free throws by Love, Cleveland regained the lead. It was back to point guard Durant. He dribbled down the left side of the court, James on him. Iguodala came to set the screen and Love chased him. But it was a diversion: Iguodala never set the screen, just kept running to the left corner. Durant whipped the ball to Draymond Green on the right, the side of the court Love had just vacated. Green bounced a pass down low to Curry, who took advantage of the open space for a layup. The Warriors had the lead again with three minutes left.

Then Iguodala stripped Love, starting a fast break that lead to a Curry 3-pointer. Warriors 101, Cleveland 97. That was five points in twenty seconds, giving the Warriors control of the game.

Curry had been struggling mightily with his shot all game. After exploding for nine 3-pointers in Game 2, he missed his first nine 3-pointers in Game 3. Meanwhile, Durant was playing a relatively perfect Game 3. Before the pull-up over Love, he had 38 points on twenty shots, with thirteen rebounds and six assists—and was playing well on defense. It was setting up to be the ideal kind of synergy between the two superstars. Durant wasn't very good in Game 1 and made a crucial mistake that nearly cost the Warriors the game. But Curry was good in Game 1, so all was well. Then Curry went off in Game 2, with Durant playing a complementary role brilliantly. And now, in Game 3, Curry was struggling and Durant was dominant. So Durant carried the Warriors, and it looked as if he was going to do it just long enough and well enough for Curry to finish off the Cavs.

But LeBron answered with a 3-pointer, cutting the Warriors lead to 101–100 with just inside of two minutes left. The Cavaliers had life. So it was back to point guard Durant. This time James fought through the weak screen by Iguodala, who was being defended by Love, and stayed glued to Durant on the right wing. The Warriors reset and re-cycled the same play with Iguodala trying to screen James so Love would have to switch onto Durant. James fought through the screen again.

So Durant, executing the Warriors' brand of offense, gave the ball up to Iguodala and the two did a dribble-handoff exchange that put the ball right back in Durant's hands. This action served as a sort of screen, since Iguodala and Durant crossed paths so closely. James couldn't fight through this time. Love was forced to switch on to Du-rant while a determined James worked his way around Iguodala in pursuit of Durant. With two players stalking Durant, Iguodala cut to the basket and received the pass, dunking over Tristan Thompson with his right hand.

That was four times Durant ran the pick-and-roll with Iguodala. The Warriors got three different looks out of them. The stage was set for the dramatic finish.

A James drive-and-dish to Tristan Thompson resulted in a miss. Warriors guard Klay Thompson scooped up the loose ball to give the Warriors a chance to take the lead. Durant demanded the ball from him. Clap. Clap. Clap. Thompson gave it up and Durant drib-bled across half-court and slowed the tempo down. He waved for his teammates to get up court and get in position. He walked the ball from the right sideline to the middle of the court. This was his time. His show.

With a minute left in Game 3, he stood dribbling on the Cavaliers logo, directing traffic with James crouched in front of him. This time Curry came to set a screen on James and he didn't fight through it.

Instead, James followed Curry away from the ball while Rodney Hood took his place on Durant. Fifty-five seconds left.

Durant kept dribbling. The capacity crowd of 20,562 at Quicken Loans Arena was on its feet. The nervous energy was palpable. The speakers blared a "De-fense!" chant, but the audience wasn't following along, too focused on the building drama.

Durant wanted Love on him, so he signaled for Iguodala to leave the painted area and set a screen for him. But the Cavaliers, wise to the Warriors' plan, made a sudden switch. Instead of Love following Iguodala, he tapped J. R. Smith, who abandoned defending Klay Thompson and followed Iguodala. Fifty-three seconds left in the game, five seconds left on the shot clock.

Durant started dribbling left, guiding Hood into the screen Iguodala was setting. Hood saw the screen and backed up, getting in position to make the switch. Smith, trying to get ahead of the screen, took the long way around Iguodala to get to Durant. The simultaneous decisions by the Cavaliers' defenders created an open pocket for Durant and a window for a historic moment to take place. Durant took advantage, pulling up from thirty-three feet away as he stepped into his shooting motion. With Durant's height, Smith didn't have a chance. His lunge with his right hand outstretched didn't enter Durant's space until the ball was already released.

As Durant hoisted, the crowd collectively gasped an inhale, holding it while the ball floated toward the rim. When it splashed the net, the exhale of the Cavalier faithful was resounding, nearly drowning out the whistle from Cleveland's immediate timeout. Green and Klay Thompson walked toward Durant with both arms extended, each mimicking the referees' signal for a made 3-pointer and symbolizing the victory.

Durant had done it again.

"Supreme self-confidence," Curry said during the postgame press conference. "He works hard at his game, at his craft. He's ready for those moments. When you have that belief in yourself, the moment is never too big for you. To have the guts and composure to take the shot last year and tonight, it was big. I think he would live with the result knowing how much work he's put into it. That's what superstars do."

Durant's reaction was noticeably still after his monumental basket.

His arms dropped lifelessly to his side as he stared blankly to his left at a sea of Cavs fans. After a second of stillness, his shoulders slumped, he let out an exaggerated exhale as he turned to head the other way. He looked more like a teenager irritated by his mother summoning him than a player who had just created a legendary moment. He kept the blank stare as he started his strut toward the bench. He didn't say a word. He didn't make an expression. His face remained stoic, immovable, his eyes piercingly empty. Durant just started walking. What looked like no reaction morphed into the loudest statement he could make.

In the twenty-three months leading up to this very moment, Durant had existed as an NBA villain. His decision to leave Oklahoma City after nine seasons and join the Warriors transformed him from beloved to reviled. His character was assassinated relentlessly. He was weak. Soft. A snake. A coward. His legacy was called into question. His status among the elite was revoked. He was unofficially banned from consideration as an all-time great in the proverbial court of public opinion. Through it all, Durant had been doing a lot of talking.

He tried to defend his decision. He barked back at his critics. He tried to explain himself. He called into question the same fans who once revered him, that same court of public opinion. He deemed analysts and commentators unworthy. He made a lot of declarations, a lot of long-winded explanations and deep-diving rationales. A lot of talking.

But in this moment, his moment, he did no talking. He walked away from the destruction he had just created as if it was inevitable and therefore unworthy of a response. The Cavs had one last hope of making this a series. Down 2–0, having lost Game 1 in overtime, Cleveland was in a must-win situation in Game 3. Once again they had the defending champions on the ropes. But Durant snatched away their hope as if the Cavs were foolish for even having it. Coolly, slowly, his eyes scanned the crowd as he strutted.

Green walked up behind Durant shouting expletives. Curry worked his way in front of Durant, backpedaling in stride, squatting down as he bellowed up at Durant in celebration. Durant slapped Curry's hand without breaking stride. Warriors bounced from the bench toward Durant. They screamed at him, gave him high-fives, hugged him. The whole time, he didn't say a word. His facial expression didn't change. The super–slow motion replay really gave Durant the appearance of an action-movie star. He was the NBA's version of Denzel Washington in *Man on Fire*. The broadcast played Justin Timberlake's "Can't Stop the Feeling" over the replay of Durant's 3-pointer and walk off. It would have been more fitting to play the spoof song the comedic trio the Lonely Island made for the 2009 MTV Movie Awards: "Cool Guys Don't Look at Explosions."

This wasn't a spoof though. This was real destruction, even though the explosion was metaphoric. On a court with at least five Hall of Famers, Durant had crafted this moment. He willed it. And the Cavaliers were rubble.

Durant did more than just yank the heart out of Cleveland—again. He did more than secure his second straight NBA Finals MVP with an epic punctuation to one of his best games ever. This was a message. A rebuttal. For about two years he'd been existing in restlessness and uncertainty. Since switching teams, he'd been under attack, grappling with the crumbling of his reputation, his new position as basketball's most hated. For a player who was a good guy most of his career, these were trying times.

So Durant resolved to wear the black hat. He prefers to be loved. Anyone who knows him knows that about him. But he had to come to grips with being hated. For years he sought and received approval. Now he was forced to embrace rejection.

He had no choice, really. No explanation for his decision would suffice. No amount of reason would muzzle his naysayers. And as long as he was with the Warriors, it was never going away. He had to come to grips with the reality that he was now, and possibly forever, the antagonist. His joining Golden State, altering the balance of power and the history of the league, was just simply not acceptable by the masses.

In his black hat and black trench coat with a cannon in his hand, Durant shot down LeBron, Cleveland, and everyone who had something to say. He played the game of his life against the player many consider the greatest. He punctuated that performance by taking and making the kind of shot that affirmed his supremacy, rubbing his greatness in the face of his detractors, trolling them with his eliteness. So many wanted him to fail, considered losing just deserts for his decision. He deprived them all of the satisfaction, then walked away to let them stew in their emotions. He created a highlight that will be played in perpetuity, etching himself in NBA Finals lore.

It was a moment twenty-three months in the making.

· · ·

After he did his introductory press conference in Oakland three days after the announcement that he was leaving Oklahoma City for the Warriors, Durant took off for a scheduled trip to China with Nike to promote his ninth signature shoe. But that was where he found the bottom of the pit. He crossed the Pacific Ocean but couldn't escape the vitriol.

He knew it was coming. He didn't know it would be *this* intense, *this* unforgiving, *this* venomous. What made it worse was that he had no home yet. He merely stopped by the Warriors facility for his press conference. NBA teammates disperse during the summer. Many of them don't have permanent residences in the cities where they work. So Durant didn't yet have his teammates to distract him from the noise. He didn't have the daily grind to consume his energy. He wasn't yet entrenched in Warriors culture. He was a man on an island watching the demolition of his reputation happen in real time.

"To have so many people just say, 'Fuck you,' that really does it to you," Durant told *San Francisco* magazine.

Many of the people who once said they loved him, who cheered for him, were now attacking him like jilted lovers. For nine years he poured his heart out for the Oklahoma City Thunder. He actually developed his game, actually put in the work to get better. He was truly part of the community.

Just like that, they reviled him. They burned his jersey. They disowned him. Hell hath no fury like a fanatic scorned.

It wasn't just Oklahoma City fans, either. It was NBA fans at large, who follow the storylines of the league like a television series. They, too, had come to admire Durant from afar. Now they lost respect for him. Analysts and experts were throwing stones. Former players and current players, who would figure to best understand the liberty he exercised, were criticizing him.

Durant was overwhelmed. He was in China with countless fans who idolized him, lined up and waited to see him, be in his presence, and he felt exiled.

It was six in the morning when he called his manager, Rich Kleiman. Durant vented from the depths of his soul.

"And he's like, 'Why the fuck did you let me do this to my life?' " Kleiman told *San Francisco* magazine. "And I'm like, 'Oh shit. I'm coming over to your room.' "

Whatever angst Durant was feeling was appeased once he got on the court. The Warriors went the extra mile to make him feel welcome—especially on the court. In the fifth game of the season, the Oklahoma City Thunder visited Oracle. The Warriors made sure Durant looked good in front of his ex.

It was needed, too. Westbrook became the pied piper of a basketball nation ridiculing Durant.

First, on the day Durant announced, Westbrook took to Instagram. He posted a picture of a three-tier tower of cupcakes decorated for Independence Day. All he wrote on the post was "HAPPY 4th YALL . . ." with three American flag emojis. The visual, though, had inside meaning, which was uncovered by then *Sports Illustrated* writer Lee Jenkins.

Durant and Westbrook used "cupcake" to describe play they thought was soft or people they thought were soft. The colloquialism was introduced to the Thunder by Oklahoma City center Kendrick Perkins, and the two stars ran with it. The whole team did. So it was obvious to Durant, and later the world, what Westbrook was saying in his post. The only way to make it more obvious would have been to have thirty-five cupcakes in the picture.

Westbrook was especially ornery when asked about Durant. It was clear by his demeanor he was angry at him, at least initially. Before the Hamptons meeting, Durant had dinner with Westbrook and Nick Collison, who had been with the franchise since it moved from Seattle. Westbrook left that dinner believing Durant was staying.

According to the report from ESPN's Royce Young, Durant told West-brook and Collison he was returning.

"It's false," Durant said, addressing the dinner in an interview with Yahoo! Sports. "I didn't say that—words about me telling Russell or Nick that I would stay or leave never came out of my mouth. We met as teammates, but no promises came out of it. In this day and age, I can't control anything people claim out there. Someone can go out and say something random right now, and people will believe it. I never told Russell or Nick, 'Alright, guys, I'm coming back to the Thunder'—and then a week later, I decide not to. Never happened. I don't operate like that. I heard people say that story, but it's not the truth."

The soap opera between the two turned up a notch when they faced off for the first time on November 4, 2016. Westbrook got the drama going early with a pregame subliminal shot.

Westbrook wore a photographer's vest to the first game against Durant. Even with his eccentric fashion taste, Westbrook's jab at KD's photography hobby was obvious, which only added to the buzz before the game.

But this was bigger than the rivalry between the two ex-teammates. This was Durant's first chance to stare down his ac-cusers. For nearly four months he'd been a piñata for hot takes and criticism. This was his chance for revenge, or validation, or both. Durant played it cool before the game, emitting his best friendly vibes. He opted out of the back-and-forth with Westbrook. He chat-ted with former teammates who didn't hold animosity. He even went to pregame chapel service, a Christian-based gathering that usually includes players from both teams, with Westbrook and several oth-ers. But despite all of his efforts Durant was nervous, antsy. No way he could lay an egg. No way he could give people a reason to pile on.

"That's one thing we always talk about," Draymond Green said. "No guy's going through anything by himself. Obviously we knew that was a huge game for him. He wanted to win that game and if you don't want to win that game, I'm questioning what kind of competitor you are."

So the Warriors propped up Durant. They fed him the ball. They ran plays for him. They stayed in his ear with encouragement and permission.

There was one sequence when the Warriors were blowing open the game. Durant missed a pull-up in the lane that Golden State center Zaza Pachulia batted back out to the perimeter, right to Durant. He corralled the loose ball and drilled a 3-pointer from the right wing. On the ensuing defensive possession, the Warriors thwarted a Westbrook drive and the loose ball squirted to Curry, who started a fast break. He jogged from the left side of the court to the middle. It seemed as if by taking his time he squandered the transition opportunity. Thunder forwards Jerami Grant and Domantas Sabonis blocked Curry's path at the 3-point line. But the Warriors MVP whipped the ball around his back as he stared down the defender in front of him. But it wasn't a dribble move. It was a pass. Durant was charging down the right side in transition. Curry had slowed to allow Durant to catch up to the play and his around-the-back pass hit Durant in stride. No dribble was necessary. He just stepped into the pass, pulled up, and drilled his second 3-pointer in as many possessions. Oracle erupted in its special way for Durant, just how his teammates set it up.

"I felt like they rallied around me," Durant said after the game, "and that was a great feeling."

There was a price for the Durant assimilation project. Curry paid it, and, as a result, so did the Warriors' offense. On Christmas Day 2016 in Cleveland, the Warriors' first showdown against LeBron James with Durant in tow, the bill was due.

Part of the Warriors' aggressively working to incorporate Durant involved featuring him in the offense. The Warriors thrived on ball movement in building into a championship franchise. The glaring shortcoming, the one that made them especially want Durant, was in isolation offense. Durant is one of the best isolation players in the league. The Warriors, especially late in games, made a habit of putting the ball in Durant's hands and leaning on his special ability. But in the process, Curry became a decoy. His combination of shooting, passing, and penetrating was the fuel for the Warriors offense for years. But with the offense running through Durant, Curry spent far more time than usual in the corner. Considered the greatest shooter ever, Curry being in the corner required a defender to join him, which gave Durant space to operate.

In this marquee showdown on Christmas, Durant was dominant. He scored 28 points on fourteen shots in the first three quarters. But in the fourth quarter, with the offense running through Durant and Curry a secondary figure (and struggling defensively), the Warriors became predictable. Durant was two for nine in fourth quarter. The Warriors managed just 21 points and lost a nail-biter. Curry was benched in the final moments for defense.

"Honestly, I can't have 11 shots," Curry told the *Mercury News* afterward. "That's nobody's fault. I've just got to figure out a way to be more aggressive in that respect. And keep the defense honest and use all the talent we have on this team, including my scoring ability."

Curry was averaging four shots fewer per game, including that Christmas Day matchup. He lost his aggressiveness trying to feature Durant and became one-dimensional as an off-the-ball component. What was brewing was the culture war between Curry and Durant. In this battle, waged in the hearts of Warriors fans, Durant was also the villain.

The Bay Area adores Curry. He is the player most responsible for lifting their beloved Warriors from doormat to dynasty. They watched him grow up on the court, morph from an undersized teenage-looking hooper to a full-fledged family man and mogul. He is to Warriors fans what LeBron James is to Cleveland, what Kobe Bryant is to the Lakers. Curry plays second fiddle to no one in the Bay Area when it comes to adoration. So watching him reduced to an extra in the Durant Show had some murmuring.

This wasn't Durant and Curry's battle. It was Durant who talked to Curry and set things in order. He told the two-time MVP to just play his game. Durant said he didn't need Curry to adjust to fit him in. Durant would instead fit into the Warriors' style of play.

Durant was right. His offensive talents are so diverse, he could play any style. The first two months of the season showed his efficiency skyrocket because of his ability to play off the ball. He averaged 27 points on 57.1 percent shooting. Of the Warriors' possessions in a game, 27 percent went to Durant. In his last season with Oklahoma City, he averaged 28 points on 50.5 percent shooting while using just over 30 percent of the Thunder's possessions. With the Warriors he was getting essentially the same production but with less work. In the Warriors' offense, all of his skills were maximized, not just his powers of isolation. So he encouraged the Warriors to get back to that.

It still wasn't an easy transition. Not even two weeks after the Christmas Day game, the Warriors had a meltdown on the court. The incumbent players had been noticing how different the offense was with Durant. Coach Steve Kerr milked Durant's height advantage and scoring prowess, getting away from their get-everyone-involved approach. And the truth is, Durant was comfortable in this style of basketball. This is what he did for years in Oklahoma City. It only made sense that his old habits would surface.

But on January 6, 2017, in a home loss to Memphis, Durant's habitual style of play and the Warriors' philosophy clashed on the court.

Golden State led Memphis by 2 with fewer than forty seconds remaining. Curry had the ball at the top of the key and the Warriors were getting ready to run a play. A score would all but end the game, so victory was one crisp execution away, especially since opponents are usually tired from the pace and having to keep up with all the Warriors' passing. But Durant had Grizzlies power forward Zach Randolph defending him. Randolph is a slow six-foot-nine, 260 pounds, and he was caught out on the perimeter away from his comfort zone in the paint. Durant was sure he could beat Randolph off the dribble, so he did what came natural to him. He clapped for the ball. That's what Durant does when he wants the rock. The louder the sound, the more he wants it.

First, Curry ignored the clap and directed Durant to the spot he was supposed to be. But Durant clapped again, demanding the ball. Curry gave it up, put his head down, and got out of the way. Immediately, Draymond Green started yelling at Durant from the other side of the court, punching the air in frustration. The Warriors had been doing so much to make sure Durant felt comfortable. Now it was backfiring.

Curry made one more attempt to create the motion the Warriors prefer by going to set a screen for Durant. But Curry was waved off. Durant knew he could take Randolph. Had no doubt. He just wanted the space to do so.

But instead of going around the slower Randolph to the rim, Durant settled for a pull-up 3-pointer and missed. The Grizzlies called a timeout and Green shouted down Durant in the huddle as they argued about what had just happened. After the timeout, Memphis point guard Mike Conley Jr. hit the shot that tied the game and the Warriors lost in overtime.

Even as a four-time scoring champ, Durant had a reputation. Sometimes he could be downright unstoppable. But he was also known for stopping himself. The best teams, the best defenses, could have success against him by baiting him. It was really the only hope against Durant. If he is on top of his game, hitting his shot, there really is no containing him. But when he doesn't hit his shot, his answer is usually to keep taking them. He has a weakness for the mid-range jumper. It's what he hangs his hat on, the by-product of learning basketball in the late '90s and early 2000s, before the 3-point shot took over the sport. Never the strongest player, Durant didn't force his way to the rim as much as he should. He was too infatuated with his own beautiful shot.

But the Warriors unlocked the rest of Durant's game and revealed him to be one of the most diverse offensive talents in NBA history. In addition to being an incredible one-on-one scorer, he proved with the Warriors he could also thrive without the ball in his hands.

Most elite scorers require the ball being in their hands, directing traffic, making decisions, creating and taking openings. It's a right they have earned by being good at scoring. They become control freaks who feel naked without grasping Spalding and don't buy in fully for the work it takes to control the game without the ball.

The art of cutting in basketball is like counterpunching in boxing in that it uses the aggression of the opponent against them. The biggest part of being a good cutter is believing it is effective. Conviction is the secret ingredient, which is hard to secure from superstars—especially after they have had the control for so long. Slashing is a sales job, and the best salespeople believe in what they are selling. The Warriors had to get Durant to see the value of playing well off the ball, then help him master it. To his credit, he took to it like coffee takes to cream.

He had height, length, touch around the basket, basketball IQ, shot-making ability. All those tools make him a threat without the ball. In the Warriors' offense, those attributes blended together perfectly. Slashing across the lane, finishing in transition, cutting back door, catching lobs, curling off screens, spotting up for threes—he did it all. It took the Warriors' offense to another level. Durant showed he can be as dominant without the ball in his hands as with it. They got him to fill their isolation void. But they also got him to play off the ball. A strong case could be made that they would have won back-to-back championships in 2015 and 2016 if Harrison Barnes was more productive off the ball. Cleveland's game plan was to trap Curry and face-guard Klay Thompson, the Warriors' two most prolific scorers. With Green serving as the secondary playmaker, once Curry gave up the ball when he was double-teamed, Cleveland determined they could afford to leave Barnes open. He got a lot of good looks and went ice-cold.

With the Warriors holding a 3–1 series lead over Cleveland in the 2016 NBA Finals, they needed one good game from Barnes to make Cleveland pay for their defensive scheme. In Game 4, he had 14 points, knocking down four 3-pointers to put the Warriors on the brink. One more big game from Barnes and the Warriors would win the championship. But over the last three games of the series, Barnes missed twenty-seven of thirty-two shots total.

If Durant was getting those shots instead of Barnes, it would be a wrap. That was the thinking of the Warriors as they coveted an upgrade at small forward. And Durant could do so much more than just hit the open shots fed to him.

Durant posted the highest offensive rating of his career—the Warriors averaged 125 points for every one hundred possessions Durant was on the court—even while averaging career lows in field goal attempts (16.5) and minutes (33.4) per game. The Warriors' style of play was what attracted Durant. He wanted to play the "right way" in a system where he watched multiple stars be productive. He wanted to be part of the beautiful symphony of five players who make music together.

They had to go through the rough patch. They had to yell at each other. They had to refocus and figure out how to make it work. What ended up happening was a manifestation of the promises they made to each other in the Hamptons. They became closer because of it. They were a better team because of it. Even Durant was better because of it.

This was why he came to the Warriors. And this spirit would be necessary for his first visit back to Oklahoma City.

. . .

They printed out blown-up versions of Durant's tweets, including one from April 28, 2009, in which he wrote "I wanna play with Oklahoma City for my whole career." They wore T-shirts and held up signs that called him a coward—spelled with a *K* instead of a *C* so his initials would bookend the taunt. "KowarD." One fan had a sign featuring a picture of a man and his pregnant wife. Green's face was superimposed on the man and Durant's on the expecting woman.

And there were cupcakes. Lots of cupcakes. Someone made white T-shirts with cupcake clipart on the front in the Thunder's colors. Signs featuring cupcakes were everywhere in Chesapeake Energy Arena. One kid paraded around in a cupcake costume.

This was seven months of energy and momentum against Durant building to a crescendo in Oklahoma City. It was his first game back and it was perhaps the closest the modern NBA game has ever gotten to an angry mob. He wore headphones during pregame warmups to block out the jeers. But he couldn't cover his eyes. The intensity of the animosity toward Durant was befitting of a courtroom with the defendant testifying. This used to be Durant's home. Now it was the most unsafe court for him.

The pregame tension escalated when Durant and Westbrook started talking trash to one another. Westbrook taunted Durant: "I'm coming! I'm coming!" Durant rebutted: "So what."

The Warriors got ahead by as much as 26 points. This time their approach was more balanced, with Durant leading the way. He finished with 34; Curry and Thompson had 26 points each, easily overcoming Westbrook's 47 points, eleven rebounds, and eight assists. The Warriors' collective approach overwhelmed Westbrook's one-man show.

But even as the game got out of hand, the intensity did not dissipate. The anger at Durant remained, heightened. The Thunder fans cheered heartily for the valiant way the Thunder fought, for the ferociousness with which Westbrook went after his former costar.

After the Warriors' 130–114 win, Green got his hands on one of the cupcake T-shirts and put it on. Curry followed suit. Other players followed suit. They traded autographed gear for T-shirts until the entire locker room had them. But while they had fun with pranking Thunder fans, Durant seethed in the locker room. He stood in front of his cubicle, his plaid shirt buttoned all the way up with a black cardigan that draped like a cape. His hurt was frothing into anger. At Westbrook's antics. At the rage from the crowd. At the cupcakes.

He had tried to lavish his former city with praises, be respectful to the hurt fan base. But his efforts were futile. He couldn't hide how much that night hurt him. Especially the cupcakes, the stinging declaration that he was soft. Durant has been fighting that label since he was a frail kid in Maryland. Undoubtedly, the cupcake reference harkened back to his childhood days when they playfully called him "Cookie." He didn't think it was so funny. But back then he was too weak to hold his ground, which helped build his work ethic and drive, hardened his refusal to be intimidated.

"I'm built for this," Durant ranted. "They think they can break me? They can't break me. You know what I've been through in my life? I gave my all to them and look how they treat me. They acted like they love me and just like that the love is gone. But you gotta be for-real tough to handle this, not that fake tough. Everybody ain't cut like this. These boys ain't really tough like that. It's all a front."

Seventeen days later, Durant was crying.

The Warriors were playing in Washington, D.C. He spent some $10,000 securing tickets for family and friends, and fifty-seven seconds into the game he was injured. Wizards center Marcin Gortat shoved Pachulia, throwing him to the hardwood. Pachulia fell backward and his head crashed into Durant's left knee.

Durant said he heard a crack, something he'd never felt. He immediately got nervous. He tried to run it off. He knew it was serious on the next possession when he left his man wide-open for a 3 because all he could think about was his knee. Fear of another season-ending injury hijacked his focus. Doctors initially told him he had fractured his tibia and he would be out four to five months. He burst into tears.

Once again, he was on the precipice of reaching the mountaintop and was knocked out by injury. He was left stewing in a dark place. Then he got another call on his ride home. It was the doctors. They had checked the scans again. They had good news.

"They told me it was just a bruise there and I sprained my MCL," Durant said on Bill Simmons's podcast. "And that reaction in the car was like second to none. That emotional roller coaster was something out of a movie."

Durant was out nineteen games. That's when things got interesting. The Warriors lost five of the first seven without him, including the Washington game—and then ran off 13 straight wins. Most important, Curry was Curry again. He averaged 27.5 points on 50.2 percent from the field. He made 64 3-pointers at a 47.8 percent clip and averaged 8.2 assists. And the Warriors outscored opponents by an average of 15.7 points per game. Fans were reminded of life before Durant, when Curry was everything. And they liked it.

Durant's arrival created a chasm in the Warriors, one perhaps felt more by fans and onlookers than on the roster itself. But there was definitely a Before Durant era and a With Durant era. The difference between the two is largely about aesthetic: style of play, entertainment value, distribution of praise. When he was out, the Warriors, to many, felt like the Warriors again.

Durant returned and reminded everyone of the Warriors' potency with him. He had 32 points and eleven rebounds in his first playoff game with the Warriors, a win over Portland. He missed the next two games with a strained calf. But his return, for Game 4, was a display of the firepower they envisioned when they signed Durant.

Up 3–0 and going for the kill, the Warriors blitzed the Blazers with a 45-point first quarter. They made fifteen of twenty-four shots, eight of them 3-pointers. It was a slaughter.

The Warriors, with Durant, ran off nine straight wins to reach the NBA Finals. Only one of those was decided by single digits. And the Finals weren't much different, largely because Durant was amazing.

He averaged 35.2 points on 55.6 percent shooting with 8.2 rebounds and 5.4 assists. He even made eighteen 3-pointers, one fewer than Curry. He captured the 2017 Finals MVP Award along with his first title. He even authored the first signature moment of his career, the original Game 3 dagger from the left wing that became legend.

The Warriors were up 2–0 in the series and Cleveland was fighting to stay alive. The end result wasn't really in doubt, but LeBron James was keeping alive a shimmer of hope. He led Cleveland from a 3–1 deficit in 2016, so no one could truly count out the Cavaliers.

The home team led 113–107 after J. R. Smith hit a three with 3:09 left in the game. Cleveland was in the driver's seat. Then the Warriors flipped a switch.

A Curry layup with 2:19 left. A pull-up from Durant about a minute later. Cleveland's lead was 113–111. The Cavaliers followed with a missed 3-pointer from Kyle Korver. Durant got the rebound and dribbled up court, sauntering down the left side of the floor. He took four dribbles, but by the third dribble he already saw his next move.

LeBron James was backpedaling and settled inside the three-point line. It was a red carpet.

Durant spent so many hours perfecting this one shot. He'd taken vast numbers of them. He knew how many dribbles. He knew how the ball spun in his hands as he stepped into his rhythm. He knew the exact distance, how much arc to put on the trajectory, and how much strength to use to get it over the front of the rim. This was the shot he'd prepared for for most of his life. And he nailed it with 45.3 seconds left.

Durant balled his fists, flexed his arms into a bow, and scowled as he backpedaled. It had taken ten years, but he got his championship. More than that, he found validation—or so he thought.

Five days later, Durant was walking up the court at Oracle, being serenaded by a frenzied crowd. The Warriors lost Game 4, missing the chance to go 16–0 in the playoffs. But they were up 11 in Game 5, and as the clock hit the 1:00 mark, the reality that the championship was theirs started to sink in. Durant got a little dizzy. He pulled his jersey up over his face, wiped the sweat off, and pinched his welling eyes. He crossed half-court and stopped. The emotion overwhelmed him. He doubled over, put both hands on his knees. Green got Iguodala's attention and pointed toward Durant. Iguodala walked over to the pending first-time champion, snapped him out of his joy-induced daze. Durant stood up and gradually strolled toward the right wing. He stopped to watch Curry on the other side of the court dancing with Kyrie Irving. Curry drilled the step-back 3-pointer, punctuating Warriors' title-clinching Game 5 win. Durant raised both arms in the air.

So much sacrifice had gone into this moment. This title cost him more than he could ever have imagined. But he was there, atop the NBA mountain. And when he left the arena that night, he was hailed as king.

Hundreds of fans were waiting outside the gate where the players parked. They chanted "MVP! MVP! MVP!" once they spotted Durant walking in the parking lot. He hopped into a Tesla and drove out of the parking lot. The crowd converged on the car and erupted. Durant got out, his Finals MVP trophy in his hand. He walked into the midst of the crowd, raised his trophy in the air, and screamed as the crowd cheered around him. He was in full bliss.

"After winning that championship, I learned that much hadn't changed," Durant told ESPN. "I thought it would fill a certain void. It didn't."

Durant thought getting a ring would silence the noise. He thought dominating would disarm his critics. This was supposed to be joyous. Winning a championship was the substance his career was lacking. He'd seen Michael Jordan crying on the floor with the trophy, Kevin Garnett screaming "Anything is possible!" and LeBron James dedicating the title to Cleveland like Rocky Balboa did for Adrian. They looked to be overwhelming moments of fulfillment.

But Durant learned a valuable lesson, perhaps one all superstar champions come to understand: The title is not an antidote. It doesn't vanquish hurts. It doesn't erase fears. It doesn't even provide the greatest reward.

Mahatma Gandhi famously said glory lies in the attempt to reach one's goal and not in reaching it. Kobe Bryant delivered a similar message when the Lakers retired his jerseys. He reserved part of his speech for his daughters—Natalia, Bianka, and Gianna—to remind them how work ethic makes dreams come true.

"Those times when you get up early and you work hard; those times when you stay up late and you work hard; those times when don't feel like working—you're too tired, you don't want to push yourself—but you do it anyway. That is actually the dream. That's the dream. It's not the destination, it's the journey."

Durant's journey had been punctured with darts all season. A product of social media, he can't stay off it. He can't *not* read the articles about him or watch the analysis. In some ways, it's fuel. In other ways, it's kryptonite.

It had an effect on Durant's second season with the Warriors, too. Still saddled with a void he couldn't just stuff the Larry O'Brien trophy into, Durant decided to liberate himself. He shed his propensity for people-pleasing in exchange for an unadulterated version of Kevin Wayne Durant. Like LeBron James did in 2010–11, after becoming public enemy No. 1 in the basketball world for his decision to leave Cleveland for Miami, Durant put on the black hat.

He opted out of his contract with the Warriors, as expected, and re-signed a new deal. It was another two-year deal with a player option to walk away following the first year. This, for superstars, is basically a one-year deal with protection in case they get hurt. But Durant took a significant discount. He signed for $25 million, some $9 million lower than he could have under the collective bargaining agreement. He did it to free up salary cap space for the Warriors to retain Iguodala and Shaun Livingston, both of whom were free agents and critical reserves for the Warriors. Giving the Warriors a discount was Durant helping to keep the Warriors together, preserving the bonds he had created and built when he joined them. It was also Durant firing back at the dart throwers.

So many didn't like him being in this position. They didn't want him on top of the NBA world, not like this, surrounded by more talent than he could ever imagine. So Durant rubbed it in the face of his naysayers. He made sure the Warriors would stay together, keep styling on the league, by taking a pay cut.

Villain Durant seemed angrier and more forceful in Year 2. He was even more willing to fire back. He was more willing to say how he felt. He was just as giving, just as down-to-earth in person—but transparent, no longer willing to erect the veneer so people would like him. He knew those days were over.

"The guy you see now is the real me," Durant sent in a text to Fox Sports personality Chris Broussard. "The guy in Oklahoma City was the phony—I was just trying to please everybody and do what I thought everybody wanted me to do."

The *real* Durant was a far cry from the lovable, cuddly seven-footer the country came to know. He seemed to be a magnet for controversy.

June 18, 2017: Bored on a flight, days after winning a championship, Durant took to Twitter to dish it back to critics.

"I got time today though," Durant said. "I ain't have time before but it's time now."

August 18, 2017: He hopped into the political discourse and announced he wasn't making the trip to the White House to celebrate his championship because "I don't respect who's in office right now." Durant said he was sure his teammates would agree with him, and it turned out they did.

President Donald Trump wound up pulling the invitation from Curry, who said publicly he wasn't going at the Warriors' media day, effectively ending any hopes of the Warriors attending. The team was in discussions with the White House, trying to figure out a way it could possibly work. One of the ways the players suggested was to visit the White House so they could be heard by the president but they wanted to nix all photo opportunities. Once the president took to Twitter to uninvite Curry, any arrangements were dead.

Instead, the Warriors took youth to the National Museum of African-American History and Culture in Washington, D.C. The players voted on this event being media-free.

"I feel ever since he's got into office," Durant told ESPN, "or since he ran for the presidency, our country has been so divided, and it's not a coincidence."

September 17, 2017: The infamous tweets from a burner account that actually wasn't from his burner account. Durant, who never acknowledged using a secret Twitter account, apologized for dissing his former teammates and coach while speaking at a technology conference in San Francisco three days later.

"I use Twitter to engage with fans. I think it's a great way to engage with basketball fans. I happened to take it a little too far. I do regret using my former coach's name and the former organization I played for. That was childish. That was idiotic, all those type of words. I apologize for that."

October 21, 2017: Durant got his first ejection three games into the season. In the final minute of an impending loss in Memphis, Curry was ejected for throwing his mouthpiece after not getting a foul call. In the commotion, Durant said something and got ejected, too.

December 1, 2017: He was ejected after complaining about foul calls. He screamed "Fuck you!" to the referee who tossed him on his first technical foul. Three days later he picked up two more technical fouls, the second one for getting into it with DeMarcus Cousins. Both of them were ejected.

January 24, 2018: His fourth ejection came against the Knicks while arguing a foul call. It was his second technical foul. Durant ended up publicly apologizing to the referee. "I was being an asshole," Durant said. "I was being a jerk."

Durant finished the season with five ejections. He had two ejections his previous ten seasons in the NBA, one of them a hard foul that was ruled a Flagrant 2, which comes with an automatic ejection.

Suddenly, Durant was a nuisance, a combatant in a war against officials. For so long, he had been what's right with the NBA. Now he was leaning into his bad-boy reputation. And the whole time, his overtones were about how everyone else needed to get used to the new Durant, the full picture. When he was wrong, he apologized. But he was done biting his tongue, putting on airs.

This new Durant, growing comfortable in his own skin and new-found freedom, became a challenge for his team. He seemed unaffected his first season. He acquiesced. He went stretches without getting shots and didn't murmur once. He spent most of his time off the ball. None of that seemed to faze him.

But in his second season, his overall disposition soured more often. There were bouts of distance with Durant, more than in his first year, enough to make members of the Warriors' organization nervous about whether he would return.

A lot was going on with Durant. The adjustment to villain wasn't going smoothly. And later in the season, the perceived Curry-Durant Cold War resurfaced.

Curry missed thirty-one games in 2017–18. This included an eleven-game stretch from a severely strained right ankle, a six-game stretch later when he sprained it again, and the final ten games of the season after he suffered a similar injury to what Durant had the previous season. It was JaVale McGee who fell into Curry's knee, spraining his MCL and knocking him out of action. Curry also missed the first six playoff games.

The Warriors' offense was always significantly better with Curry on the floor. And that form held true even with the greatness of Durant. Curry missed sixteen of the last seventeen regular season games. The Warriors went 6–10 in those games. Durant was back in the driver's seat, running the show. But the Warriors are crafted for Curry. His DNA is in the genetic code of the offense. The players whom the Warriors have are intended to complement him. So Durant carrying the team didn't look nearly as fluid. On top of that, the Warriors didn't have much to play for. Injuries thwarted their chance at the No. 1 seed in the Western Conference. Houston ran away with the best record in the West, leaving the Warriors resigned at No. 2. They were unmotivated and their offense, which was heavily weighted on Durant isolations, sputtered noticeably.

The fodder for debate in the Bay Area was centered on Curry and Durant and who was best to steer the dominant offense. Durant was being made the scapegoat for the Warriors' struggles. The outside talk seeped into the Warriors locker room in New Orleans.

The Warriors beat the Spurs in five games and blew out the Pelicans in Game 1. But all of it was secondary to the question hovering over the entire playoffs: When would Curry return? It was Game 2 against New Orleans. He came back majestically: 28 points, seven rebounds, five 3-pointers. Curry was back. The Warriors were back.

The Warriors lost Game 3 in New Orleans, though. Curry operated off adrenaline in his first game back. But then rustiness surfaced. He was six for nineteen in Game 3. The Pelicans routed the Warriors and changed the tide of the series. And Durant was not happy. It was visible. He screamed at his teammates for freezing him out in Game 3, yelled at Steve Kerr for pulling him out. He dragged the injury-plagued Warriors across the finish line, carried them to a 5-1 start in the playoffs. And suddenly Curry returned and Durant was second fiddle in the offense again.

Durant's approach wasn't without merit. Curry needed more time to get his legs under him. Durant had developed a groove running the offense. Why go away from that? So the Warriors went back to it, in part to appease Durant, a pending free agent. He took twenty-seven shots in Game 4, torching New Orleans for 38 points as Jrue Holiday looked helpless to defend him. The Warriors bounced the Pelicans in five games.

In Game 1 of the Western Conference Finals at Houston, Durant was magnificent again: 37 points on twenty-seven shots. The Rockets could not defend him and the Warriors stole home-court advantage right back. But all wasn't quite right yet. The Warriors were up 2–1 in Game 4 at Oracle. This game was the difference between a close series and an easy one. As they had been doing relentlessly, the Warriors leaned on Durant's isolation in the fourth quarter, often getting him the ball in the post against shorter defenders. He didn't deliver. The Rockets used Chris Paul and P. J. Tucker, who are strong, with low centers of gravity, and they gave Durant problems. He failed to hit the clutch baskets and the Warriors lost. They now had a series on their hands—and a raging dialogue about who should run the Warriors' offense.

The series, and the season, climaxed in Game 7. The Warriors trailed by 11 in a must-win game on the road. It had to become less about who should run the show and more about winning. Curry struggled and Durant struggled at times against the Rockets' defense. They went from stressing about who should be the lead of the high-powered offense to figuring out how to stay alive in the playoffs.

They all found their center—especially Durant, who was starting to feel like the outcast even on the Warriors. The desperation forced him to get back to center, as he put it. His mind was diverted from "stuff that don't matter." This was the first time the Warriors were tested. They hadn't faced elimination since they got Durant. They had to figure it out together

A monster second half put away the Rockets. They did it the way they had been doing it—together. Curry was playing his game, being aggressive, while Durant thrived off the ball. And when they needed him to be the once-in-a-generation scorer, he was.

"I just feel like the way our team is built," Kerr explained, "Steph is kind of the engine and KD is the guy who just keeps us going when things go bad or puts us over the top. It's a unique team, obviously, with Steph and Klay and KD and so many high-ball screens for Steph. Sometimes, KD gets lost a little bit. And I don't think we've done as good a job this year of integrating it all. Like last year, it felt integrated. The first couple months of the season were tough, then it was just like, we clicked and everything was smooth. This year has not been smooth."

The Warriors easily handled the Cavaliers and Durant authored his Hollywood ending. But the questions lingered. Are the Curry-Durant comparisons and offensive tug-of-war a fixture in their union? Can they find a happy medium?

Most important: Can Durant, who bares the stripes from verbal and keyboard lashes that never seem to stop, exist in a setting where he will always be No. 2 in the hearts of the fervent? Pretty much everywhere outside of the Bay Area, he has to hear the slights and the jabs. Can he stand being a prisoner to Curry nostalgia? Will he be the perennial scapegoat when things don't go well, shoulder the blame in the unlikely event the Warriors get bounced from the postseason early? Or will it just take time, adversity like they faced in Game 7, and moments like he created in Game 3 of the Finals? Even villains need a safe space.

Durant made it clear that the second championship hadn't softened his resolve to be unadulterated. He was back in Las Vegas in July 2018 for Team USA training camp. The throng of media gathered around him, just like they did in this same gym two years earlier. But the questions weren't about his decision to leave Oklahoma City anymore. They were about the person he'd become since.

This time he wasn't smooth. He was defensive. He was biting. He challenged the motives behind the questions and the intent of the questioners. His proverbial black hat was on. He was comfortable in it now. It was even tilted to the side a little bit.

Even his toenails were painted black. Literally.

"If I got something to say," Durant said, half a smile on his face, as if he enjoyed the sparring, "don't get mad because I say something and then you catch feelings when I call you out on it. Then I'm insecure and everyone run with it? Now people come to me, like, 'Damn, I didn't know you were so cool' when they meet me in person. Why? Because of what y'all say. That goes for everybody around here."

The questions were about technical fouls and social media gaffes. But Durant was calling B.S. He was certain those inquiries were symptoms of a central issue. There is a reason, he believes, media and critics analyze his technical fouls or his social media habits. He believes he is being intentionally painted as an angry person or a bad teammate.

He snickers. Then asks the media about who are really the sensitive ones. The way he sees it, he is confronted with premises that paint him in a certain light. He gives his honest response. A firestorm ensues. So, is he sensitive for speaking honestly, or is everyone else sensitive because they can't handle his honesty?

And this is all because of his decision to leave Oklahoma City and join the Warriors. That is the genesis, the core. It's the root of all that has happened, all he has had to endure. There is a fundamental dislike of the choice he made, and he can't escape it. The criticism. The amateur psychology they perform from afar. The deep dives and analysis on his motivation and purpose. The constant, relentless talk about him and what he did. He knows that's the root of this new world he inhabits.

The consensus simply doesn't like that he went to the Warriors, changing the landscape and history of the league. Because of that, they want to pick him apart, to hurt him. Because of who he is, he feels it.

"I know y'all trying to make me look crazy and discredit me, strip me of my credibility. But I see what y'all doing."

10 | THE NEXT CHAPTER

DURANT INTERRUPTED HIS PREGAME WARM-UPS to acknowledge the royalty sitting courtside. He had a long embrace with Gary Payton, the Hall of Fame point guard who once starred in this arena. He talked with Lenny Wilkens, the only coach to bring an NBA championship to Seattle. He thanked Spencer Haywood, the former Sonic most famous for his legal victory that opened the NBA to underclassmen being drafted. Before long, Durant was surrounded by a crowd of people, many of them Seattle's elite. He towered above the well-wishers, his full grin beaming above the crowd around him, as they all sought to get a word, a moment, with him.

And then Durant walked over to half-court. He dropped down on one knee so he could be eye level with Bill Russell. The two had met before, several times. Two of those encounters happened on a stage after the Warriors clinched a championship, as Russell handed Durant the NBA Finals MVP trophy. But this occasion was unique. They were both on what they would consider special ground.

The Boston Celtics great sat back in his chair. His attire—a tan jacket, sky-blue button-up shirt, and navy pants—was as casual as the smile he flashed when they shook hands. Durant smiled like a nephew talking to his cool uncle as Russell gently placed his eighty-four-year-old left hand on top of their clasp. Neither spent much time with the SuperSonics organization. Durant played just one season before the new owners moved the franchise to Oklahoma City in 2008. Russell coached the Sonics for four years, between 1973 and 1977. He made Seattle his home, retiring from the sidelines to Mercer Island. Yet Durant and Russell are both important figures in Seattle basketball lore. This latest connection between the modern marvel and the storied legend was significant because of where they were: in Seattle. Their presence underscored the magnitude of this night.

The whole city had been buzzing about the return of the NBA to Seattle for the first time in more than a decade. The weather this weekend was picturesque, with blue skies, beaming sun, and evergreen trees. From Amazon tech bros to Starbucks baristas to mothers and hipsters walking dogs in Capitol Hill to power suits in Bellevue, everyone was talking about the Sonics and Durant's homecoming. The Seahawks, kings of the market, were in full swing. Jay-Z and Beyoncé were in town for a stop on their popular On the Run II tour. But all of it took a back seat to the NBA coming back. The Warriors were in town on October 5, 2018 to face the Sacramento Kings, which meant Durant was back in Seattle. Even though the rain and gray skies returned that night, nothing could dampen the spirits of an NBA game back in Seattle, of Durant coming home. The whole town was charged.

"It did not feel like a preseason game," Klay Thompson said. "You could almost touch the energy with your hands."

A sea of green and yellow buzzed around the perimeter of Key Arena as the line started developing hours before the doors opened. It seemed every other person at the game was wearing a Durant jersey. Each member of one family of five had on his No. 35. The parents wore the white Sonics jerseys from the 2007–2008 season. The three children wore Durant's Warriors jersey. The nine-year-old in the bunch wasn't even born the last time KD played in Seattle, but he was bouncing down Warren Avenue, bursting at the seams over the chance to see his favorite player.

Once the doors opened, it was a fever pitch inside. Placards reading "We Got Next" were all over the place. Former Sonics star Detlef Schrempf got the place rocking when he was seen on the video board and peeled open his sweater like Superman to reveal the Sonics logo on his T-shirt. Slick Watts, a Sonics basketball legend who played under Bill Russell, looked as if he was ready to take the court at sixty-seven, with his green sweatsuit with yellow trim and yellow headband.

Seattle used this night as a way to plead for the Sonics to come back. They displayed how much the passion for NBA hoops and their long-lost franchise was thriving more than ever, intensified by efforts to do what was done to them: buy up a franchise and snatch it up from the roots. Hedge fund manager Chris Hansen led a Seattle-based group that tried to buy the Sacramento Kings and move them to the Northwest. The statuses of franchises in New Orleans, Memphis, and Milwaukee were being watched closely for opportunities to swoop in and snatch up a vulnerable team.

There is rampant support for the resurrection of the Sonics. Many professional athletes are trying to throw their money behind such a venture: Seahawks quarterback Russell Wilson, NBA stars Jamal Crawford and Dwyane Wade. There is a growing consensus that Seattle should have a team.

But this night was also about Durant. It was a tribute to him as the last Sonics star and they serenaded him with adoration. They also anointed him as the hope of their future, the star they want to be the next face of the franchise. And Durant felt every ounce of the love.

"I never felt that way going into a game," he said. "Especially a preseason game."

The Warriors' 122–94 win over Sacramento may have been irrel-evant, since it was a preseason game, but it will long be remembered as being more about reparations than results.

The highlight of the night didn't even come during the game but before the opening tip-off. The lights went down in Key Arena as the Warriors' starting lineup was announced. It was a home game for the two-time defending champions, which meant they got the use of the video board and the musical introductions. They even brought their pregame tradition with them: the electronic dubstep remix to 2Pac's "California Love" by British producer Rusko.

Klay Thompson, the Washington State graduate who spent part of his childhood in Portland, was announced first. This was a home-coming of sorts for him. The next three players were relative un-knowns. Curry didn't make the trip, staying back home with his wife, who had thyroid surgery. Draymond Green was in attendance, but he sat out with a sore knee. So the only All-Stars available were Thomp-son and Durant. And that meant Durant went last.

The last name called in the starting lineups is an honored position in the NBA. At Oracle, Curry gets the last spot, reverence for being the founding piece of the Warriors' sudden dynasty. But this wasn't Oak-land and this night wasn't about the Warriors.

"And now! In his twelfth NBA season!" the public address an-nouncer blared. His yelling faded into the background, behind the roaring wave of cheers from the crowd. The hype that had been build-ing all weekend in Seattle was coming to a head as the sellout crowd rose to its feet.

Durant, who was the last player on the bench, stood up from his seat. On his way up, he pulled his blue shooting shirt over his head. But the Warriors' home white jersey was still covered. The cheers went from ecstatic to historic once Durant's surprise was evident. He was wearing a Shawn Kemp jersey.

Durant hit up Don Crawley, a popular designer of urban wear known as Don C. His clothing line, Just Don, which carries high-end throwback sportswear, has a partnership with Mitchell & Ness Nostalgia Co., chief producer of classic jerseys. They came through with a vintage Kemp throwback. It was the Sonics road jersey, the one they wore in Chicago during the 1996 NBA Finals, the franchise's last great team. The spotlight followed Durant as he walked through a tunnel of high-fives from his teammates. Not even they knew he had it on. They laughed at the big reveal while Durant kept a stoic expression. His green jersey with brick-red and bronze accents popped among the Warriors blue. The old-school logo featured Seattle's famed Space Needle serving as the *I* in the "SONICS" across the chest, with Kemp's name and No. 40 in white on the back. The Warriors players bounced around in a huddle, their pregame ritual featuring an unexpected zest, with Durant in the center.

The ovation went up another notch as Durant made his way to center court after the huddle. He had to know the fans would love the gesture of the Kemp jersey. He had special green and yellow versions of his KD 11 Nike shoe. Still, he looked nervous as he went to speak, as if the raucousness of the cheers overwhelmed him. The lights in Key Arena returned as Durant made it to the Sonics logo at half-court. He took a moment to soak in the serenade. He put the microphone to his mouth, but the ovation wouldn't let him speak yet. He paced in the center of the logo, giving in to the moment. He raised his right hand in the air, signaling he was about to speak, then waited some more before the crowd gave him the floor.

"First off," Durant said, "I want to give a shout out to the Seattle Storm for holding it down and winning a championship."

Another eruption ensued. Durant nodded his head in approval. He had the crowd eating out of his hand. The last time he played on this court was April 13, 2008. He had 19 points on eighteen shots in a

win over Dallas, the final NBA game at Key Arena. Durant's last time
wearing a Sonics jersey came three days later in Oakland. He closed
out his rookie season and his Seattle tenure with 42 points, thirteen
rebounds, and six assists at Oracle Arena, torching a dispirited Warriors squad that was just eliminated from the playoffs.

But Seattle hadn't forgotten. The absence of the Sonics has made
their heart grow fonder for Durant, their last star, the future that was
ripped away from them.

"I know it's been a rough ten years," Durant said to the crowd. "But
the NBA is back in Seattle for tonight but hopefully it's back forever
soon."

In Seattle, Durant is preeminent. Time has only exalted him. An
entire heartbroken market has watched their child be adopted by
another city. He was raised by another family in another town. They
watched with pride as he became a star but it was bittersweet because
he was supposed to be theirs.

The then-new Sonics general manager Sam Presti traded All-
Star guard Ray Allen to the Boston Celtics, officializing the rebuild-
ing of the franchise on the day of the 2007 NBA Draft. Allen had led
the Sonics to a 52-win season and the second round of the playoffs
two years earlier. But after two straight years of missing the playoffs,
Seattle was starting from scratch. Minutes after news of the Allen
trade broke, the Sonics scooped up Durant with the No. 2 pick of the
2007 NBA Draft. Durant scored 18 points on twenty-two shots in his
debut. He then rattled off three straight games with at least 24 points.
Though the Sonics lost the first eight games of Durant's career, it was
clear they had found a gem. He scored 35 points on twenty shots twice
in the span of eight days, the second time just his twentieth pro game.
His knack for scoring was obvious. He became the hope and future
of the Sonics. And then he was gone. Packed up and shipped to Oklahoma City.

In all those years, Seattle has never forgotten Durant. The rekindling of SuperSonics fervor, the five or so years of talk about the NBA returning to the Emerald City, has also stirred up the region's adoration for Durant. The Sonics are not short on legendary figures. But Durant is the rightful heir to the throne of Seattle hoops, and they anointed him as such in his return to Key Arena.

It was this moment, as they sent him off the court with musical cheers, that crystallized what Durant's career has lacked. He has never had this before. Not in the NBA, not like this—which explains why he called this night in Seattle one of the top moments of his career. The greatest players in the game enjoy the perk of being the sole face of their franchise and the apple of the fan base's eye. They are the centerpiece of the show. The legions are loyal to them. In the age of social media, where alliances are drawn and debates rage perennially, a player's legion and its size carries weight. This is what Kobe Bryant enjoyed with the Lakers, what LeBron James enjoyed in Cleveland and pretty much everywhere he goes. It's Dirk Nowitzki forever in Dallas. The same is true for Dwyane Wade in Miami and Stephen Curry in the Bay Area. James Harden has it in Houston.

Durant, though, has always had to share the top spot. He climbed the ladder of superstardom with Russell Westbrook. A strong case could be made that Durant was 1A to Westbrook's 1B. But once Westbrook became an All-Star in 2011, they were a duo perennially thrust into a competition by the outside world, and if you believe reports and murmurs over the years, even they jousted for supremacy at times over shots and hub of the offense. When Durant came to the Warriors, he joined forces with Curry, and it didn't take long to become clear that Curry's stranglehold on the world of the Warriors is eternally binding.

How much this all matters to Durant is a truth he keeps relatively close to his vest. On the scale of importance, it ranks somewhere between his desire to be No. 1 and his affinity for the purity of basketball and teamwork. But one thing is undisputed: Durant deserves such reverence, as these things go. He has been a worthy ambassador of the game who for most of his career has been a likable figure. His talent has always warranted such a level of adoration. His list of accomplishments usually comes with undying loyalty. Durant's popularity is elite. His name has never been more known. But what Seattle showered on him underscored what he's never really had. And now he is at the peak of his powers with no kingdom of his own. It's the last thing left for him to accomplish in what is already a storied career.

It begs the question about Durant's legacy. What happens next could define him. It's certainly on his mind as he weighs his next move. When he signed with the Warriors in 2016, he had given a two-year commitment to Golden State. So when he opted out, the expectation was for him to return. After Year 2, though, he signed another two-year deal with an option to terminate the deal after one year. So it is decision time again for Durant in 2019.

But what will motivate Durant? What will weigh most valuable to him on this next move? The options are aplenty.

"I am thinking about the money I'm going to get," Durant said. "I never got the [massive] deal. I've just seen a bunch of dudes around the league making so much money—and I'm happy for them. But I know I deserve that, too. That's the only thing I'm probably thinking about, to be honest."

Because Durant has more than ten years of experience, he is eligible to sign for 35 percent of the salary cap no matter where he plays. But the Warriors have the advantage of being able to pay Durant the most money, if that is the deciding factor. Because he has been with them for three years, the Warriors have some critical rights under the collective bargaining agreement. They can sign him to a five-year deal, while other teams are limited to four. They can also give him 8 percent raises each year. Other teams can offer just 5 percent.

As a result, Durant has what projects out to be a five-year contract worth more than $221 million waiting for him with the Warriors should he want to commit long term. It will be the largest contract in NBA history if Durant signs it.

Durant could sign a shorter deal with the Warriors, such as a three-year, $123 million contract. It would give him the fourth-highest average salary in the NBA—behind James Harden, John Wall, and Russell Westbrook—but also give him the flexibility he has seemed to like. LeBron James awakened superstars to the power of flexibility by not signing long term, hitting the market every two years or so. The ability to leave is an elite player's greatest power. Durant could follow that model and sign a three-year deal with a chance to opt out and become a free agent after two years. Durant would hit the market again a few months shy of his thirty-third birthday, presumably still in his prime. Here is another tantalizing speculation: a three-year deal with an opt-out could leave the door open for a return to Seattle. Should a miracle happen and the Sonics land a franchise in the next few years, when a refurbished Key Arena reopens, Durant might want to be available.

If Durant signed with another team, the most he could sign is a four-year contract worth $164 million. That's nearly $60 million less than the total value of the contract he could sign with the Warriors. However, the disparity is not as drastic as it first appears. The attractiveness of the Warriors offer is that it is all guaranteed. But, barring injury, Durant is going to get a contract for the 2023–24 season. So adding that estimated salary to the $164 million he could get from another team is a more accurate picture of the disparity between what the Warriors could offer and what he could get elsewhere. If after four years Durant gets $40 million on the open market, that would give him $204 million over the five-year span—still nearly $20 million less than the Warriors can pay him but not as astronomical a difference as the numbers look on the surface. Plus, Durant makes a ton of money off the court, and where he lands could mitigate the losses he would take in NBA earnings. In a market like New York he could potentially reap enough dividends outside of his contract to make up for the money he left on the table if he leaves the Warriors. Of course, Durant could get injured and diminish what he could demand on the free agent NBA market in 2023. He would also be thirty-five entering that season, so there is a reasonable chance he won't be as elite a player. So he would be facing some risks if he did take the four-year option with another team.

Either way, Durant is making more than $40 million per year over the next four or five years. The prime of his career will pay him the kind of ransom it deserves. So if that is enough to satisfy his financial appetite, the question becomes: What else does he want? If the money is good enough no matter what he does, what becomes the most important factor?

The general consensus among NBA fans is that adoration is high on his list. It's a hypothesis fed by Durant's own behavior. From his self-defense tactics on social media to his public despising of being No. 2, it seems as if Durant wants his rightful perch. He might call it respect, which sounds more like an earned benefit. But NBA elitism is largely a measuring of clout in the hearts of fans and in the presentation of media. The money is the primary delineator of that clout. But in the rarified air where Durant exists, the salaries are often locked in by the collective bargaining agreement. That's life in a sport with a salary cap. So the players whose ego and confidence have pushed them to the heights of the sport end up jousting for supremacy in other areas, such as endorsement deals, commercial branding, social media love, and praise from sports debate shows.

Durant, more than any other player in the NBA, is seen as an antagonist. His move to the Warriors cost him a significant portion of the respect and adoration he spent building. It is not just his decision to leave the Thunder that drew the ire of the basketball community; it was joining the Warriors. For many, including former and current players, as long as Durant is on the Warriors, his legacy is tarnished. Valid or not, his success won't ever carry the same weight as his peers' because he joined a championship team featuring three All-Star players. The not-so-kind critics of Durant regard him as a snake, a sharp rebuke suggesting he was underhanded in how he left the Thunder. Durant knows some NBA fans hold this opinion. In November 2017, months after his first championship, he was seen in his interview with the media wearing a T-shirt featuring the legendary wrestler Jake "the Snake" Roberts. A few mornings after the game in Seattle, Durant made a less subliminal acknowledgment to his harshest critics. The Barstool Sports twitter account posted a picture of a snake slithering across the green of a golf course. Durant commented on the post—"my bad, lemme get out your way"—with some self-deprecating humor.

Perhaps the only way to silence those critics is for Durant to leave the Warriors and go win a championship under different circumstances. Instead of winning with a ready-made championship contender, Durant dissenters want him to carry a contender from the ground up, winning as an underdog. In essence, finish the work he left behind in Oklahoma City.

That's where the New York Knicks come in. The counterbalance to joining a championship team is to join a team whose championship hopes are but a pipe dream. Whatever ill will created by his success with the Warriors could be washed away by Durant resurrecting the Knicks, one of the NBA's most storied franchises in the country's No. 1 market. New York hasn't won a championship since 1973. If Durant delivered that, he'd be a deity in New York basketball.

But a championship in New York is more than a long shot, as titles aren't won exclusively on the court. Championships are choreographed from the ownership levels and executed by the front office. Leadership, roster construction, and culture of the franchise are also relevant factors in NBA success. The Knicks for decades have been a magnet for dysfunction, which suggests they would have a hard time putting the pieces around Durant to win a title.

Such a challenge might be appealing to Durant. Modern NBA stars have become unofficial general managers. They politic their way into what they feel are the best situations. They strike deals with each other, adjust their salary demands to make alliances work. Even if many believe Durant went too far by joining the Warriors, few of the NBA's best players are actually looking for a fixer-upper of a franchise. Kyrie Irving forced his way out of Cleveland. Chris Paul left the Los Angeles Clippers and teamed up with James Harden in Houston. Paul George forced his way out of Indiana and Kawhi Leonard out of San Antonio. DeMarcus Cousins signed for cheap with the Warriors just to spite the rest of the league. Durant taking the New York route would be atypical for the modern player, as the Knicks aren't the most inspiring franchise.

But would five championships exalt him just as high? Basketball culture, especially in the wake of Michael Jordan's success, emphasizes championship rings in the hierarchy of elite players. It's part of why Durant left Oklahoma City in the first place. The prospect of going an entire career without winning a championship is even more disconcerting these days as even Hall of Fame players, such as Charles Barkley and Patrick Ewing, are summarily downsized because of their lack of championship glory. So what would be said about Durant if he stayed with the Warriors and racked up championships? A five-year deal with the Warriors would give Durant an eight-year stretch in the Bay Area. What if at the end of that he had five championships, more than LeBron James and as many as Kobe. Would that be enough success to muzzle the criticism over his move? Most basketball experts would agree that Durant winning five championships in eight years with the Warriors is more likely than winning one in New York in the same time frame.

There are other places Durant could go where a championship would drown out the detractors of his legacy. The Los Angeles Clippers have never won a championship and exist in the shadows of the Lakers. Winning there would make him an icon.

Philadelphia hasn't won a title since 1967. They have the young core ready made for Durant to lead to championship levels. Milwaukee hasn't won a championship since 1971, when Kareem Abdul-Jabbar was their star center. Portland's last championship was in 1977. But the 76ers already have two young stars in Ben Simmons and Joel Embiid. The Bucks have a superstar already in Giannis Antetokounmpo. The Trail Blazers have a face of franchise in Damian Lillard. Those situations aren't nearly as established as the Warriors were when Durant signed. But if supremacy is a priority for Durant, joining the 76ers or the Bucks, both of which have incumbent stars who made the franchise relevant before Durant, could lead to the same totem pole issues.

Durant could join franchises already with modern championship pedigrees. Miami, San Antonio, Boston—they'd all take him and be legit championship contenders with him. But with those franchises, he'd just be the next in a line of Hall of Fame legends.

There is a real possibility that rebutting his critics won't be the deciding factor. Durant has emerged from the criticism much more defiant. It would not be shocking if he stayed with the Warriors and won championships just to flaunt in the face of his most strident naysayers.

But what about the other parts of Durant? The humble, regular guy who is addicted to basketball and deep down just wants to have fun playing with people he likes might take over at decision time. When he was struggling with the choice to stay with Oklahoma City or join the Warriors, his father gave him some advice that pushed him over the edge. Wayne Pratt told Durant to be selfish, to do what he wanted to do. A self-professed people-pleaser, Durant struggled making decisions independent of outside influence. If he were to be selfish again, perhaps he'd still want the same things that drew him to Golden State in the first place.

"You talk about all the different reasons somebody would look to go to another franchise," former Cleveland general manager David Griffin said on NBA TV in November 2018. "Fit oftentimes comes into play. Market size comes into play. The ability to win comes into play—stop me when I say something that's not perfect in Golden State for Kevin Durant. Playing with Steph, he's selfless, Draymond's selfless, Klay Thompson's selfless. They all want to do whatever is required to win basketball games. If that can't be your expression of joy and fit, I'm not quite sure what it is you're looking for that would make any sense."

But the Warriors' joy underwent an incredible test on November 12, just fourteen games into the 2018–19 season. The team was at Staples Center visiting the Los Angeles Clippers. Curry was back in the Bay Area recuperating from a groin injury, one of the reasons the Warriors were struggling with the Clippers.

The game was tied at 106 when Green swooped in front of Durant to rebound a missed jumper from Lou Williams. Green turned up court and led the fast break. Durant clapped for the ball as he skipped up court. He clapped harder. Green kept dribbling up court. Durant angrily waved for the ball. Green wound up losing control and turning it over. The Warriors never got a shot off. When the team returned to the bench, an argument ensued that threatened the very dynasty they created.

Durant screamed at Green for not giving him the ball. Durant was sitting on a game-high 33 points and had it rolling. He wanted the ball in his hands. He slapped the chair, pounded his chest. Already embarrassed by the mistake that cost the Warriors a chance at a game winner, Green retaliated.

He unleashed a profanity laced tirade at Durant. Green took objection to Durant's tone, the suggestion that he wasn't capable of pushing the ball in that situation and making a play. And all the pent-up issues Green had been holding in were unleashed.

Green made it clear he has been making plays in the same fashion for years and shouldn't be treated like a trivial role player. He reminded Durant the Warriors were champions before Durant and they didn't need him: it was Durant who needed the Warriors. Green accused Durant of making the whole season about him even though he was certain he was just going to leave at season's end. He also mixed in some very pointed personal insults.

The core issue with Green centered on Durant's handling of free agency. Durant gave the Warriors an unofficial two-year commitment when he agreed to sign. He even gave the team a $9 million discount after the first year so it could retain Iguodala and Shaun Livingston. But as his second season with the Warriors progressed, the uncertainty about what Durant would do became a growing curiosity if not concern.

There were stretches where Durant was distant off the court. On the court, he was falling back into his Oklahoma City habits. The stylistic differences between Curry's style of play and Durant's preferred style seemed to be at odds more than ever. Durant carried the Warriors for stretches with the ball in his hands, as most superstars do in the NBA. But the Warriors' philosophy is motion, to move bodies and the ball and play with pace, which runs best with Curry dominating the ball. The way the Warriors play, the offense runs through Curry, opens the floor, and loosens the defense for the entire offense. It also occasionally ices out Durant for stretches. The tension between the two philosophies was palpable in the playoffs. In the first-round series against San Antonio, Durant carried the Warriors without Curry.

In the six games Curry missed to start the 2018 playoffs, thanks to a Grade 2 sprain in his left MCL, Durant used at least a third of the Warriors' plays in four of them. When Curry returned, in Game 2 against New Orleans in the second round, Durant's usage dropped to 27 percent. Then it was 25.5 percent in Game 3. His displeasure was obvious. With Curry rusty, the Warriors put the ball back in Durant's hands and he dominated Game 4, scoring 38 points while using 36.7 percent of the plays.

The same back-and-forth happened in the series against Houston. But adversity brought them together. Down 3–2 in the series and facing elimination, the Warriors rallied together to win the series and then blitzed the Cavaliers in the Finals. All was well that ended well, but the season wasn't nearly as smooth.

"Last year was the honeymoon. It seemed like he was engaged all year last season," Kerr said about Year 1 on the *Lowe Post* podcast after the Warriors won their second title. "Whereas this year everything was harder, everything was more difficult. Not only was that true as a group but for individuals.

"I thought it was a harder season for Kevin. . . . It hasn't always been easy for him—even though he makes it look easy—it hasn't always been easy for him to blend into the team and blend his talents into the style that we have had here for many years."

That reality led to questions about whether Durant would be back. Eventually, he decided to take another one-year deal. That clearly bothered Green. After two years and two championships, Durant still wasn't sure he wanted to be a Warrior, and Green took exception. And he went off.

Warriors' management deemed Green's actions unacceptable. They suspended him for a game and chose to do so publicly, which left Green feeling betrayed.

It seemed for a time as if the Warriors wouldn't survive this. Things were said that couldn't be unsaid. If Durant was leaning toward leaving Golden State, Green's verbal attack figured to send him packing.

But then something happened. Durant and Green sat down together and talked it out over some wine. Green expressed his concerns to Durant with civility while accepting responsibility for handling it all the wrong way. Durant explained himself more clearly and demanded more from Green. Explosions are nothing new for Green—his fire is what makes him such a great player. And though he has been known to burn the people around him, the Warriors benefit from Green's passion, edge, and bluntness. They simply have to swallow it when these same characteristics cause problems, especially since the positives of his approach always seem to outweigh the negatives.

Given this pattern, Green was ready to frame the situation as an acceptable casualty of his passion. But Durant wasn't buying it. He told Green he'd seen him keep his composure on the court in the most intense of situations. He told Green he believed he could control his rage and was going to hold him accountable. And Green couldn't argue with Durant's logic. The two embarked on a journey of working out their issues.

Green did what he always does: accept responsibility and work to get better. Durant did what he has always done: reconcile. He opened himself to be forgiving and understanding, for doing the difficult work it takes to mend fences. He did it with his father. He did it with Westbrook. Now with Green.

But for the rest of the season, the pervasive question involved Durant's free agency: whether he could reconcile enough to remain with the Warriors. The nation wondered if Durant would leave and break up one of the most dominant teams in history. Analysts, color commentators, talking heads, writers, and podcasters couldn't get enough of speculating and pontificating about what Durant would do. It was indeed a paramount decision; Durant's choice would shape the next five years of the league. But it frustrated him to no end, given that he routinely complained about the media and fans' refusal to focus on basketball.

Durant and his camp did nothing to help this cause, though. Their actions had a way of fueling the speculation. Some inadvertent. Some blatant.

On February 2, 2018, as the Warriors were pursuing their second championship, Rich Kleiman, still Durant's confidant, business partner, and a die-hard Knicks fan, tweeted his desire to run the Knicks one day.

In July, Durant opted to sign a one-year deal.

In late September 2018, when asked about the one-year deal, Durant said he wanted to keep his options open, kick-starting the dialogue about his options.

In early October 2018, shortly after training camp began, Chris Haynes of Yahoo! Sports reported that the New York Knicks had a good chance to land Durant in the following offseason. The thought of Durant resurrecting the beleaguered Knicks was nothing short of juicy.

In late October 2018, the Warriors played the sixth game of the season at Madison Square Garden. Durant was greeted by Knicks fans with their own recruitment tool: a billboard that said "Can You Make NY Sports Great Again?" with a cartoon image of him and Kristaps Porziņģis below the hashtag #KDNY2019. Durant potentially coming to the Knicks was the storyline that most captured the New York media during Durant's visit as a throng of reporters surrounded him and peppered him with questions about a possible future in New York.

Then, on February 1, 2019, the New York Knicks traded their future. Porziņģis—the lone hope of the Knicks, a seven-foot-three forward with the skills of a guard so unique he's been nicknamed "Unicorn"— was shipped to Dallas. The move was shocking because the bounty they received for Porziņģis, despite his recent ACL injury, was a net loss in the talent department. But the whispers behind the scenes suggested that the Knicks were clearing salary-cap space to make room for two superstars. The Knicks, many thought, were operating based on a promise from the Durant camp that he would make Madison Square Garden his home court. The other superstar expected to join Durant was Kyrie Irving.

Durant, anticipating another round of questions about New York, stopped talking to journalists after the Porziņģis trade, stiff-arming requests from Warriors PR to fulfill his media obligations. For eight days, he refused to do pregame or postgame interviews.

On February 11, in a collaboration with ESPN to promote Durant's new show, *The Boardroom*, a feature on the network's website about Durant's business endeavors revealed that his media company was relocating to New York City. This fueled further speculation.

On February 17, during NBA All-Star Weekend, Durant and Irving were filmed chatting with each other in the hall of Charlotte's Spectrum Center. It wasn't small talk, either. They looked like close friends. The visual was evidence, albeit circumstantial, that Durant and Irving had a unique bond, giving even more credence to the rumors.

It sure felt like Durant was leaving the Warriors. He went stretches where he distanced himself from his teammates off the court. He barely talked to anyone, just kept to himself.

The entire 2019–2020 season became tiresome due to the endless speculation about Durant's free agency and attempts to read the tea leaves of his relationship with the Warriors. Despite this, the Warriors managed to have the best record in the Western Conference and get the top seed in the playoffs. And the playoffs have a way of making NBA consumers forget about what happened in the regular season. Toward the end of the eighty-two-game schedule, Durant not only reinserted himself into the locker room, becoming more vocal and displaying an energized presence—he also doubled down on his commitment to being a leader and teammate.

But the tension flared up again in the playoffs. During the first two games of the first-round series against the Clippers, Durant's performance was pedestrian by his standards, and the underdog Clippers stole Game 2 from the two-time defending champions. Patrick Beverley, a loquacious and pesky point guard, made up for the foot Durant had on him by pressing up on Durant, being physical with him and taking every occasion to try to steal the ball. It was hard to tell if Beverley had prompted Durant to be less aggressive or if Durant was silently and subliminally protesting the Warriors' approach. Either way, Durant taking just eight shots in Game 2 was jarring for a player of his caliber. After three seasons of being indoctrinated with the Warriors' philosophy of ball movement, Durant was now passing too much, seemingly in defiance, instead of obliterating an inferior player like Beverley.

"Absolutely he needs to be more aggressive," Steve Kerr said after their Game 2 loss. "It's the playoffs. He can get any shot he wants, anytime. I want him to get twenty shots, thirty."

Usually it was Durant who would contradict or disagree with Kerr in interviews. One of the most noteworthy instances happened on March 5, 2019, when Boston came to Oakland and destroyed the Warriors by 33 points. Kerr called the loss "embarrassing" and chastised the team's effort, especially on defense. He said that he himself needed to do a better job with defensive schemes, but that "it starts with a passion and an anger and an intensity, and it wasn't there tonight." Kerr's commentary was presented to Durant during his postgame interviews.

"I thought we move off of joy? Now anger?" Durant asked.

"That's what your coach said," the reporter responded.

"I disagree with that one," Durant said.

Over the years, the Warriors head coach has said many times that the Warriors run on joy, a quality he attributes to the demeanor and spirit of Steph Curry. Durant, who'd heard a lot about the Warriors way of doing things, had seized the chance to highlight the contradiction in Kerr's dogma.

But after their loss to the Clippers, it was Kerr who positioned himself opposite his star. Kerr made it clear, publicly, that Durant was choosing not to play his usual game.

In the playoffs, every storyline gets blown up. But storylines involving Durant and the Warriors tended to take on a life of their own. After two days of hearing about it, Durant appeared fed up with the narrative. And when queried again about his lack of forcefulness against Beverley, Durant made the proclamation that would define his postseason, his time with the Warriors, and how dominant a player he'd become.

"I'm Kevin Durant. You know who I am. Y'all know who I am."

He then went out and scored 38 points in Game 3, another 33 points in Game 4, then 45 in Game 5, before ending the series on the Clippers home court with a majestic 50-point performance in Game 6.

After the game, Beverley and Clippers star Lou Williams underscored the greatness of Durant with the kind of praise rarely given by players after a series.

"I mean, he's Kevin Durant," Beverley said.

Williams: "I promise we tried."

Beverley: "We didn't roll over. We didn't just say, 'Come on, man, just give us fifty tonight.' Of course not. He's a hell of a player. The shots he took, he made some tough shots. If you were a coach, what would you tell us to do?"

Williams: "We tried everything. We had several different coverages for KD."

Beverley: "It didn't work."

Beverley and Williams were part of a chorus in the NBA universe praising Durant. Finally, Durant was getting his due, the anointing that had been in the making since he picked up a ball as a little boy.

. . .

Over the next eight playoff games after his "Y'all know who I am" declaration, Durant took at least 21 shots in each game and averaged 38.8 points on 51.5 percent shooting. And even though the top-seeded Warriors needed six games to oust the No. 8 Clippers, even though they were tied 2-2 in the second-round series against Houston, Durant wasn't being blamed. Instead, he was being revered as the leader of the Warriors, their best player and best hope.

Kerr took it one step further and began regularly hailing Durant as the best player in the NBA. The same talking heads who derided him for coming to the Warriors were professing him the unofficial king of the league.

But then in Game 5 against Houston—one of the most anticipated matchups of the postseason, as it was a rematch of the 2018 Western Conference Finals and the Rockets pinned their entire season, their franchise, on beating the Warriors—everything shifted because of one injury.

In the third quarter in Oakland, with just over two minutes left and the Warriors up a point in the most pivotal game in the series, Durant was suddenly limping. It was a simple move he'd done a million times. He swiped the ball from left to right, under the reaching arms of Rockets swingman Iman Shumpert, as he drove to his right. Then after one dribble he suddenly stopped for a pull-up jumper from the right baseline, rising up over Shumpert's outstretched hand and making the sixteen-foot shot. He landed cleanly, missing the defender's feet. But as he jogged back toward the defensive end, having put the Warriors ahead 68–65, he felt a pull in his right calf. His jog immediately turned into a hop as he looked back to see if something had hit him from behind. But nothing was there.

This meant that Durant had hurt his leg running, a noncontact injury that usually suggests serious internal damage. People who have suffered a torn Achilles' say it feels like being kicked in the back of the foot in the area just above the heel. When it happened to Kobe Bryant in 2014, he looked back and asked Warriors forward Harrison Barnes, "Did you kick me?" after he felt a pop in his leg. So when Durant turned to look behind him, it immediately signaled to the millions watching that he'd torn his Achilles', one of the most devastating injuries in basketball.

But it was his right calf that Durant immediately grabbed. So although it looked like an Achilles'—and the mood in Oracle Arena certainly felt as if twenty thousand people had just watched Durant get robbed of his prime—when the Warriors diagnosed it as a strained calf, it made some sense; Durant had injured this muscle before. Even though conspiracy theorists instantly began chattering about how the Warriors were hiding a more serious injury—dialogue that was bolstered by photos of Durant wearing an ice bag noticeably below his calf—Durant's return was expected because of the routine nature of the injury.

Curry scored 12 points in the fourth quarter to lead the Warriors to victory. Then he scored 33 points in Game 6, all in the second half, as the Warriors pulled off a stunning win in Houston over the Rockets, thereby eliminating their biggest rival. The Warriors advanced with KD on the sidelines.

They had a sense of urgency; they were focused on finishing the job and extending the season so that Durant could return and join them on the court. The reverence for Durant was overt and persistent in the Warriors locker room, where they dedicated each game to him. But outside of it, the tide of the dialogue in NBA circles and sports media had turned against Durant. The Warriors completing the ouster of Houston without him regenerated talk about his decision to join the Warriors and restarted the social media–driven debate about whether he or Curry was the Warriors' best player. Two weeks hadn't passed since he'd dropped fifty on the Clippers and been crowned the best, and already he was back to being questioned, second-guessed, psychoanalyzed.

This turmoil only increased as the Warriors swept Portland in the 2019 Western Conference Finals without Durant, earning a fifth consecutive trip to the Finals. And when Durant still wasn't ready to return, the noise grew louder. After Klay Thompson sprained his ankle and missed Game 3, and Kevon Looney fractured his collarbone, and the banged-up Warriors lost Game 3 at home to trail in the series, Durant still couldn't return to the action. All the drama and speculation and opining that shrouded his Warriors tenure had reached its highest level in three years. Depending on what corner of the NBA landscape you listened to, Durant either had a torn Achilles' after all, was trying to prove that the Warriors still needed him, had already checked out because he knew he was leaving the Warriors, or was going stir-crazy from his inability to play.

It all proved to be a setup for the NBA history that was about to unfold. The Warriors were down 3–1 heading into Toronto and facing elimination. And Durant returned. Never had a player of Durant's caliber been inserted for the first time into an NBA Finals this late. And it couldn't have come at a better moment.

Durant instantly reminded the world what the Warriors were missing. He scored 11 points in the first quarter, playing fewer than ten minutes, and made all three of his 3-point attempts. The Warriors looked like a different team, controlling the Raptors from the outset and sending a wave of nerves through Canada, which was already on edge as their team was so close to the country's first NBA championship.

Durant started the second quarter. Two minutes in, he had the ball on the right wing and was being defended by Raptors big man Serge Ibaka, his former Oklahoma City teammate. Most of what Durant had done in Game 6 up until this point was catch and shoot; with the bigger player on him, he decided to attempt to drive around Ibaka. But as soon as he pushed off on that right foot, he stopped suddenly, let go of the ball, and collapsed to the ground. It was instantly clear: his worst nightmare had come true. His face said it all. The reaction from his teammates said it all. And if that wasn't enough, the area Durant was holding, down by his heel, while he sat on the floor in Scotiabank Arena, made it unmistakable. It wasn't his calf.

This time, Durant tore his Achilles'.

Initial cheers from the crowd, which were deemed by most to be unsportsmanlike and disrespectful, quickly turned into a standing ovation for Durant as he limped off the court, clearly for the last time in those playoffs. Warriors forward Andre Iguodala, who had been starting in Durant's place, joined the Warriors' head athletic trainer, Rick Celebrini, in helping Durant off the court, past the Raptors bench, and through a showering of encouragement from their players. An emotional Curry left the bench and followed them, walking behind Durant to the locker room.

The tendon-tearing ended Durant's season. It effectively ended the Warriors' bid for a third straight championship, as they lost the next game after Klay Thompson also suffered a season-ending injury. And now we know it ended Durant's tenure with the Warriors.

But that tendon tear also made him a legend. It reshaped the narrative around him, elevated him to hero status in a way that his play alone never could. The tear suggested that he shouldn't have been playing, that he was indeed not yet ready to come back. For the conspiracy theorists, it was evidence that his initial injury wasn't his calf. Either way, Durant risked it all and played. He sacrificed himself to help the Warriors get a championship. It was such a moment of clarity that his motives for doing so weren't even questioned.

Three doctors had cleared Durant to play: the Warriors' team doctors, Durant's second opinion, and a third independent doctor. They all gave the green light. Inside sources say that Durant was always told that Game 5 of the NBA Finals was his most reasonable target, and he was pining to get back on the court. He wanted to be in the NBA's premiere showcase. He wanted to silence the naysayers. Durant chose to play, and that was enough to end the questions about him.

"I heard the Warriors pressured me into getting back," Durant told Chris Haynes of Yahoo! Sports. "Nobody never said a word to me during rehab as I was coming back. It was only me and Rick working out every day. Right when the series started, I targeted Game 5. Hell, nah. It just happened. It's basketball. Shit happens. Nobody was responsible for it. It was just the game. We just need to move on from that shit because I'm going to be back playing."

. . .

Klay Thompson usually exists above the fray, or below it, depending on perspective. Either way, he usually avoids making statements. He has opinions and thoughts. Sometimes they slip out because he is so carefree. But usually his emotions stay so close to his vest it seems as if he doesn't have them, as if he's perennially unaffected. It's arguably Thompson's most endearing quality, this ability to exist in the bubble of NBA drama and never seem to be impacted by it, or even notice it. His persona is the epitome of unbothered.

But what happened to Durant seemed to touch Thompson. When they first met in the Hamptons, Thompson welcomed Durant by declaring he wouldn't change his game. Thirty-five months later, he was stepping out of his comfort zone and lavishing praise for Durant on Instagram, where he barely posts outside of endorsements. Before Game 6, Thompson took to social media and spoke up for Durant. Emotively. Publicly. Unprompted.

But DubNation, I need you to reflect on the fact that we would not be in this position if it weren't for this man and his sacrifices. He's the reason there are banners hanging in the rafters of Oracle. I'm gonna need every Dubs fan in the building tonight to bring the same fire K brought everyday to the court!! It's not gonna be the same running out that tunnel without u bro. We all know this is a minor set back for a major comeback !! Nothing can impede this mans greatness.

One of the most poignant gestures of how emotionally invested they were in Durant, and what would be their last run, came in the visiting locker room of Scotiabank Arena. Curry was getting dressed after Game 5 of the NBA Finals, visibly stunned by the sudden turn of events in Durant's life. When he learned from reporters that Durant's injury was indeed an Achilles' tear, he was overcome with emotion. He turned his back to the media gathered at his locker so he could pray and fight off the tears.

Warriors general manager Bob Myers, who was Durant's confidant in Golden State's front office, didn't bother hiding his tears. He faced the media on behalf of the franchise after Game 5 to answer questions about why Durant was playing and to reveal it was an Achilles' tear. He choked up dramatically, sniffling, his voice cracking and hands shaking.

"Let me tell you something about Kevin Durant," Myers said. "Kevin Durant loves to play basketball. And the people that questioned whether he wanted to get back to this team were wrong. . . . He's one of the most misunderstood people. He's a good teammate. He's a good person. It's not fair. I'm lucky to know him."

Members of the franchise had begun heaping the love on Durant earlier in the playoffs. A transition of power seemed to happen as the Warriors began to lean on his playmaking ability as a counter to the opponents pressing physical defense. And Durant was producing in a way that left even his teammates impressed. Even Draymond Green, who prides himself on being a leader in the locker room, praised Durant for his leadership. Durant was carrying the Warriors.

By the end of the season, it seemed that Durant was being showered with all the admiration and respect that he could ever want by an organization and fan base that wanted him to stay. It was as though the three years of emotional and psychological struggle, trying to merge this collection of Hall of Famers in a sustainable fashion, had finally paid off. Maybe it was an ambitious recruiting method as Durant headed into free agency. Or maybe it had just been a matter of time all along, the completion of a bond that required forging through adversity. It all seemed set up for Durant, who became a legend for playing in Game 5, to sign long-term with the Warriors so they could ride off into the sunset together.

The Warriors, despite Durant's significant injury, still offered him the maximum contract—five years, $221 million—though he would miss the first year while recovering. Myers flew out to New York to get Durant's decision in person. Curry was in China on tour with Under Armour and flew from Shanghai to meet with Durant before free agency began. Thompson, rehabbing his torn ACL in Los Angeles, was planning on FaceTiming in on Curry's visit. Green went to New York to visit Durant shortly after the season ended to spend some time with him.

But hindsight revealed this to be less of a recruitment strategy than it was a group of teammates who decided to end a historic run amicably. They weren't trying to convince Durant to stay, but they were committed to concluding their time together on a high note. Now that it's over, it is clear that they all knew Durant was leaving. They weren't changing his mind, but rather changing the narrative about what he meant to them. Curry wasn't going to recruit Durant. He was going to look him in the eye and speak from the heart.

"There was no need to pitch," Curry said. "He knows what we're about and what we accomplished. He just had to make a decision that makes him happy. That's what everybody wants to do in this league. It was more about a respect factor, not letting the BS of this league get in the way of our relationship, and not let it change who I am or anything like that. I feel like he just knew what he wanted. And at the end of the day, that's all you can ask for as a player."

. . .

Durant was expected to return a proud franchise to glory, to make the Knicks—one of the NBA's most historic and important franchises—relevant again. Sources said some in Durant's own camp expected him to go to the Knicks. The Mecca of Basketball, formally known as Madison Square Garden, was supposed to be Durant's new home.

But Durant shocked the league, and broke the hearts of Knicks fans, by choosing the Brooklyn Nets. The Knicks are the historic power whose success is a boon for the league because of their massive following. The Nets are transplants from New Jersey who play second fiddle to the beloved Manhattan club.

Durant chose the start-up over the established. He thumbed his nose at nine months' worth of speculation by opting for the unconventional route to resurrect New York basketball.

"If I was leaving the Warriors," Durant told Yahoo! Sports, "it was always going to be for the Nets."

There is something fitting about Durant ending up in New York. This union, between this player and this metropolis, feels like the inevitable conclusion to a winding journey of more than twenty years—all designed to land him in the Big Apple. A game like Durant's seems crafted specifically for the biggest stage, under the brightest lights. Phenoms like him belong on display, deserve to be marveled at. Appreciated. And there is no bigger display case than New York City: the NBA's largest market, the epicenter of buzz, the land of countless basketball legends. Since he was a young buck, Durant has worked to be the greatest basketball player in the world. He has put in innumerable hours of grind to that end, suffered and sacrificed in this pursuit to maximize his unprecedented talents. He's climbed his way to the top of the modern NBA, accumulated coveted individual accolades, won two championships, and become a needle-mover in the sports landscape. Now all that's left is where he finishes among the legends in the history of the sport.

New York gives him the largest and loudest bullhorn to refute his critics, to acquit himself of the one remaining slight on his basketball résumé. He is one of the most scrutinized and vilified basketball players of the modern era. He has been doubted and criticized, chided and ridiculed. All because he chose to sign with Golden State, already an established power, thereby undermining his reputation in the minds of many and derailing his trajectory as successor to the throne of LeBron James.

New York is his refuge. New York is his revenge.

Durant fits in a big city. Raised in the D.C. area, he's always had the towering presence of the National Mall as a beacon for his dreams. He was shaped by the energy and pace and progress of the nation's capital. His mind-set was fashioned by a cosmopolitan vibe. The urge to do something and be part of something major. The inspiration of being around success and people who are striving for it. The diversity of the people, of the opportunities, of the ideologies. He often likes to be in the middle of the action, soaking up the dynamism of his environment. This is what drew him to Los Angeles every summer and is part of what lured him from Oklahoma City to the Bay Area. It is the impetus behind moving his media company, Thirty Five Ventures, to New York. It is probably an unspoken factor in why he was so drawn to and connected so strongly with Rich Kleiman—a New York native who has grown from friend-of-a-friend to agent to copartner of the Durant empire. Yeah, Durant is about that cosmopolitan vibe.

It also makes sense, knowing the man, why he chose Brooklyn over the Knicks. He does have a chill, understated side. He appreciates simple things. He loves being connected to a community, loves hip-hop, and has an affinity for grimy, blue-collar charm. In that vein, Brooklyn fits his soul. Manhattan is about loftiness, about bright lights and big dreams. Its aura screams business and commerce and money. But Brooklyn is about people, where families and schools and small businesses make up neighborhoods. He's got the big-city aspirations of New York City, but he also has an antiestablishment streak that draws him to the 'hood. Durant has grown to love defying what's expected of him, bucking against the grain, and then fighting to validate this defiance.

Plus, Brooklyn offered something that the Warriors couldn't. By the end of his three-season stint in Golden State, Durant wasn't as immersed as he'd expected. The connection that had attracted him, that he saw when the quartet of Warriors showed up to the Hamptons, never fully materialized. The bond he'd anticipated having with Curry suffered due to their different lifestyles. Curry is married with three kids. Any time he has left over after basketball and business is devoted to his family. Conversely, Durant is single with no children. Curry can't hang out like Durant, and Durant wasn't trying to be an extra in the Curry family.

Green and Iguodala, both fathers, had similar constraints. Even Thompson, who is also unmarried with no children, has his circle of friends and a routine of behavior. While it seemed that he and Durant could have bonded, the execution proved to be less than organic, as Thompson already had his life and way of operating established. Timing proved to be a pivotal factor.

What Durant walks into with Brooklyn is precisely the kind of relationship he'd hoped to build with the Warriors. He'd already been close friends with Kyrie Irving and DeAndre Jordan for years before joining the team, easing the transition.

Durant's move prompted more fervor and dialogue. The conversation among fans and media went from speculating about where he was going, to digesting his choice of the Nets, to deciphering his reasons for leaving the Warriors. And because Durant remained silent, not commenting on the issue, former players and media analysts continued to fill the void with their opinions and inside information.

The day after he announced his decision, Durant took to Instagram and declared he was his own man. "No man can speak or make decisions for me," he wrote.

That's what New York is getting in Durant: a superstar with something to prove. A man who has discovered who he wants to be and given up trying to be anything else. Take him or leave him. A legendary player with a legendary game looking to add the climax to his legendary résumé. He comes to the Big Apple a controversial figure in an era of hypercoverage and relentless discourse. He comes nursing his wounds, looking for a place to call home. He comes looking to reclaim his post as the face of today's NBA and remind everyone he is one of the greatest of all time.

That's his relentless pursuit now.

ACKNOWLEDGMENTS

The first and greatest acknowledgment must go to my wife.

Confession: this book was incredibly hard. The timeline, the subject, the frenzy that is Warriors' world, the princess being in middle school—it all conspired to make this book quite the grind, admittedly. Of course, that doesn't matter to most people. Book writing is hard. But it's relevant solely because the only way I was able to pull this off was because my wife, Dawn, put a cape on and saved me and our family from my process of stress and insanity. The long nights swimming in words followed by a pruned state wasn't fixed by quadruple lattes. It was her patience, support, love, accountability, and multitasking. After one all-nighter, I was determined to take my daughter to school as I do every morning. I had thirty minutes, so I took a little nap. Next thing I know, I woke up in a quiet house in the afternoon, breakfast waiting and the seemingly endless list of morning tasks already handled.

I must acknowledge my daughter, too. She did an excellent job respecting the hustle while also making sure there was fun and joy during the grind. The minibreaks having shooting contests on the office hoop were everything.

Writing a book about someone's life has a way of forcing you to reflect on your own. Diving into Durant's history and upbringing, I found the similarities were undeniable and moving, reviving an appreciation for my little family and the biography we are currently crafting.

When it came to the execution, some others were tangibly instrumental. Chief among them is Darnell Mayberry, a veteran NBA writer and my friend for years. There is arguably no better source on Durant's tenure with Oklahoma City than Mayberry, who covered the Thunder since the franchise moved from Seattle and is the author of *100 Things Thunder Fans Should Know & Do Before They Die.* He was a critical resource for learning about Durant during his Oklahoma years and their context. Mayberry was so clutch, allowing me to tap into the vast knowledge in his brain.

Two other women were valuable in my process. Ryan Lindsay, a future force in the journalism industry, was invaluable with her research help and expertise on the D.C. area. And Danielle McNamara, my longtime friend and colleague, was nothing short of a godsend with her consultation, editing, advice, and professionalism.

I've come to learn well the difficulties of writing unauthorized biographies. They are not possible without access. Learning the history and background, getting the details and stories—those are all essential elements. But there is another key element that leads me to a couple other acknowledgments. Writing biographies requires an interest in people. In what makes them tick. In what their passions are. In their emotions. In how life and circumstance alters and impacts. That, for me, is why I like them. It is a chance to peel back the layers and reveal the person behind the athlete.

I leaned on a couple of people especially for the digesting of the complex figure that is Kevin Durant. They are my usual muses on all things pertaining to humanity. Anthony Nelson and Ammar Saheli, the latter being my minister, are two of my best friends and two of the most thoughtful men I know. And not just thoughtful in the sense of considering others, but in forgiveness, introspection, and philosophy and prayer. Our conversations unpacking life and our experiences, what they mean and how they impact us, were like years of unintended prep work for this book. But they put in overtime for me on *KD*. They endured my questions and analysis, waded out with me into deep waters of dialogue, read excerpts, and chatted some more. I should also mention my colleague Ethan Strauss, who ventured out into the depths with me, too. I wanted to present the genesis and essence of Durant, and I couldn't begin to understand that without the benefit of their intelligence and perspective.

INDEX

245

ABOUT THE AUTHOR

Marcus Thompson II, an Oakland, California native, is a lead columnist at *The Athletic*, covering the Golden State Warriors, San Francisco 49ers and Giants, and the Oakland Raiders and A's. He has been a sportswriter in the Bay Area since 1999, previously for the *Contra Costa Times, Mercury News*, and *East Bay Times*. He covered the Warriors exclusively as a beat writer for ten seasons. Thompson is also an adjunct professor at Las Positas College in Livermore. He lives with his wife, Dawn, and daughter, Sharon, in Oakland. He is the author of the national bestseller *Golden: The Miraculous Rise of Steph Curry*.

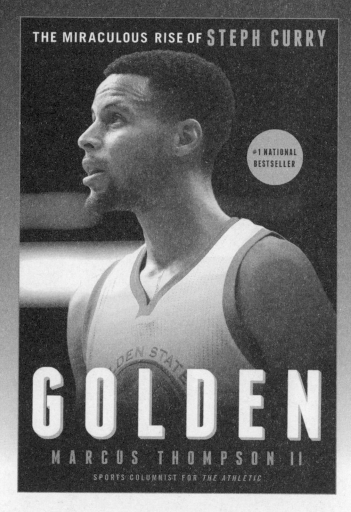